PATHS
WITHOUT GLORY
RICHARD FRANCIS
BURTON
IN AFRICA

Also by James L. Newman
Imperial Footprints: Henry Morton Stanley's African Journeys

PATHS
WITHOUT GLORY
RICHARD FRANCIS
BURTON
IN AFRICA

JAMES L. NEWMAN

POTOMAC BOOKS, INC.
WASHINGTON, D.C.

Library of Congress Cataloging-in-Publication Data
Newman, James L.
  Paths without Glory : Richard Francis Burton in Africa / James L. Newman.
     p. cm.
  Includes bibliographical references and index.
  ISBN 978-1-59797-287-1 (hardcover : alk. paper)
  1. Burton, Richard Francis, Sir, 1821–1890. 2. Explorers—Great Britain. 3. Africa—Description and travel. 4. Travelers—Africa—History—19th century. I. Title.
  G246.B8N49 2010
  916.04'23092—dc22

                                                        2009038259

Printed in the United States of America on acid-free paper that meets the American National Standards Institute Z39-48 Standard.

Potomac Books, Inc.
22841 Quicksilver Drive
Dulles, Virginia 20166

First Edition

10 9 8 7 6 5 4 3 2 1

CONTENTS

ILLUSTRATIONS

PREFACE

DURING THE FINAL STAGES of preparing *Imperial Footprints: Henry Morton Stanley's African Journeys*, I faced the daunting issue of what to research and write about next. A literary agent suggested doing something similar, saying readers tend to expect this of authors. That sounded appealing, since I'd enjoyed time traveling with Stanley. It taught me a great deal, and I could build upon the experience, while staying anchored in Africa, where most of my career thoughts have been directed.

So, who would the person be? Herbert Ward came to mind. He'd been part of Stanley's Emin Pasha expedition "rearguard" disaster and afterward became renowned for his African sculptures, which told me an artist or art critic would be needed to do him justice. I'd written a paper on the discovery of gorillas, and so thought about Paul Du Chaillu. Although he was and still is an interesting figure, his journeys to Africa were few and each covered pretty much the same ground as the last. A book, thus, seemed most unlikely. All the while in the back of my mind lurked Richard Francis Burton. He stayed there because so much had already been written about him. Further reading, though, convinced me a niche still existed that hadn't yet been well filled, namely the theme of Burton and Africa. Yes, his biographers have written about this, but with eyes predominantly on him. So, I continued on, hoping to refine the theme by bringing the Africa he visited more to the fore. Late one night, for whatever reasons I can't say, the title of a great World War I film starring Kirk Douglas flashed before my mind and, voilà, I had it.

Books like this one cannot be written without the assistance of others, and I would like to single out Mary Lovell for a special thank you. She'd combed the world searching for information to write *A Rage to Live* and graciously suggested that I pay a visit to go through her files and use what I wanted. When that became impossible, she directed me to the Orleans House Gallery. Being able to consult the files there saved me much time and not a little money. And, of course, I have to thank the gallery staff, led by Mark De Novellis, for allowing me to work in a quiet place with all the items completely at my disposal.

Four people at the Royal Geographical Society need to be mentioned for their kind and invaluable services: the archivist officer, Sarah Strong; the map librarian, David McNeill; the picture library manager, Jamie Owen; and the collections and enterprise assistant, Julie Cole. And I can't forget now-retired Francis Herbert for his valuable advice and council. Unfortunately, I don't have the names of the many people at The National Archives who assisted me. All I can do, therefore, is thank them, one and all, for their kindness and amazing efficiency in providing requested documents.

At the Huntington Library the Avery chief curator of rare books, Alan Jutzi, always found time in his busy schedule to say hello and pass on valuable information. I'm particularly indebted to him for bringing to my attention Burton's hand-drawn map of the journeys Dr. Livingstone made while he was presumed lost. Culled seemingly from newspaper accounts, it is reproduced here. And there's no way I can thank Gayle Richardson enough for allowing me to work in her office while she recatalogued the library's Burton collection.

I must thank the staff of Syracuse University's Special Collections Research Center of Bird Library for hunting through the stacks to find my many requests. The super hunter of all is Nicolette Dobrowolski. And the Interlibrary Loan Department never once failed to locate a book or article I needed. Indeed, in several instances they found items I thought impossible to find.

Personal thanks are owed to Joe Butler for stimulating conversations about Burton over beers in London. I owe a debt of gratitude to David Robinson for assistance with research in London and at the Huntington Library. Once again, Joe Stoll provided excellent cartographic assistance. And many thanks to Don McKeon for his meticulous editing of my manuscript.

AFRICA

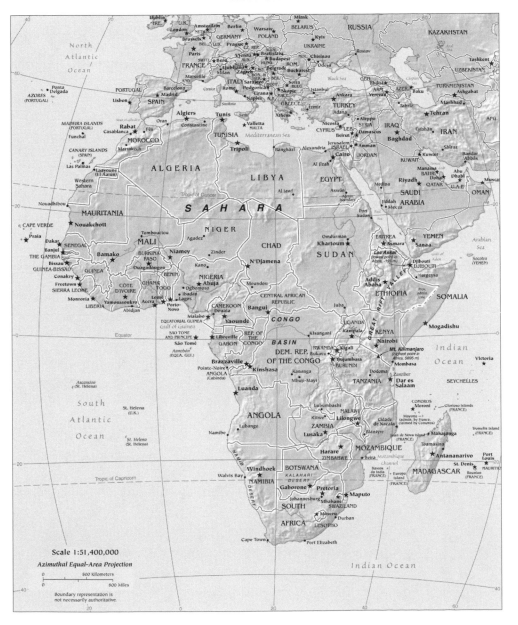

Scale 1:51,400,000

Azimuthal Equal-Area Projection

| 0 | 800 Kilometers |
| 0 | 800 Miles |

Boundary representation is
not necessarily authoritative.

INTRODUCING
RICHARD F. BURTON

ON MONDAY MORNING, October 20, 1890, Sir Richard Francis Burton bade farewell to this world. His was a comparatively peaceful ending to a remarkable and often highly turbulent sixty-nine years of life. Bold and brilliant, Burton made contributions to such fields as exploration, linguistics, ethnography, geography, and literature, and more esoteric ones like fencing and falconry. Some credit him with being the founding father of sexology, both from life experiences and translations of erotica, notably the *Kama Sutra* and *Anaga Ranga*. Not to be forgotten are his military service and many years as a consul for the British Foreign Office in four locations. In the words of admirer and collector Quentin Keynes, Burton "lived and experienced enough for a dozen lives."[1] In the process, he generated about as much controversy as it is possible for any one person to do. And the years since his passing haven't witnessed much change in this regard. With all Burton left behind, and all he didn't, it's been possible to use many different epitaphs to characterize him—genius, hero, misfit, egomaniac, madman, bigot, revolutionary, misanthrope, gypsy, to cite a few that have some ring of truth to them. Two others, though, perhaps come closer to the real Burton. One is that of explorer, at least as defined by historian Daniel J. Boorstin, namely a "seeker," someone "who risks *un*certain paths to the *un*known."[2] For Burton, the "unknown" included mind and spirit, as well as physical places. The other is "actor."[3] His most famous role was that of impersonator, but there were others, such as provocateur and victim, the two sometimes conflated, which he played on many occasions. To this must be added the epitaph cultural critic. Sometimes an outsider looking in, at other times he was an insider looking out.

1

Little wonder, therefore, that Burton continues to be a subject of interest. There are two active websites, http://burtoniana.org/ and http://www.isidore-of-seville.com/burton/, devoted to him, and the Orleans House Gallery in Twickenham, England, has held three exhibits focused on Burton and his wife Isabel in the last two decades—A Blaze of Light Without a Focus (1990), Lady Burton's Gift to the Nation (1998), and Burton, the Case For and Against (2005). He's even wound up being featured in five novels and made it to the silver screen in the 1990 epic *The Mountains of the Moon*, based on William Harrison's fictionalized account *Burton and Speke*.[4] Just recently a documentary of sorts, *The Victorian Sex Explorer*, appeared on British television. Additionally, many of Burton's books are being reissued.

Burton's rise to fame started with the successfully completed pilgrimage to Mecca in 1853. Prior to this time, while he had demonstrated an array of talents, especially with languages, and experienced more than his fair share of adventures, only family, a few friends, and colleagues knew of him. But newspaper reports of the deed and his subsequent book, *Personal Narrative of a Pilgrimage to El-Medinah and Meccah* (1855–56), turned Burton into a celebrity. Further adventures and a penchant for outspokenness helped keep him in the limelight. In addition, he wrote prodigiously. Depending on exactly what's counted, some fifty books, many with multiple volumes, carry his name. The best known, and certainly most profitable, *The Book of the Thousand Nights and a Night* with supplements ran to sixteen volumes. Articles, letters to the editor, reports, and speeches flowed from his pen as well. Nonetheless, in many ways Burton lived an unfulfilled life. His dream of becoming a high level diplomat remained just that, a dream: he spent the final seventeen years of his life as Great Britain's consul in Trieste, hardly a top posting. As Burton himself noted, "Professionally speaking, I was not a success." He pointed his finger characteristically at others' inadequacies, not his own, for the reasons why. "It is hard for an outsider to realise how perfectly is the monopoly of commonplace, and to comprehend how fatal a stumbling-stone that man sets in the way of his own advancement who dares to think for himself, or who knows more or who does more than the mob of gentlemen-employés who know very little and who do even less."[5] As for financial fortune, it pretty much passed him by, and the family kitty was all but empty when he died.

That his outspoken and often sarcastic to insulting style played an important role has been well documented. It created enemies, many in high places, who would strike back when opportunities arose. Gordon Waterfield hit it pretty much on the head when he remarked, "At every stage of his life Burton puzzled, shocked, and exasperated people."[6] Yet, there was also something else involved that has been less commented upon. I'm speaking of Africa, where Burton traveled extensively from 1853 to 1864. Indeed, he once called it his "adopted home."[7] But like many such homes, Africa didn't provide a nurturing environment. Injuries and sickness sapped Burton's strength, and few things worked out as intended. Indeed, failures spoke louder than accomplishments. In their wakes he became increasingly frustrated and bitter, with alcohol a frequent remedy. I would even venture to suggest that his time spent in Africa and its aftermath distracted Burton from what proved to be his real attributes, those of literary translation and commentary. Even his language proficiency may have suffered. He never did become fluent in any African language. Effort could very well have been better placed on furthering his knowledge of those languages he had learned earlier. Fairness, of course, requires that I note his accomplishments, some of which were significant. Overall, though, a promising future after the Mecca pilgrimage hit the skids and never really got back on track.

For his part, Burton proved to be a troublesome adopted son of Africa. While there he went from being merely a servant of British imperialism to one of its strongest advocates. His voice in favor of developing more decisive and aggressive policies grew ever louder, with economic and geopolitical concerns top priorities. If Great Britain didn't seize the opportunities presented, then, Burton argued, other European powers, especially France and Bismarck, would to the country's detriment. Despite having once said, "England is the only country where I never feel at home," he was steadfast in promoting the interests of his natal land. Any attempt to portray Burton as someone less than a red-blooded imperialist, as Greg Garrett has, runs at odds with the facts.[8]

Africa was also where Burton turned from being a man with strong, often prejudicial beliefs about people into a leading proponent of the new "science of race." Based on crude morphological measures, such as skin color and phrenology, it argued that evolution triggered by the environment had created a hierarchy of human races. When Burton began thinking in such terms is unclear; the best one can say is that the rudiments were formed before he went to Africa. They can be seen in two early books, *Goa and the Blue Mountains* (1851) and *Sindh, and the Races that Inhabit the Valley of the Indus* (1851). For example, in the latter, he referred to the Baluchi as being "far superior to the common Sindhi in appearance and morals. He is of fairer complexion, more robust frame and hardier constitution." Accordingly, "the dark complexion of the Sindhi points him out as an instance of arrested development."[9] One can also see here the rudiments of what would become an obsession in later books: making comparisons, whether well-founded or not. Less in doubt is that experiences in Africa led Burton to give race greater and greater prominence as an explanation of human differences more generally. What he called "true" Africans, or Negroes, ranked near the bottom of the hierarchy, primarily because they inhabited tropical climates, which supposedly produced lethargy and degraded physical forms. In line with the ideas of philosopher Herbert Spencer, who coined the phrase "survival of the fittest" in 1864, Burton at one time thought they would probably disappear in the not-too-distant future because they would be unable to compete in the new world facing them.

Burton's embrace of this stance contributed to a number of stereotypes. One linking the imperial agenda to race was that of Africans being "children" who needed guidance from more advanced peoples to grow into "adults." Another involved Africans' supposed lack of creative abilities. Consequently, anything seen in tropical Africa smacking of a higher stage of development, whether physiological or cultural, had to, in Burton's mind, have come from outside sources, notably lighter-skinned people from the north. Relying on these stereotypes, his work contributed to a long-held "Hamitic hypothesis" that would not be exposed as fallacious until the mid-twentieth century.[10]

While Burton's imperialist and racist leanings, a common tandem in the nineteenth century, have received attention, the role Africa played in their development has not been subjected to close scrutiny. Noticeably missing is how these biases evolved over time as Burton interacted with Africa and Africans, and so my procedure will be to follow him, looking at where he went and why, what he saw and did, what happened to him along the way, and, most important, what, in the end, he said about everything, whether fact or fiction, right or wrong. Although a man of action, it was primarily through words that Burton confronted the world. And, unlike some others who wrote about distant lands, he was his own wordsmith, one who didn't bother about making revisions to please publishers and the public.

A subtheme that I feel needs to be pursued is Burton and women. Simply put, he used them, whether for pleasure, for enlivening stories, for making points, or as subjects for his fascination with sex, more generally. Even his wife Isabel seems to have mattered more for her usefulness than anything else. Furthermore, some of Burton's comments on African women rank among his most racially charged. They well illustrate the point made by Patrick Brantlinger about the close links that developed between imperialism, racism, and sexism, or better, perhaps, in Burton's case, misogyny, in the nineteenth century.[11]

This task requires an understanding of the Africa, or more accurately the different Africas, into which Burton stepped. Although he made many astute observations that stood the test of time, others did not, and, despite his mental acuity and wide-ranging study, he couldn't know everything. And, like each of us, what he saw was filtered by experiences and preexisting biases. Today, we have much more information at our disposal to get closer to the realities of time and place Burton encountered. This doesn't mean that I'll be providing detailed historical, ethnographic, and environmental accounts of the lands through which he passed. To do so would require a book of several volumes and lead to numerous diversions of attention along the way. Instead, I'll concentrate on those matters that seem most pertinent to achieving a better understanding of what it was about Africa that led Burton to say what he did, how experiences there affected him, and what impacts his presence had.

This book, therefore, is not a biography of Richard F. Burton, per se. Quite a few have been written over the years, with *The Devil Drives* (1967) by Fawn Brodie, *Captain Sir Richard Francis Burton* (1990) by Edward Rice, *Burton: Snow Upon the Desert* (1990) and *From the Sierras to the Pampas* (1991) by Frank McLynn, and *A Rage to Live* (1998) by Mary Lovell being required reading for anyone interested in Burton, the person. Also of significance is *The Highly Civilized Man* (2005) by Dane Kennedy. Kennedy uses a thematic approach to investigate Burton, contending "we can make more sense of the man if we work harder to situate him in the multiple contexts that gave shape and direction to his life."[12] His choice is the Victorian world surrounding Burton; mine the various

African worlds he entered. The newest addition is *The Tangled Web* (2008), in which Jon R. Godsall seeks to challenge many previous "givens" about Burton's life. More of a fact check and an exposé than a biography, it still must be read by all Burton scholars and enthusiasts.

Nonetheless, to tell the story properly requires that I present the salient features of Burton's days before Africa, connect the threads between times spent there, and bring his life to a close. Structurally speaking, therefore, what follows does resemble a biography. Such an approach, I believe, is especially useful for nonspecialists, as they can better see how Burton's life and thoughts evolved. For his devotees, this will mean traveling familiar grounds and at times slighting what might be of most interest to them. If fortunate, I hope what I say will both inform and, on occasion, provoke them.

An indispensable source of information is *The Life of Captain Sir Richard F. Burton*. Compiled by Isabel Burton and published in 1893, it contains what he related to her during a sea voyage to India in 1876, plus extracts from his writings, letters, diaries, and an array of other materials. Everything up to 1861, save editorial comments and some insertions, she put in his voice. In 1861 a warehouse fire destroyed virtually all of Burton's possessions, including manuscripts, letters, and journals. After that date the book is as much about her as him. His biographers have uncovered further details and corrected errors in *The Life*. Isabel sanitized much and left out more in her attempt to tell the story of the man she considered her "earthly god and king."[13] The book must, therefore, be read with caution and judged in the light of other evidence whenever possible.

Mention of *The Life* brings up Isabel's pyrotechnics shortly after her husband's death. She decided it was best to burn many of Richard's papers, and when word got out, it caused an immediate and enduring outrage. Burton scholar James Casada has called it "a damnable act" that "denigrated his memory and rendered a singular disservice to students of the man and his milieu."[14] Mary Lovell has been somewhat less critical, noting that Isabel didn't burn as much as many people have assumed and most of the items, like bills and receipts, were useless, while others Richard himself wanted destroyed. According to Isabel, he signed the following: "In the event of my death, I bequeath to my wife Isabel Burton, every book, paper, or manuscript, to be overhauled and examined by her only, and to be dealt with entirely at her discretion and in the manner she thinks best, having been my sole helper for thirty years."[15]

Much of the initial reaction centered on the pages of *The Scented Garden* that went up in smoke. An update of the earlier *Perfumed Garden of the Cheikh Nefzaoui*, Richard was working on the book at the time of his death. According to Isabel, he called it a "pot-boiler," and she determined the work was beneath his standards.[16] The more critical losses comprised letters and diaries. The logical assumption that she kept most, if not all, of these at hand for writing *The Life* would mean they were included in another burning that took place later.

Several other books of the time deserve brief mention. *A Sketch of the Career of Richard F. Burton* by Alfred Bate Richards, Andrew Wilson, and St. Clair Baddeley appeared in 1886. Just ninety-six pages long, it's of interest mainly for some personal reflections and observations about Burton's early life. The following year saw the publication of *Richard F. Burton, K. C. M. G.: His Early, Private and Public Life* by Francis Hitchman. The Burtons allowed Hitchman access to their papers in anticipation of the book being an "official biography." Overall they weren't happy with the results, despite its largely sympathetic tone, and much of what Hitchman wrote would later appear in *The Life*. Then there's *The True Life of Capt. Sir Richard F. Burton, K. C. M. G., F. R. G. S.* by Burton's niece Georgiana Stisted, which came out in 1896. While containing some interesting reminiscences on her uncle's life, much of it was designed as an attack on Isabel. Finally in 1897 W. H. Wilkins published *The Romance of Isabel Lady Burton: The Story of Her Life*. It was in some ways a response to Georgiana Stisted and contains much of personal interest about Isabel and Richard.

An array of important primary documents fortunately have survived. The Royal Geographical Society archive in London contains a number of letters and reports that are especially relevant from the time of the Mecca pilgrimage to the early 1860s. Burton's consul years are well documented in the Foreign Office files housed in The National Archives (formerly the Public Record Office) at Kew, England, and the Huntington Library in San Marino, California, is home to Burton's personal library and the newly recataloged Sir Richard Francis Burton Papers, which includes the extensive collection of letters and other items assembled by Edwards Metcalf. Another private collection, that of Quentin Keynes, who died in 2003, is now housed in the British Library. Fortunately, much of it of relevance to Africa can be found in Donald Young's MA thesis, "The Selected Correspondence of Sir Richard Burton 1848–1890," and his edited volume *The*

Search for the Source of the Nile. Mary Lovell also dug deeply into the Keynes's collection, occasionally producing more accurate transcriptions of Burton's notoriously bad handwriting. These and other documents she assembled for the writing of *A Rage to Live* are currently available at the Orleans House Gallery. The British Library, Trinity College Library at Cambridge University, and the National Library of Scotland also house documents related to Burton, as does Special Collections in the Syracuse University Library. The Wilton and Swindon History Centre is the primary source for Isabel's papers, a microfilmed version of which exists at the Huntington Library.

Three highly useful bibliographies have been published, the first being Norman Penzer's *An Annotated Bibliography of Sir Richard Francis Burton* in 1923. Penzer also had his own Burton collection, which was unfortunately destroyed in the 1939 London blitz, making a fourth Burton burning. In 1978 B. J. Kilpatrick released *A Catalogue of the Library of Sir Richard Francis Burton, K. C. M. G.*, at that time in the possession of the Royal Anthropological Institute. Then, in 1990 came James Casada's invaluable *Sir Richard F. Burton: A Biobibliographical Study*.

By necessity, I've had to use the place names recorded by Burton. Some of these no longer exist and in other instances they've changed. When that's the case, I include both. I will do the same with names of peoples that have changed between then and now. I decided not to use "*sic*" to indicate misspellings in quotes. It's distracting, and besides, readers can tell for themselves. Since they were the units employed at the time, U.S. customary and imperial weights and measures are used throughout.

Burton's books have appeared in many different editions. In general, I've used the first ones, but once in a while you'll see later editions cited because they contain valuable information added by editors. Also, quotes by Burton often appear in multiple sources. When this is the case, I reference the most readily available one.

1

THE TIME BEFORE AFRICA

NOTHING UNUSUAL MARKED the birth of the boy, baptized as Richard Francis, to retired Lieutenant-Colonel Joseph and Martha (née Baker) Burton in the South Devon town of Torquay on March 19, 1821. Nor was it at all unusual in those days for new parents to move in with one of the families, as the Burtons did by taking up residence at the substantial Baker home in Hertfordshire. Right from the start, though, one thing did differentiate Richard: his looks. With an olive complexion, bright red hair that eventually turned coal black, and penetrating, dark eyes, he hardly fit the English norm. These traits he attributed to his father, whom Richard described as being "of very mixed blood," without ever specifying the mixture.[1] Might the mixture include Gypsy? Burton is a common Romany name, and Richard would become fascinated with Gypsies later in life, enough so that a few years before his death he helped found the Gypsy Lore Society, which thrives today. Burton never claimed Gypsy lineage, and no evidence has been unearthed to say otherwise.

In 1826 Richard's parents decided to move the family, now enlarged by Maria (b. 1823) and Edward (b. 1824), to Tours, France. The exact reason for the move is unclear. It may have been health (both parents suffered from asthma and Joseph complained of numerous other disorders), or perhaps they just wanted a change of scenery to start a home of their own. Finances likely played a role. As a result of having gone off active duty, Joseph was on half pay and the family's only other income came from a trust fund left to Martha at the death of her father in 1825. Since the end of the Napoleonic Wars, exchange rates allowed British pounds to buy more on the continent than at home, and as a result expatriate communities had formed in an array of places such as Tours. Moreover, Joseph had developed a fondness for the Continent from his days in the military. The opportunity to hunt the likes of wild boar was especially attractive to him.

Early on Richard showed the spark of brilliance that later became a flame. Seeing this, Joseph hired tutors to teach him, among other subjects, Latin and Greek. At age six Richard began attending school and from the outset demonstrated another lifelong quality, a combative nature that often led to fights with so-called French gutter boys. In particular, he didn't take well to teasing and insults, which came with the territory of being an outsider. Backing down wasn't his style from the very outset, and he himself seems to have started a fair share of the rows. The brothers also enjoyed playing the vandal, doing things like breaking windows and defacing structures. In this context, it's worth noting Richard's later statement about developing the habit of lying:

> Moreover, like most boys of strong imagination and acute feeling, I was a resolute and unblushing liar; I used to ridicule the idea of my honour being anyway attached to telling the truth, I considered it impertinence. . . . Being questioned, I never could understand what moral turpitude there could be in a lie, *unless it was told for the fear of consequences* of telling the truth, or one that would attach blame to another person. The feeling continued for many a year, and at last, as very often happens, as soon as I realized that a lie was contemptible, it ran into quite the other extreme, a disagreeable habit of scrupulously telling the truth whether it was timely or not.[2]

In fact, lying remained a habit of the adult Burton. He liked to shock people with tales of his supposed horrible deeds, such as killing someone or engaging in cannibalism, and as noted earlier, outright fabrications were not beyond the pale.[3] Furthermore, his disguises have to be considered lies of a sort. And while Burton did often speak the truth as it appeared to him, no matter the consequences, the final sentence above can be taken as another instance of rationalizing why his career aspirations had faltered. He was just too honest for his own good!

In 1829 the Burtons moved back to England, settling in Richmond in hopes of preparing the children for formal education. Richard hated virtually everything there—weather, people, food and drink, and especially the school, where, according to him, "instead of learning anything" he and Edward "lost much of what we knew, especially in French, and the principal acquisitions were a certain facility for using our fists, and a general development of ruffianism."[4] In 1831, with the intended educational benefits nowhere in sight, the Burtons returned to France, following Richard's recovery from what he later claimed was a serious case of measles. If, as he also said, several boys at the school died from the disease, a better bet would be that it was scarlet fever, since measles had long since ceased being fatal in England. The family first went to Blois, but stayed only a year before beginning a phase of nomadic existence that lasted through most of the decade. By now both parents' asthma attacks had worsened, and so they journeyed to Provence and from there to Italy, with stops in Pisa, Siena, Florence, Sorrento, Rome, and Naples. From Italy they traveled to Pau, in the Basses Pyrenees region of France, and then to the spa town of Bagni di Lucca, Italy, looking for better climes, both health-wise and socially. Martha also suffered from an unspecified nervous condition. This nearly constant moving about set the stage for Richard's later life of restlessness. No place held him for very long.

Tutors schooled the children in an array of subjects. These included manual arts, two of which, how to sketch and shoot, would serve Richard well later in life. The streets taught other things. Both boys started smoking and drinking, and they continued to get into fights. To better defend himself, Richard learned how to box. He tried opium and visited brothels, taking Edward with him on one such trip in Naples. During a cholera epidemic in the city, the boys disguised themselves as undertakers in order to observe firsthand the death carts as they took victims from workhouses to burial pits.

As the 1830s came to a close, Joseph and Martha decided the time had come for their overly rambunctious and frequently disobedient sons to settle down and prepare for future careers. For Richard this meant enrolling in King's College, Oxford, with the intent of becoming a parson in the Church of England. Edward headed off to Cambridge for the same kind of training. To say Richard didn't care much for Oxford would be putting it mildly. The "mean little houses" surrounding the "fine massive and picturesque old buildings" of the campus instantly put him off. He described the Isis River as a "mere moat," and its Cherwell tributary seemed like a "ditch." The countryside was "flat and monotonous" and the sky "brown-grey," with the air constantly smelling of smoke.[5] The college hardly suited him either. Classes proved boring, as did most of the other students, who had had conventional English upbringings he didn't share. His way of speaking Greek and Latin made him stand apart, as did a moustache, which he was forced to shave off. While in a way he relished being different, it also frustrated him, or at least his ambitions. As he later related to Isabel,

> The conditions of society in England are so complicated, and so artificial, that those who would make their way in the world, especially in public careers, must be broken to it from their earliest day. The future soldiers and statesmen must be prepared by Eton and Cambridge. The more English they are, even to the cut of their hair, the better. In consequence of being brought up abroad, we never thoroughly understood English society, nor did society understand us. And, lastly, it is a *real* advantage to belong to some parish. It is a great thing, when you have won a battle, or explored Central Africa, to be welcomed by some little corner of the Great world, which takes a pride in your exploits, because they reflect honour upon itself. In the contrary condition you are a waif, a stray; you are a blaze of light, without a focus. Nobody outside your own fireside cares.[6]

Richard did find some enjoyable diversions. There were plenty of opportunities for playing pranks, carousing late into the night, and spending time in the fencing room. Another favorite pastime involved visiting "a pretty gypsy girl (Selina), dressed in silks and satins, [who] sat in state to receive the shillings and the homage of the undergraduates."[7] One can surmise that Richard did more than admire her dress and have his fortune read. To take on something different from the Oxford norm, he also started to learn Arabic, first via self-study and then under a tutor.

After failing to receive a scholarship, Richard gave up on the idea of getting a First Degree, and since a Second would not do, he asked Joseph during a family summer vacation in Germany for permission to leave Oxford for the army. Richard also put forth the possibility of immigrating to either Canada or Australia. The answer to both was a firm no. As he later told it, the rebuff led him to think about ways to get "rusticated," or suspended from school, as opposed to being "sent down," or expelled, which would prohibit returning at some future date. The opportunity came the following year when he and several others attended a steeplechase against college policy. Called the next day to explain their actions, Richard's sharp responses to questioning prompted the committee to tell him to pack his belongings, leave forthwith, and not return, although apparently the option of returning remained open.[8] He did so gleefully, proclaiming,

> I leave thee, Oxford, and I loathe thee well,
> Thy saint, thy sinner, scholar, prig and swell[9]

At least, this was how Richard remembered it. It is more likely that he was asked to leave for reasons of poor performance and bad attitude.[10] While at Oxford, Richard sharpened another aspect of his personality: a disdain for and rebellion against authority. Cocksure, at least on the outside, he made a habit of challenging superiors, often arrogantly, and had little sympathy for those with differing views. This penchant would cost him many times over.

At age twenty-one and more or less footloose Richard went to London to stay with his aunts on the Baker side. During moments off from having fun, he considered employment options and decided joining the army of the British East India Company (John Company to initiates) looked like the best bet. It was a choice made by many young men of lesser means searching for adventure and a way up the career ladder, and the situation in Afghanistan made the prospects for achieving both all that more promising. The British had just suffered a humiliating defeat, and troops were being mobilized to retaliate. A nomination from an anonymous friend led to Richard being granted the rank of cadet in the Eighteenth Native Bombay Infantry regiment.[11] It was technically illegal to buy commissions, but according to Richard, five hundred pounds changed hands. No paper trail has ever turned up to indicate giver and taker, if indeed there were such. Before leaving for India, Richard began studying Hindustani, having, he said, developed his own system of language learning.

I got a simple grammar and vocabulary, marked out the forms and words which I knew were absolutely necessary, and learnt them by heart by carrying them in my pocket and looking over them at spare moments during the day. I never worked more than a quarter of an hour at a time, for after that the brain loses its freshness. After learning some three hundred words, easily done in a week, I stumbled through some easy book-work . . . and underlined every word that I wished to recollect, in order to read over my pencillings at least once a day. Having finished my volume, I then carefully worked up grammar minutiae, and then chose some other book that interested me. The neck of the language was now broken, and progress was rapid. If I came across a new sound . . . I trained my tongue to it by repeating so many thousand times a day. When I read, I invariably read out loud, so that the ear might aid memory . . . and whenever I conversed with anybody in a language that I was learning, I took the trouble to repeat their words inaudibly after them, and so to learn the trick of pronunciation and emphasis.[12]

Aboard the *John Knox* he had the services of several Hindustani speakers for the nearly five months it took to reach Bombay via the journey around the Cape of Good Hope. As will be seen, Burton, as I shall now call him, except on occasions when it might be unclear if it's he or Isabel in question, found another method that proved to be invaluable for learning colloquial speech.

India provided a stage upon which Burton honed skills and attitudes that he would take with him to Africa. It did not, however, lead to glory on the battlefield because the military campaign was over by the time he arrived on October 28, 1842. With war off the table, Burton chose the interpreter route as the way to advance in rank. Already well versed in Hindustani, further study allowed him to pass the exam first among twelve. When posted to Baroda, he moved on to study Gujarati, again earning a first on that exam. He continued developing his Arabic and before leaving India added Maratha, Sanskrit, Persian (Farsi), Sindhi, Telegu, and Toda to his list of languages. On many days, there wasn't much to do beyond drilling, which left Burton time for study. He often spent it with local scribes called *munshi*, who served as tutors. Curiously, Burton claimed to have also studied the language of monkeys, learning sixty of their "words" from animals he kept at one time. The supposed vocabulary list went up in the warehouse flames. Some years later American Richard Garner set about to do the same thing. He didn't get very far.

India sharpened Burton's interest in women. He certainly enjoyed the sexual side, and by all accounts his partners in India were numerous and varied. Some may have been British, for he noted a common activity among cadets like himself was "peacocking," a euphemism for midday dalliances with the wives of superior officers. The strain of sneaking around, however, led most who partook to turn their attentions eventually on the "dark fair." This, he said, had its advantages and disadvantages. "It connected the white stranger with the country and its people, gave him an interest in their manners and customs, and taught him thoroughly well their language. . . . On the other hand, these unions produced a host of half-castes, mulattos, 'neither fish nor fowl, nor good red herring,' who were equally despised by the races of both progenitors."[13]

The woman at any given time could be a live-in lover, *bubu* (temporary wife), mistress, or prostitute. Burton especially liked the company of young, seductive singers and dancers known as "nautch girls," some available for sex at a price, some not. He talked about his affairs openly and created a portly Mrs. Grundy as a foil to shock Victorian attitudes. According to Isabel, Richard often recited a favorite poem:

> They eat and drink and scheme and plod;
> They go to church on Sunday,
> And many are afraid of God,
> And more of Mrs. Grundy.[14]

While in India, Burton became a regular user of *bhang* (hemp), marijuana, and opium, and as with his enjoyment of women, he never hid the fact. In addition, he drank a lot of port, claiming it helped prevent and cure malaria, which, of course, it didn't, although enough port may have induced a state of mind oblivious to malaria's symptoms. In the long run, alcohol would prove to be his most serious addiction.

In 1844 Burton joined the Survey Department headquartered in Karachi, then often rendered as Kurrachee, at the time no more than a small town plagued by sand, dust, and foul odors from raw sewage and decay. The work of assaying and mapping took him throughout the territory of Sindh, centered on the strategic lower reaches of the Indus River Valley, often as the lone Englishman. He became fascinated by the land, its peoples, and most especially, Islam, and threw himself to their study, using an extraordinary eye for detail and abilities to interrogate informants to good effect. He did most of this in the guise of Mirza Abdullah the Bushiri, a Persian/Arab seller of linens and jewelry. As such, he could wander about at will, gaining access to such venues as markets, homes, parties, inns, and mosques. In addition, Burton operated several small shops that provided opportunities to carry on conversations with those who stopped by. Looks helped him pass—he darkened his skin with walnut juice and henna and grew a great beard—as, of course, did language skills. The Bushiri identity came from a need to cover his accent.

All the travel and information gathering wasn't just about ethnography. Indeed, Burton would hardly have been given the time to wander as he did unless another reason existed, in this instance that of being part of the so-called Great Game of intelligence gathering.[15] In other words, like many officers he spied for British authorities, most particularly for Sir Charles Napier, the conqueror of Sindh and its then-governor, for whom he served as regimental interpreter. Napier was especially interested in being informed about infanticide and *suttee*, the practice of widow suicide by immolation on the husband's funeral pyre, both of which he hoped to ban. Beyond what Burton saw with his own eyes, he was able to listen in to gossip, rumors, and conversations in ways few others could. There's precious little information available to say anything of substance about how much time he actually spent on such missions and what he might have provided in the way of information. It's doubtful Burton ever engaged in any significant political espionage.

One purported investigation, however, has had a life to it, that concerning the use by troops of Karachi's homosexual brothels. Years later Burton claimed having "passed many an evening in the townlet, visited all the porneia and obtained the fullest details, which were duly passed to Government House." He would further claim that enemies discovered what was supposed to be for Napier's eyes only and used it to slander him, thus effectively short-circuiting his career ambitions then and afterward.[16] In-depth searches by several biographers and others have failed to locate such a document, and Hitchman made no reference to it in his biography. In addition, nothing has turned up to indicate a reprimand or other blot on Burton's official record because of such a report. So, he could have invented the whole thing as a convenient way of blaming others for his failures, or, perhaps, as James Casada has said, it was "nothing more than figments of Burton's fertile imagination."[17]

The year 1846 turned out to be a bad one for Burton. Desperately wanting combat, he resigned from the Survey Department to join a unit destined for the Great Sikh War in the Punjab. This went against Napier's wishes, and in any event, Burton's unit turned back after three weeks of grueling march. Burton was now in the doghouse for disobeying orders and reassignment had to wait for matters to be "settled."[18] Before this happened, he became ill from what could have been cholera, an epidemic of which had ravaged the army. A venereal disorder is also a possibility.[19] Whatever the cause, Burton managed to convince authorities he needed time to recover, and so they sent him to the hill station of Ootacamund (Ooty to initiates) in the Nilgiris (Blue Mountains) of southern India. The four months he spent there plus a visit to the Portuguese enclave of Goa en route led to his first true book, *Goa and the Blue Mountains*. It began his serious writing career and demonstrates the style and structure Burton would use in books about Africa, being part travelogue, part history, part geography, part ethnography, part critique of what others who'd written about the area had said, all in a kind of mish-mash. Burton never was one for editing. He preferred throwing information at readers almost straight from his notes. And liberally sprinkled throughout were his opinions. Among the latter he'd formed and take with him was the inadvisability of marriage between Europeans and natives. In his mind it produced inferior half-castes, such as those in Goa, of whom he said it would be "difficult to find an uglier and more degraded-looking race" in Asia. As for character, Burton went on to say that theirs "may briefly be described as passionate and cowardly, jealous and revengeful, with more of the vices than the virtues belonging to the two races from which they are descended."[20] Another developing trait was a preference for people untouched by Europeans, since according to Burton, it almost always meant degradation. He cited the once "noble unsophisticated Toda" of the Blue Mountains as an example, noting, "They have lost their honesty: truth is become almost unknown to them; chastity, sobriety, and temperance, fell flat before the temptations of rupees, foreign luxuries, and ardent spirits.[21]

Although Burton finally did get reappointed to the Survey Department, his usefulness ended in May 1847 with an eye infection, most likely a severe form of infectious conjunctivitis. It plagued him the rest of his days in India and flared up on occasion later in life. He managed, however, to continue his studies and in the process amassed a huge library on Oriental life and thought. Religions, particularly the more mystical versions, fascinated him, not for purposes of salvation—he doesn't seem to have worried about an afterlife—but instead for what they might reveal concerning the deeper meanings of existence. This led him to the Nagar Brahmin sect of Hinduism, then to Sikhism and Sufism, a version of Islam noted for its scholastic and poetic paths to reaching the Divine. He also worked on two tasks that would be completed much later on: compiling *The Arabian Nights* and translating *Os Lusiadas* by the sixteenth-century Portuguese poet/traveler Luís Vaz de Camoëns, whom Burton would come to look upon as a life model.

Burton continued to make enemies in India right up to the very end. Going native alienated some in the ranks, who took to calling him "White Nigger," a common epitaph for those who dared to cross social boundaries. And he often offended superiors with an opinionated, acerbic tongue. He left one such moment in the form of a brief doggerel:

> Here lieth the body of Colonel Corsellis;
> The rest of the fellow, I fancy, in hell is.

The colonel and Burton then purportedly went at it "hammer and tongs."[22]

Burton's India era ended in March 1849. Still suffering from bouts of conjunctivitis and intestinal problems, he'd been given a two-year-long home leave. Friends who carried him aboard the sixty-year-old tub *Elisa* thought it unlikely he'd survive the journey. On top of the physical pain rested the mental. After nearly six and a half years of service and in his twenty-eighth year of life, Burton had managed to achieve only the rank of lieutenant, and under current conditions no further advancement seemed likely, especially since in the previous year he'd been passed over to be the interpreter for a unit scheduled to see action in the Second Sikh War. Burton couldn't fathom this and other slights as having been in any way his fault. As he later put it while playing the role of victim, "My career in India had been in my eyes a failure, and by no fault of my own; the dwarfish Demon called 'Interest' had fought against me, and as usual had won the fight."[23] And in another context he penned the lines,

A fatal land that was to me
It wrecked my hopes eternally[24]

The departure from India came just in time. Under the care of a servant during the voyage to England, Burton's health slowly improved, enough so that after a brief stay in London he traveled to Pisa to visit his parents and sister. The thought of re-enrolling at Oxford crossed his mind. If that had happened, the name Richard Francis Burton probably would have become no more than a footnote to history, perhaps garbed in the robes of a "dyspeptic don."[25] Instead, he set about completing book manuscripts and by the end of 1850 had *Goa and the Blue Mountains* off to the publisher. Two on Sindh, *Scinde; Or, The Unhappy Valley* (1851) and *Sindh, and the Races that Inhabit the Valley of the Indus* (1851), quickly followed. In the former Burton related events and opinions to a fictional and thoroughly disliked traveling companion named Mr. John Bull. Reviews were decidedly cool owing to Burton's sloppy writing and penchant for inserting asides and lengthy footnotes, often on arcane matters. The second was much better and is still used in Pakistan for its ethnographic observations. But, like the other, most copies at the time remained on store shelves.

Burton also produced *Falconry in the Valley of the Indus* (1852), a slender monograph that derived from dabbling in the sport during his teenage years and time at Oxford. In a postscript Burton provided both some pointed commentary on book critics and biographical information, the most interesting being about his activities as Mirza Abdullah the Bushiri. Neither here nor in the two books on Sindh did the brothel investigation and report come up for mention.

Burton led a mostly quiet life, with much of the time spent in Boulogne, France, living with his mother and sister. He was still unwell: a urethral stricture and swelling of the left testicle adding to his miseries. Georgiana Stisted attributed the genital issues to an attack of mumps, something neither Richard nor Isabel ever mentioned in print that survives.[26] Or it may have been complications of a venereal disease, perhaps syphilis.[27] Despite continuing health problems, Burton finished writing another book, *A Complete System of Bayonet Exercise* (1853). Referring to himself as one of his "ancient subalterns," Burton sent a copy to Napier, noting that it resulted from "rather long study."[28] For exercise, he put on fencing exhibitions at the Salle d'Armes, wowing the French audiences with his deft skills, and in spare moments he thought about taking a wife, which led to more than one amorous affair.

While in Boulogne, Burton learned of an opportunity to explore the Arabian Peninsula under the aegis of the Royal Geographical Society (RGS). Negotiations with renowned Finnish explorer Dr. Georg A. Wallin had recently broken down, and Burton offered to take his place. Such a journey held out the possibility of making the pilgrimage to Mecca, something that seems to have been in the back of his mind since India. Starting with Lodovico Bartema in 1503, several Europeans had already managed to do it, the last of note having been Swiss scholar-cum-adventurer Johann Ludwig Burckhardt in 1814–15. None, though, had entered the *Ka'abah*, the holiest of holy sites, which Burton planned to do in the guise of a born rather than converted Muslim. The strategy certainly carried risks, maybe even death, if he were exposed as an infidel passing for a Muslim, but Burton felt there were important benefits to be had. As he later wrote in his account of the pilgrimage, "The convert is always watched with Argus eyes, and men do not willingly give information to a 'new Moslem,' especially a Frank; they suspect his conversion to be feigned or forced, look upon him as a spy, and let him see as little of life as possible. Firmly as was my heart set upon travelling in Arabia, by Heaven! I would have given up the dear project rather than purchase a doubtful and partial success at such a price. Consequently, I had no choice but to appear as a born believer."[29] Furthermore, pulling off such a stunt would heighten the dramatic appeal, and thus sales, of a book he planned to write. In addition, the journey fit his desire to use experiences in exotic lands and among different peoples for personal growth.

Burton needed two things in order to undertake the pilgrimage. One was financing. Stressing exploration to fill in the "white spaces on the map of the Arabian interior," he received two hundred pounds from the Royal Geographical Society. Burton felt he could make some additional money in the process. "When I started my intention had been to cross the all but unknown Arabian Peninsula, and to map it out either from El Medinah to Maskat, or from Mecca to Makallah on the Indian Ocean. I wanted to open a market for horses between Arabia and Central India, to go through the Rubá-el-Khali ('the Empty Abode'), the great wilderness on our maps, to learn the hydrography of the Hejaz, and the ethnographical details of this race of Arabs."[30]

He also needed more leave time and thus asked the East India Company for three additional years. They refused but did grant six months to study Arabic, giving him a total of ten to work with. Burton seems never to have mentioned the Mecca visit to them. Indeed, he told the Court of Directors he wanted to be "in some way useful to the promotion of science." To do so he said he would survey the resources and tribes, and beyond that "attempt to remove the obstructions which the ignorance or the apathy of the natives may have opposed to the establishment of direct commercial relations with the Western coast of our Indian Empire." In Burton's mind, knowledge of Islam and "personal appearance" made him the right man for the job.[31]

Burton left Southampton on April 4, 1853, aboard the Peninsular and Oriental (P&O) steamer *Bengal* disguised as a Persian prince. At Alexandria he took residence for five weeks at an outbuilding on the estate of John Thurburn, who'd also accommodated Burckhardt, with most days spent on study and "remembrance of things oriental."[32] At some point while there Burton dropped the prince identity for that of a Persian *sufi* who dispensed health advice and folk medications. He then went to Cairo, staying six weeks in the Greek quarter. There he befriended Haji Wali, who convinced him that being Persian was a bad idea because it would brand him a Shiite in largely Sunni territory. So, Burton became Abdullah Khan, a footloose health provider of Pathan descent who'd been educated in far-off Rangoon, which would explain away his less-than-perfect accented Arabic. Interestingly, records indicate Burton failed an Arabic proficiency exam upon his return from Mecca, and there's no evidence to suggest he passed a later one.[33] He also added the identity of dervish to cover any out-of-the-ordinary behavior. As Burton explained it,

> No character of the Moslem world is so proper for disguise as that of the Darwaysh. It is assumed by all ranks, ages, and creeds; by the nobleman who has been disgraced at court, and by the peasant who is too lazy to till the ground; by Dives, who is weary of life, and by Lazarus, who

begs his bread from door to door. Further, the Darwaysh is allowed to ignore ceremony and politeness, as one who ceases to appear on the stage of life; he may pray or not, marry or remain single as he pleases, be respectable in cloth of frieze as in cloth of gold, and no one asks him—the chartered vagabond—Why he comes here? or Wherefore he goes there? He may wend his way on foot alone, or ride his Arab mare followed by a dozen servants; he is equally feared without weapons, as swaggering through the streets armed to the teeth. The more haughty and offensive he is to the people, the more they respect him; a decided advantage to the traveller with a choleric temperament. In the hour of imminent danger, he has only to become a maniac, and he is safe; a madman of the East, like a notably eccentric character in the West, is allowed to say and do whatever the spirit directs.[34]

The journey finally began in July, when Burton joined some 130 other pilgrims on the rickety sambuk *Golden Wire* for a miserable twelve-day voyage from Suez to Yambu on the Arabian Peninsula. From there he traveled to Medina and stayed a month taking in the sights before joining the large Damascus caravan for Mecca, which it reached on September 10, 1853. The story, enlivened by liberal doses of dramatic license, is well known and therefore doesn't need repeating here.[35] Two things, though, are of note because they reveal ideas Burton would bring with him to Africa. One was his romance with the desert.

In such circumstances [desert] the mind is influenced through the body. Though your mouth glows and your skin is parched, yet you feel no languor,—the effect of humid heat; your lungs are lightened, your sight brightens, your memory recovers its tone, and your spirits become exuberant. Your fancy and imagination are powerfully aroused, and the wildness and sublimity of the scenes around you, stir up all the energies of your soul, whether for exertion, danger, or strife. Your *morale* improves; you become frank, and cordial, hospitable and single-minded; the hypocritical politeness and the slavery of Civilization are left behind you in the City. Your senses are quickened; they require no stimulants but air and exercise; in the desert spirituous liquors excite only disgust.[36]

Costumes for the pilgrimage to Mecca as portrayed in Personal
Narrative of a Pilgrimage to El Medinah and Meccah.
*(Reproduced with permission of the Special Collections Research
Center, Syracuse University Library.)*

He would react quite differently to the African tropics.

The second involved a growing respect for Arabs, notably the Bedouin, and Islam. The former appeared pure and noble to Burton; the latter, in many respects, was better suited than Christianity to non-Europeans as a way forward. Both would often be used as standards to judge what he observed in Africa in the coming years.

2

AMONG THE SOMALIS

PUBLIC RECEPTIONS FIT FOR A HERO, fetes with the rich and powerful, and well-paid speaking engagements awaited Burton in London. Instead, he chose to go to Cairo, where he took a room at the popular Shepheard's Hotel in the city center to recuperate from a case of dysentery and to begin two papers about the Mecca adventure for the RGS. He wrote fitfully. The first paper wasn't read to members until June 12, 1854, and the reading of the second was delayed until March 12, 1855. Both disappointed geographers. Because Burton had failed to do any of the intended exploration, the white spots on the map remained just that, white spots. He blamed this on unsettled conditions in Arabia, citing the existence of obstacles only someone with "unlimited time" at his disposal could eventually overcome. What obstacles he didn't say, but a good bet is that they involved undue risks to life and limb.[1] Burton also failed to get his horse scheme off the ground, calling the animals he'd seen "slender stunted bloods" available only at "fabulous prices," should owners wish to sell any.[2] Still, even with these geographical and financial shortfalls, the name Richard Francis Burton had achieved national prominence and the future of its bearer looked bright indeed.

For purposes of both comfort and unconventionality, Burton continued to dress in Bedouin garb, sometimes fooling those who knew him from India days as "Ruffian Dick." He coined the epitaph himself. After a while, though, the hotel routine grew tiresome, and to spice things up, Burton moved into a house he described as a "precious scene of depravity" owing to its hosting virtually nonstop "fornication."[3] By this Burton clearly meant homosexual relations because he noted it as something forbidden by the pasha. Anyone caught in the act could expect a severe penalty, perhaps even death. Given Burton's penchant for sexual adventure, it's likely he joined the "depravity" from time to time, at least as a spectator. Even more likely were dalliances with Cairo's renowned prostitutes.

Burton was thinking about making a follow-up Arabian journey in order to do some of the missed exploring, but Zanzibar caught his attention. Zanzibar at this point in time encompassed not just the island and city but also the stretch along the eastern coast from Mogadishu to Cape Delgado that its sultan claimed to be under his jurisdiction, however loosely. Burton wrote two letters to the RGS secretary and editor of its journal, Dr. Norton Shaw. In the first he wrote, "I hear that the Geographical has been speaking about an expedition to Zanzibar. Dakhilak as the Arabs say—'I take refuge with you'. I shall strain every nerve to command it, or rather get the command—and if you will assist me I'm a made man." In a postscript he added, "Could you get my arrival in Egypt reported in some London papers, just to warn my friends that my throat is safe."[4] Given all the newspaper coverage of the pilgrimage, he needn't have worried about friends being concerned.

The second letter contained greater detail. His "wish," Burton wrote, was "to attack [scientifically] Zanzibar & if I can only get pay from Govt. for a few good men to accompany me (one to survey, another for physic and botany) I doubt not of our grand success." A little further on he returned to the subject:

> About Zanzibar I have plenty of sound practical reasons why a mission is highly advisable. A scientific mission of course. It is one of the headquarters of slavery—the Americans are quietly but surely carrying off the commerce of the country—and it has very great resources quite undeveloped. As a native I found out a spy of old Mohamet Ali who let me into all kinds of secrets about the country and wanted me to accompany him. I should have done so if I had not been bound for Arabia.
>
> You will ask why I now prefer Zanzibar to Arabia. Because I have now tried both sides of Arabia & see no practical results. Travelling is a joy there and nothing would delight me more than leave for 3 or 4 years to the Eastern Coast. But nothing except more discoveries of

desert valleys and tribes would come of it; no horses, no spices and scant credit.[5]

The comment about Americans "carrying off the commerce of the country" refers to the many ships from New England trading along Africa's eastern coast. Indeed, by the mid-nineteenth century, the Stars and Stripes outnumbered all other colors calling at Zanzibar.[6]

While passing through Cairo, Dr. John Ellerton Stocks paid Burton a visit. Friends from Karachi days, the two had shared quarters for a while and later cooperated on an article about Sindh.[7] Stocks mentioned a botanical exploration of East Africa he hoped to organize and was "one of the few good men" Burton had in mind. A meeting with German missionary-cum-explorer Johann Ludwig (confusingly sometimes called John Lewis) Krapf led Burton to think about an even more ambitious adventure. Affiliated with the Church Missionary Society (CMS) headquartered at Rabai just outside Mombasa, Krapf and his colleague Johannes Rebmann were the first Europeans to sight Mounts Kilimanjaro and Kenya and, not too far distant, according to informants, lay the fabled Mountains of the Moon and a great sea that could be the source of the White Nile. An opportunity thus existed to make history by solving mysteries that had baffled scholars since the time of Herodotus. As Burton later told the authorities in Bombay in his sometimes colorful and rambling style,

> It may be permitted me to observe that I cannot contemplate without enthusiasm, the possibility of bringing my compass to bear upon the Jebel Hamar, those "Mountains of the Moon," whose very existence have not, until lately, been proved by the geographers in 2000 years—a range white with eternal snows even in the blaze of the African summer, supposed to be the father of the mysterious Nile, briefly a tract invested with all the romance of wild fable and hoar antiquity, and to this day the [most] worthwhile subject to which human energy and enterprise could be devoted. For unnumbered centuries, explorers have attempted the unknown source of the White River by voyaging and travelling metaphorically against the stream. I shall be the first to try by a more feasible line to begin with the head.[8]

Mission success would bring great fame and likely much money from a book and lectures. In his desire for both, Burton was a conventional man of the times.

At the moment, though, the RGS's members were more interested in unexplored Somaliland, and the East India Company had already approved a venture there, should a "fit and proper person" come along to serve as leader.[9] As part of its more aggressive Red Sea/Gulf of Aden policies to counter French activities, the British had annexed Aden in January 1839. An old center of some importance, it fell into decline following discovery of the Cape of Good Hope route to the Far East and by the nineteenth century was no more than a rundown village. Burton called it and the surrounding countryside "the abomination of desolation."[10] Still, Aden had a strategic location and harborage ideal for a coaling station.

The taking of Aden led to greater interest in the Somali coast, a source of trade goods and much-needed fresh meat. Nothing could be had from countryside behind Aden, as hostile tribes were in control. Indeed they basically held the city hostage, the only outlet being via the port. To secure the produce from Somaliland, in 1840 the East India Company negotiated a treaty that allowed its ships access to the strategic port of Berbera, home to a six-month-long annual trade fair. Some knowledge of the coast west from Cape Guardafui had been garnered from two expeditions earlier in the century, but many unknowns still existed.[11] Charles J. Cruttenden, a lieutenant in the Indian Navy and assistant political agent at Aden, helped fill some of the gaps. A man with considerable experience in the Red Sea region and fluent in Arabic, he engaged in survey research, both via observations and interviews, while overseeing a six-month-long ship salvage operation during 1843–44. A political mission took him back in 1848, and as a sidelight he conducted an even more detailed study of the coast and its immediate hinterlands.[12] Cruttenden was enthusiastic about the possibilities for trade, noting that the people seemed especially disposed to English merchants, as long they brought the goods themselves in order to avoid the extra costs imposed by middlemen.[13] A variety of circumstances scrapped a follow-up expedition by Dr. Henry Carter to penetrate the interior, and so Burton took the opportunity to propose a new one, with him, naturally, in command. Afterward, he intended to head for Zanzibar to arrange for the journey westward, which might, if conditions permitted, reach all the way to the Atlantic Ocean.

Burton left Cairo for Bombay on January 16, 1854, to report for duty, which, if all went well, would involve gaining company permission and financial support for his expedition. During a two-week-long layover at Aden, he stayed with Dr. John Steinhaeuser, another old India hand. Mutual literary interests led to a fast friendship, and they decided to collaborate on producing "a full, complete, unvarnished, uncastrated copy of the great original" version of *The Arabian Nights*.[14] In 1704 French scholar Antoine Galland had begun translating the tales, but he was highly selective, and over the years the best-known stories had become mostly children's fare.

Fortune smiled on Burton when he boarded ship for the remainder of the journey—Bombay City Council member James Grant Lumsden would be a traveling companion. The two men had met in Egypt, and Burton stayed at Lumsden's house in Bombay after arriving on February 21. The congenial surroundings devoid of unwanted interruptions provided an ideal environment in which to complete a draft of *Personal Narrative of a Pilgrimage to El-Medinah and Meccah*. Lumsden also interceded with the company on behalf of the Somaliland plan and helped gain the support of Bombay's governor John Elphinstone, while Burton waited for reassignment.

The possibility of visiting the city of Harar (Hárer) heightened Burton's interest in the venture. Several earlier attempts by Europeans, including one by Krapf, ended in failure, and thus, the only information about the city came from second- and thirdhand sources. Uncertainty even existed as to where exactly it was located. Such a journey would be like the pilgrimage to Mecca all over again, as Harar was considered to be the holiest of the region's Islamic centers and supposedly forbidden to infidels, especially Europeans who, according to what Cruttenden had gathered from informants, "would be exposed to much insult and ill feeling from the bigoted ruler and inhabitants of the place."[15] The person might be imprisoned and even beheaded. As Burton told RGS members, "I could not suppress my curiosity about this mysterious city. It had been described to me as a land flowing with milk and honey; the birthplace of the coffee-plant, and abounding in excellent cotton, tobacco, saffron, gums, and other valuable products. But when I spoke of visiting it, men stroked their beards, and in Oriental phrase declared that the human head once struck off does not regrow like the rose."[16]

Getting there and back would break the city's so-called guardian spell, which was said to protect it from nonbelievers. Furthermore, the inhabitants reputedly spoke a distinctive language, whose affinities Burton hoped to unravel. Harar was also known as a major slave mart, and the sight of slaves in Arabia had prompted him to remark, "And here I matured a resolve to strike, if favoured by fortune, a death-blow at a trade which is eating at the vitals of Eastern Africa. The reflection was pleasant,—the idea that the humble Haji, contemplating the scene from his donkey, might become the instrument of the total abolition of this pernicious traffic."[17]

By this time slavery and its eradication had come to define Africa in the minds of most Britons, Burton clearly being one of them, despite his Arab garb. To him, though, eradication was always about slavery's deleterious economic consequences, especially on free trade. Humanitarian concerns entered in hardly at all, and as we shall see, he often scoffed at their proponents. Regarding this particular journey, Burton later admitted it was about "curiosity and for display of travelling savoir faire" more than anything else.[18]

Although Harar's exact beginnings are still murky, research has uncovered its founders—migrants from Aksum, centered in Tigray, and the forerunner of Christian Abyssinia (now Ethiopia), who reached the fertile Harar highlands around the middle of the first millennium CE. Derived from a many-centuries-long fusion of Semitic speakers from the Arabian Peninsula with indigenous Cushitic (formerly Hamitic) peoples, the Aksumites created a powerful state that by the second century dominated the Red Sea region. In an effort to broaden its realm, Aksum established colonies and military garrisons at favorable locations throughout the Ethiopian highlands. It sought not only economic gain but also converts to the Monophysite version of Christianity, which became the official state religion during the mid-fifth century. Today it is known as the Ethiopian Orthodox Church.[19]

When Islam arrived at the coast in the late seventh century, it found a receptive audience among traders. A vast Islamic world extending from Iberia to India was forming, and being part of it opened up all kinds of opportunities for increased profits from an array of products, including coffee (deemed superior to mocha), ivory, gum arabic, myrrh, frankincense, ghee, ostrich feathers, and, of course, slaves, of whom the most highly prized were Oromo (formerly Galla) and

Somali women destined for the harems of the Middle East. One of the routes to the sources ran from Berbera across the Harar Plateau, and by the twelfth century virtually everyone in the area claimed to be a Muslim. Nonbelievers were excluded from participating in the highly lucrative trade, and conversion, therefore, had obvious appeal. A person didn't have to practice Islam so much as proclaim he or she was a follower of Allah, a condition still prevalent in much of East Africa. Starting out as a commercial center, Harar became the capital of Adal, an Islamic state bent on destroying Abyssinia. It almost succeeded in 1520 as part of a holy war led by the legendary Somali Ahmad Grāñ ("The Left-handed"), but then met a reversal of fortune in the guise of a Christian resurgence under the Amhara in the 1540s and the coming of the Oromo, who coveted the plateau's rich pastures for their livestock. The formation of an independent Emirate of Harar in the mid-seventeenth century failed to halt the decline, and eventually only the walled city remained to the Harari. The Oromo could have sacked it but refrained from doing so. As herders, they had little interest in cities beyond exacting payments, which the Harari willingly made to protect their commercial interests. They even minted a special currency for transacting business with permitted traders, mostly operating out of Berbera and Zeila. By the mid-nineteenth century three caravans per year left for the coast laden with their precious commodities.

The "master of disguise" this time planned to go as El Haji Abdallah, an Arab merchant. Besides Dr. Stocks, Burton found another good man in G. E. Herne, who'd made a name for himself in India as a first-rate surveyor and mechanic. Lord Elphinstone gave his seal of approval to the project, and Burton went back to Aden to make preparations for the journey while waiting for the official letter of permission to arrive. Soon thereafter he learned that Stocks had unexpectedly died in London from a brain hemorrhage. Stocks's death was a personal as well as professional loss to Burton. Lieutenant William Stroyan replaced him. Like Herne, Stroyan was a surveyor with India experience.

Colonel James Outram had recently been appointed Aden's political resident. Burton also knew him from India, where he was a vocal critic of Napier's Sindh policies, which he considered overly harsh. Indeed, locals referred to Napier as the "Devil's Brother." This didn't sit well with Burton, both because of his respect for the general and his belief that Britain needed to show a strong hand in its overseas territories. As he told his imaginary traveling companion in *Scinde*, humiliation was the essential punishment in eastern lands: "Mind, Mr. Bull, I don't want permission to erect minarets of skulls, or to hang my hostages. But I think we may claim, and you should concede to us, some slight relaxations of prejudice; for instance, free leave to modify and proportion punishment to the wants of a newly conquered people, of course avoiding such barbarities as massacre and torture. I would always flog and fine where you imprison. I would never hang a man without burning his corpse with some solemnity."[20]

Outram questioned the wisdom of the expedition, feeling it dangerous and potentially inflammatory, a position widely shared within the Aden expatriate community. Conflicts between Somali clans had destabilized wide areas of the interior, and bandits roamed the countryside. Attacks on the expedition thus seemed likely, and any deaths among the Europeans would certainly have undesirable political repercussions. Burton expressed disdain at such thoughts: "The rough manners, the fierce looks, and the insolent threats of the Somal— the effects of our too peaceful rule—had pre-possessed the timid colony at the 'Eye of Yemen' with an idea of extreme danger. The Anglo-Saxon spirit suffers, it has been observed, from confinement within anything but wooden walls, and the European degenerates rapidly, as do his bull-dogs, his game-cocks, and other pugnacious animals, in the hot, enervating, and unhealthy climates of the East."[21] Burton also suspected that Outram harbored intentions of making his own expedition. Perhaps, but his stay in Aden hardly lasted long enough to plan anything. After only four months on the job, Outram was recalled to India, where he became one of the British heroes at Lucknow during the Indian Mutiny.

According to Burton, the original plan called for everyone to go to Berbera, then proceed to Harar, and afterward head for Zanzibar. As matters eventually turned out, the journey wound up being split into three parts. Burton would make the Harar trip, while Herne and Stroyan surveyed Berbera's resources. Rumors, which proved to be untrue, suggested there were coal deposits in the vicinity. Herne and Stroyan were also to report on the extent of the slave trade, inquire into the caravans that came to the annual trade fair, and obtain information about the best route to take to Zanzibar.

A new member of Burton's party, Lieutenant John Hanning Speke, was instructed to strike inland from Bunder (Landing Place) Gori to explore the

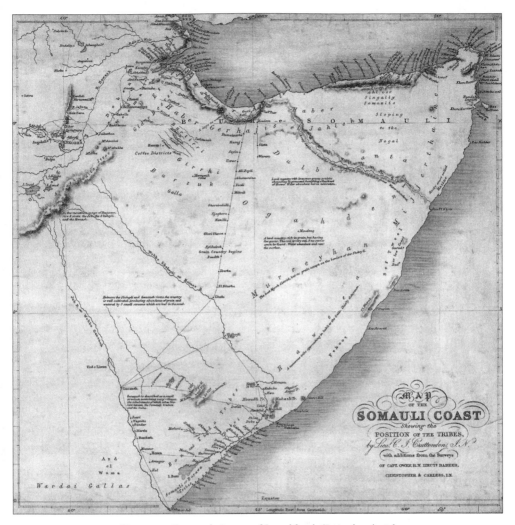

Lieutenant Cruttenden's map of Somaliland. (Reproduced with permission of the Royal Geographical Society.)

countryside around the Wadi Nogal, which Cruttenden described as "a very fertile and beautiful valley" and an important artery of commerce. It was suspected also to be a source of gold, and thus Speke also had instructions to collect soil samples. His other tasks included making detailed notes and measurements along the way, buying camels and donkeys, and establishing relationships with the reputedly warlike Dulbahante Somali before joining up with Herne and Stroyan in Berbera. At age twenty-seven, Speke had been given three years' leave from the Forty-sixth Regiment of the Bengal Infantry after a decade of service. Known as fearless and an excellent shot, he had come to Aden with the intent of mounting an African safari for sport and to provide specimens for an intended museum collection at his father's place in Somerset. Speke had already bagged an array of Indian and Tibetan animals for exhibits and thought equatorial Africa would yield species yet unknown to the outside world. He later claimed to have had in mind a Nile journey, starting with its presumed source in the Mountains of the Moon and from there sailing downriver to Egypt.[22] That's doubtful since Speke knew next to nothing about Africa in 1854. Outram refused to endorse his plan because he felt "the risk of life would not be compensated for by any discoveries that would be made."[23] Speke repeatedly tried to get him to change his mind, but Outram wouldn't budge. Instead, the colonel told him to contact Burton, who agreed to take Speke on. Because of a shortage of funds, Speke would have to use his own money to purchase required supplies and wait to be compensated at a later, unspecified date. In addition to needing another European, Burton feared that if Speke set off on his own before him, he might be killed, which would be reason enough for Outram to terminate the whole expedition.[24]

The opportunity pleased Speke, especially since the year contracted for would not count against leave time. But one thing he didn't like from the outset was Burton's recommendation to travel as an Arab merchant in order to ease suspicions about his true intentions. Speke described the outfit as "anything but pleasant to feel," consisting as it did of "a huge hot turban, a long close-fitting gown, baggy loose drawers, drawn in at the ankles, sandals on my naked feet, and a silk girdle decorated with pistol and dirk."[25] As a good Victorian, he found the whole idea demeaning, and in truth, it was ridiculous, given Speke's appearance—tall, fair, blue-eyed—and with only a smattering of Hindustani at his command. So, he shed the turban at the first opportunity and dropped any pretense about being someone other than an Englishman.

Burton attributed the change in plans to Outram and said a visit to Harar would serve as a "preliminary" to quiet the voices raised against the larger expedition.[26] However, as Jon Godsall has pointed out, there's no evidence Outram ever sought to block the expedition as proposed.[27] A better explanation is that Burton wished to save Harar for himself, so as to avoid having to share the glory. In addition, how could the disguise ploy be carried off with three European traveling companions in tow? And lacking this dramatic gesture, he'd have a far less interesting story to tell.

During the interlude in Aden, Burton spent time studying the Somali language. He started with "An Outline of the Somauli Language, with Vocabulary," written by Christopher P. Rigby, a rival from India days.[28] Burton had bested Rigby on the Gujerati exam. More advanced language skills were better learned from intercourse, in both meanings of the word, with Somali prostitutes. When not so involved, Burton queried everyone he could about conditions in the interior. Aden also introduced him to *khat*, or *qat*, in a closer rendering of the Arabic. Derived from the leaves and young shoots of the evergreen tree *Catha edulis* and grown in the same areas as coffee, qat produces, upon ingestion of its alkaloid juices, mood changes ranging from euphoria to contentment, depending on the person. It also relieves hunger pains. Normally chewed, qat sometimes is added to liquids and foods. Burton said it produced little or no effect on him, which is doubtful, since he seems to have indulged in qat liberally when opportunities arose. Because of its widespread use throughout the region, he may have done so for social reasons, but one suspects that qat did give him at least a little buzz. Another of Burton's pastimes involved further discussions with Steinhaeuser about their *Arabian Nights* project.

With official permission in hand for the expedition to proceed, Burton left on October 29 destined for Zeila, a two-day sailing trip across the Gulf of Aden. Furloughs had been granted for a year at full pay, with expenses, supplies, and transport also covered. The four men would, however, be traveling as private citizens, not government representatives, although clearly they were expected to report back on their findings. The East India Company insisted no undue risks be taken in order to avoid a backlash that could jeopardize future British activities in the Horn of Africa region.

An ancient trade center, Zeila was listed in the *Periplus of the Erythraean Sea*, a commercial seafaring guide written in Greek sometime around 120–30 CE. Although the town achieved a boost in prosperity with the arrival of Arab merchants in the tenth century, the widely traveled Ibn Batuta was hardly impressed during a visit in 1331. He called it "the dirtiest, most abominable, and most stinking town in the world" owing to the "quantity of its fish and the blood of the camels that they slaughter in the streets."[29] As a show of force in their abortive imperial adventure in East Africa, the Portuguese burned Zeila in 1516, after which it passed into Yemen's hands and later wound up a possession of the Ottoman Empire. Caught in a downward spiral, it appeared to Cruttenden as nothing more than "a miserable mud-walled town, containing some twelve to fifteen stone houses, 100 huts, and 750 souls."[30] Although cooler than Aden, Zeila suffered from a lack of nearby freshwater. And because there was no real harbor, ships of any size had to anchor about a mile from shore and off-load their cargoes onto small boats. As a result, most trade went through Berbera. Still, Zeila seemed to offer the most direct route to Harar, and while there Burton could also stay at a home owned by Governor Sharmarke bin Ali Salih, a Somali who'd negotiated the 1840 treaty with the East India Company. While officially in the Ottomans' employ, Sharmarke had pretty much become a servant of British interests after he helped protect the brig *Mary Ann* from attacks by Somali plunderers in 1825.

Burton had met Sharmarke in Aden, and he fully expected him to have all in readiness for the journey to Harar upon his arrival. Nothing of the kind, however, had been done. Burton fumed, noting, "Travellers, like poets are an angry race: by falling into a daily fit of passion, I proved to the governor and his son, who were profuse in their attentions, that I was in earnest."[31] The wait consumed twenty-six days, which Burton described as "quiet, similar, uninteresting—days of sleep, and pipes, and coffee."[32] Two women neighbors helped ease the monotony. One was a young Indian woman whom he described as a "person of fast propensities." The sight of her brought to mind a little verse:

> Without justice a king is a cloud without rain;
> Without goodness a sage is a field without fruit;
> Without manners a youth is a brideless horse;
> Without lore an old man is a waterless wady;
> Without modesty woman is bread without salt.

The other was an Abyssinian matron, brightly dressed and sporting facial tattoos, who watched over the slave girls while weaving mats. Burton said they exchanged salaams after a while. But controversy surrounded her—"more than once she was detected making signals to distant persons with her hands," something done with men, not other women.[33] He didn't indicate if she signaled him and if so what he did about it. A whiff of scandal would likely have made her all the more alluring.

Another way to pass time involved excursions into the surrounding countryside. During one such venture, some Afar (Danakil) herders came into view. Linguistically related to the Somali, they'd been squeezed by the latter's expansion into a small area centered on the arid Danakil Depression, inland from the city of Djibouti. Burton wasn't impressed, calling the men "wild as ourang-outangs, and the women fit only to flog cattle."[34] On another occasion, he and two Arab traveling companions encountered a group of Somali women leading donkeys and camels laden with water skins. "The sturdy dames," Burton observed, "indulged in many a loud joke at our expense."[35] While he didn't say what caused their amusement, the answer may have had something to do with his skin color and their doubt about him being a Muslim. Burton claimed the Arabs jumped to his defense, saying he was "a Shaykh of Shaykhs," and then, in the lighthearted spirit of the moment, "translated to the prettiest of the party an impromptu proposal of marriage." She reportedly asked for some gifts, including ones for her father, and promised to come back the next day to inspect them.[36] She didn't return, and so the game ended there.

Arabs sometimes came to the house, and when they did Burton usually read from *The Arabian Nights*. Discussions with them of the Qur'an earned him the reputation of being a true *haji*, or maker of the pilgrimage. He would be remembered for many years afterward as Haji "Abdallah."[37] No women were allowed at these meetings. As Burton explained it, "El Islam seems purposely to have loosened the ties between the sexes in order to strengthen the bonds which connect man and man."[38]

Burton left for Harar on November 27, 1854, with a party of nine, four mules, and five camels in tow. At Aden he'd hired three Somali as personal guards. Two, Mohammed Mahmud, nicknamed El Hammel (The Porter), and "Long" (because of his height) Guled were former policemen, while the third, Abdy Abokr, was a traveler known for the plethora of sayings and riddles that peppered his speech. It earned him the reputation of "hedge priest," in essence an illiterate vagabond with no formal religious standing who spoke to whatever audiences would listen. They called him "End of Time" after "the prophesied corruption of the Muslim priesthood in the last epoch of the world."[39] Two women cooks joined in Zeila. They were given names from personages in *The Arabian Nights*: Samaweda Yusuf became "Shehrazade" and Aybla Farih, "Deenazarde." Burton described them as "buxom dames about thirty years old [who looked] like three average women rolled into one, and emphatically belong to that race for which the article of feminine attire called . . . a 'bussle' would be quite superfluous."[40] He quickly learned to appreciate their stamina and willingness to help with tasks such as carrying loads and leading the camels in addition to cooking.

The success of any journey in this part of Africa required the presence of an *abban*, a person with knowledge and connections to act as guide, settle disputes, and broker sales. Burton described the position as "a primitive and truly African way of levying custom-house dues. Your 'protector' constitutes himself lord of your life and property; without him you can neither buy nor sell; he regulates your marches, and supplies you, for a consideration, with the necessaries of the road."[41] In a more sarcastic vein, Burton labeled an abban as one who "takes his money and . . . runs away."[42]

Two routes led to Harar. Sharmarke advised against taking the most direct one because much of the way went through territory held by Isa Somali and Oromo, both known to mutilate and murder for the sake of manly esteem. A blood feud then in progress would make travel even more dangerous. The governor thus suggested the other route, which followed the coast for a while before heading inland. That way, most of the journey would be in lands under the control of the supposedly friendly Gadabursi Somali, among whom Sharmarke had important contacts. Still, they would have to deal with the Isa for about fifty miles at the outset, and thus two different abban were needed. Burton surmised another reason lay behind Sharmarke's recommendation—feuds had actually closed that route to travel, and the dispensation of "British cloth and tobacco" might serve to reopen it.[43] Whatever the truth of the matter, Burton decided to follow that route.

Just as in Aden, people in Zeila warned him about the dangers of the journey ahead. Six murders had recently been committed near the town, and therefore every stranger in the desert had to be considered an enemy. According to End of Time, "Man eats you up, the Desert does not."[44] Burton once again dismissed such fears and longed to get under way. This finally happened on November 27.

The first days took the party across a desert coastal plain, termed *guban* in Somali. Burton said the sun above "singed as through a burning-glass," while "the rare wells yielded a poor supply of bitter bilge water."[45] He wondered how anyone could exist in such surroundings during the summer. The truth is that except for those in coastal settlements, Somali didn't live here permanently. Those in possession of home wells came seasonally when the brief rains produced a short bloom of vegetation for the animals to graze upon. Although nighttime brought fresh breezes, it also carried the danger of attack from Isa bands, and so guns were placed at the ready and sentries posted. While traveling, Burton sat atop a donkey with a double-barreled shotgun and two Colt pistols ready for action. He relished the adventure: "Thus it happens, that he who feels a thrill of fear before engaging in a peril, exchanges it for a throb of exultation when he finds himself hand to hand with the danger."[46]

At the sight of Burton, people often shouted out *Faranj*, the Somali rendering of Farsi *Farangi*. Literally a "stranger," it came to mean "Frank," a widely used derogatory epitaph for Europeans in Muslim lands. As had the women near Zeila, they'd seen beneath the disguise. For some unknown reason, Burton hadn't, unlike on occasions in India and during the pilgrimage, darkened his complexion with walnut juice and henna.

Late in the day on December 1 the party turned inland toward the barren hills backing the coastal plain. Instead of people, gazelles and ostriches looked on with curiosity. For extra security, some additional escorts had been added, bringing the total of armed men to twenty. Night travel was possible, the main concern being accidental encounters with scorpions and poisonous snakes. For long stretches, sharp thorns tore at ankles and feet, making the journey even more taxing. Once through the hills, they entered the better-watered *ogo*, where settlements of both Isa and Gadabursi appeared with regularity. The constant stares accompanying his arrival annoyed Burton, as he knew by now the jig was up. "This fairness, and the Arab dress, made me at different times the ruler of Aden, the chief of Zayla, the Hajj's son, a boy, an old woman, a man painted white, a warrior in silver armour, a merchant, a pilgrim, a hedgepriest, Ahmed the Indian, a Turk, an Egyptian, a Frenchman, a Banyan, a sherif, and lastly

a Calamity sent down from heaven to weary out the lives of the Somal: every
kraal had some conjecture of its own, and each fresh theory was received by my
companions with roars of laughter."[47] When crowds followed asking for tobacco
or simply to make what he thought were derogatory comments, Burton dispersed
them by firing shots overhead.

Beyond the ogo lay the *hawd*, where broad acacia trees topped steep ravines
and sections thick with termite mounds looked to Burton like Turkish cemeteries
or ruined cities. Although lacking permanent water, the hawd provided crucial
grazing grounds when the spring rains broke in April and the fall ones in
October–November. This was mainly Gadabursi country, and although they did
appear more "hospitable and docile" than the Isa, Burton found these qualities
"obscured by knavery, thievishness, exceeding covetousness, and a habit of lying,
wonderful even to Eastern travelers." The girls, though, had their attractions. He
said he gave "one of the prettiest a bead necklace." She responded by describing
him as "painted white."[48]

The Somali's insatiable appetite for news and how rapidly word from far
away reached them surprised Burton. Even at this distance, they knew about war
in Russia and a violent storm that had struck Bombay only a couple of weeks
after it happened. Before the advent of modern communications, nomads had
a capacity for spreading information over great distances that settled villagers
lacked. Furthermore, many Somali spoke several languages, having traveled to
lands as distant as India. Contrary to European assumptions, this was not an
isolated part of the world. As an upshot, Burton's movements, as well as those of
Herne, Stroyan, and Speke, were known far and wide.

On December 7 the travelers faced a tough uphill climb that required
repositioning the camels' loads on a regular basis so they would not to slip off.
For Burton, this meant dismounting his mule, and while he was seated on the
ground at one point, biting black ants attacked him with vengeance. Later that
day fatigue forced everyone to take refuge in an abandoned kraal, where a warm
fire helped soothe the cold of night that came with being at over 3,300 feet above
sea level. The ten tough days so far had taken a toll on the animals: the camels
could barely walk, and the donkeys were reduced to skin and bones. Still, travel
itself now proved to be much easier, as desert and rugged terrain gave way to
a vast open savanna, which was at this time of year covered with dry grass. In

addition, the Gadabursi provided warm welcomes, replete with milk, ghee, meat, honey, and water, which would seem to be at odds with Burton's description of them. The presence of lions and hyenas, not hostile people, required the posting of nighttime sentries. Earlier Burton had found himself being stalked by a lion. A double-barreled blast saved the day.

Burton couldn't enjoy the changes, as he suffered from severe stomach pains and diarrhea, probably another case of dysentery, picked up in Zeila. Nothing reduced the symptoms, including a remedy cooked up by End of Time. It got bad enough on one occasion that Burton thought the end might be near. But rest worked its magic, and by December 11 he was good to go again.

The journey halted at a place called Agjogsi, where Burton hoped to meet with the region's *gerad*, or clan leader, Adan bin Kaushan. Duties kept him from coming, and so after four days of waiting around Burton merged his party with a small caravan and headed across country occupied by some Isa and Habr Awal Somali. Robbery and plunder thus became possibilities, although the caravan carried little in the way of temptations.

As December drew to a close, the party left the lands of the nomads. No attacks occurred, and Burton took much of the credit for this: "Every now and then we got into difficulties with the Bedawi, who would not allow us to proceed, declaring the land was theirs. We did not deny the claim, but I threatened sorcery, death, and wild beasts and foraging parties to their camels, children, and women. It generally brought them to their senses. They would spit on us for good luck, and let us depart."[49] Instead of a parched countryside dotted with temporary kraals, the scene now consisted of settled Somali villages, with flowering hedges in between fields of sorghum. It looked to Burton like a part of "rustic England." Presently, they reached the village of Wilensi, another hoped for meeting place with Adan. Once again he was occupied elsewhere.

On December 29, disappointed, but undeterred, Burton and his three trusty companions set out for Harar, now less than forty miles distant. Camels couldn't make the trip because they were unable to navigate the steep, narrow paths along the way. That meant limiting supplies to those the more sure-footed donkeys could carry. As chance would have it, the party came across Adan at the village of Sagharrah. Although he struck Burton as "ambitious and wild with greed of gain" because of his constant begging for goods, he reportedly held the reins of power from here to Harar, and therefore his cooperation would be necessary to reach the city. The next morning found Burton too ill to get out of bed. He couldn't, however, complain about the hospitality extended him: Adan sent ahead for millet beer, some qat was located, and a sheep was sacrificed as propitiation for his return to health.

Whatever may have done the job, Burton felt well enough on New Year's Day to palaver with Adan about clearing the way for the final leg of the journey to Harar. But the gerad had recently lost control over the villages just outside the city and so couldn't guarantee anything. Burton then asked Adan to accompany him and again received a negative response. Instead, Adan promised to send his eldest son as guide; he never did show up. During the wait, several Somali warned Burton's three companions that continuing on would put their lives at risk. Rightfully scared, they wanted to turn back. Having come this far, Burton was prepared to complete the journey alone, but that proved unnecessary as both Long Guled and El Hammel were cajoled into accompanying him. End of Time was allowed to stay put to look after supplies, undoubtedly to his great relief. And Burton was relieved by not having his company; he called him "a caution—a bad tongue, a mischievous brain, covetous and wasteful, treacherous as a hyena, revengeful as a camel, timorous as a jackal."[50] Burton claimed to have abandoned his Arab disguise at this point. As he explained it, "All the races amongst whom my travels lay, hold him nidering who hides his origin in places of danger; and . . . my white face had converted me into a Turk, a nation more hated and suspected than any Europeans, without our *prestige*."[51] The latter would appear to have been the more important consideration for two reasons: Burton had had no such compunction about hiding his origin up until now, and Turks, used as a synonym for Ottomans of all backgrounds, were truly despised by the Somali for their at times brutal imperial style. Anyway, the disguise had failed to fool anyone, and so for legitimate cover, Burton forged a letter from the powers that be in Aden about Great Britain's desire to establish friendly relations with the emir of Harar.

After a few hours on the road Burton and his two companions entered Oromo country. Also present were Midgan, who occupied a caste-like position, performing such tasks as hunting and metal- and leather-working that the Oromo and Somali considered beneath them. Just before setting out on the final approach to Harar, Burton gave his journals and sketches to a Midgan elder for forwarding to Adan. Carrying such items might raise suspicions about his claim of being there in an official capacity, and there was always the chance that he would not return alive. To reinforce what had been said over and over again, the villagers at Sagharrah told Burton they were "dead men."

On January 4, 1855, Burton got his first view of Harar from about two miles away. Although sitting atop a hill, the city was hardly what he expected, since "nothing conspicuous" appeared beyond "two grey minarets of rude shape."[52] No Medina or Mecca to the eye, for sure. By spurring on the mules they reached the gates an hour later and then waited while Burton's greetings were forwarded to the emir. All the while, he said, the three of them were "scrutinised, derided, and catechized by the curious of both sexes, especially by that conventionally termed the fair."[53] But the wait didn't last long, for within a half hour they'd received permission to pass through one of the city's five gates. Reaching it required walking between rows of armed Oromo warriors, whom Burton remembered as "half-naked savages, standing like statues, with fierce movable eyes, each one holding, with its butt end on the ground, a huge spear, with a head the size of a shovel."[54] Although he was told to enter at a trot as custom dictated, Burton chose to walk at a leisurely pace. Once inside, he also refused a request for them to put down their weapons. It wasn't just Mrs. Grundy he sought to rankle, even if this meant upping the danger, which to Burton increased the thrill anyway. Such acts also, of course, served to establish personal dominance, an important imperial symbol.

The emir, Ahmad bin Sultan Abibakr, hardly struck an imposing figure, appearing more like "a little Indian Rajah, an etiolated youth of twenty-four or twenty-five years old, plain and thin-bearded, with a yellow complexion, wrinkled brows and protruding eyes." Burton greeted him with "peace be upon ye!" in Arabic but didn't kiss his extended fingers, remarking that he was "naturally averse to performing that operation upon any but a woman's hand."[55] A wry smile from the emir broke the tension, and he offered accommodations as a token of friendship. After that Burton translated his forged letter about Great Britain's peaceful intentions. With that out of the way, he next met with the *wazir*, or prime minister, of Harar. Despite a reputation for cruelty, he too seemed kindly disposed. That Burton spoke Arabic undoubtedly helped with both men. Yet, he claimed feeling anxious about being in an African city, describing them as veritable prisons that "you enter by your own will, and, as the significant proverb says, you leave by another's."[56] This could hardly have been based on experience, as Harar was the first truly African city he'd visited.

Burton spent ten, mostly tedious, days in town. Although he could wander at will and speak with people, constant surveillance precluded sketching and taking notes, since these activities would give away his ruse. Among the things he asked about was the Nile. The source of the Blue Nile in Lake Tana wasn't far from Harar, but James Bruce had been there long ago. It seems that Burton picked up nothing useful about the White Nile, although he claimed to have heard about an open east-west route through the continent.[57] Naturally enough, women caught his attention. Their "pretty Abyssinian features" surprised him, as did an "utter ignorance of bashfulness." Less appealing were their "harsh" voices, tobacco chewing, and beer drinking, by which, he said, they "demean themselves."[58] Still, this doesn't appear to have dissuaded him from pursuing a couple of dalliances.

Inside the city looked as unimposing as it had from the outside. It housed about ten thousand people, split among the Harari, Arabs, and Somali, most living in simple, sparsely furnished houses. The so-called palace turned out to be "a mere shed, a long, single-storied windowless barn of rough stone and reddish clay, with no insignia but a thin coat of whitewash over the door."[59] Burton described the streets as "narrow lanes, up hill and down dale, strewed with gigantic rubbish-heaps, upon which repose packs of mangy or one-eyed dogs, and even the best are encumbered with rocks and stones."[60] No signs of riches could be seen, and without previous descriptions, it's hard to know if it had always looked this way or not. Clearly, Burton would have wished for something much more substantial and exciting to tell people about.

Within a short while, Burton's thoughts centered more and more on finding a way to leave Harar gracefully. He'd accomplished half of what he wanted to do by getting there and now needed to complete the journey by returning safely to the coast. The presence of smallpox made a quick departure all the more desirable. Word of its existence in the city had been reported while he was still in Aden, but Burton considered this just another scare tactic. The opportunity to leave came with a request to summon a doctor and have medications sent to treat the emir's

People of Harar as portrayed in First Footsteps in East Africa.
(Reproduced with permission of the Special Collections Research Center,
Syracuse University Library.)

infirmities, which included tuberculosis, and those of a prince suffering from
an attack of bronchitis. Severe storms made travel impossible for two days, but
finally just after dawn on January 13, Burton and his two companions started on
their way. Upon passing through the gates he said "a weight of care and anxiety
fell from me like a cloak of lead."[61] They rode quickly to Sagharrah, where shouts
of joy greeted their arrival. Contrary to rumor, they'd not been "imprisoned,
bastinadoed, slaughtered."[62] A similar response awaited them at Wilensi, where
Burton found Adan in possession of his papers. Since it would take at least a

fortnight to reach Zeila, Burton decided to spend a week making the necessary preparations.

In a 1912 book, Ralph E. Drake-Brockman, who'd served in the Colonial Medical Service of British Somaliland, claimed Burton fled Harar after blowing his disguise by incorrectly washing his hands at the end of a meal.[63] As noted, Burton said he dropped the pretense before entering the city, and even if untrue, people knew he wasn't an Arab. Furthermore, fleeing under conditions of tight security would have been next to impossible, and should he have somehow managed to get outside the walls, there was no place to hide. So, unless some startling new evidence comes to light, we're left with Burton's account of events.

The party that departed from Wilensi on January 22 consisted of some twenty men, thirty women, camels, donkeys, and a few sheep. After several agonizingly slow days of travel, Burton decided to leave the main caravan and strike out for Berbera in order to find out what Stroyan, Herne, and Speke had accomplished. He'd heard nothing about them since leaving Zeila and figured a small party moving quickly could get there in less than four days. They would, though, be going through uncharted desert under control of the Habr Awal, whom Burton described as "enemies." Instead, water, or the lack thereof, proved to be the real enemy. After a day on the road without it, Burton wrote, "As I jogged along with eyes closed against the fiery air, no image unconnected with the want suggested itself. Water ever lay before me—water lying deep in the shady well—water in streams bubbling icy from the rock—water in pellucid lakes inviting me to plunge and revel in their treasures."[64] During another long period of thirst, he calculated that they could last but a few more hours before perishing. Fate then intervened in the form of a sand grouse that pointed the way to water. Farther on the men threw caution to the wind and drank lustily from muddy pools infested with tadpoles and insects. Food also ran short, with small quantities of dates and other sweetmeats the only sustenance available. Rain and mist in the foothills relieved thirst somewhat and provided much-needed grass for the donkeys to graze on, while clusters of berries helped ease human hunger.

For three days they'd struggled along without seeing signs of human presence. This changed on the coastal plain, but the people were hostile and denied them water. Fifteen hours went by before they found a potable source in a dry streambed. With donkeys and men barely able to walk after covering nearly forty miles in one day, the party limped into Berbera in the wee hours of January 31. How much fact and how much fiction there is in all of this can't be told. Whatever the case may be, Burton found reasons to be pleased. He'd completed another journey to a forbidden city, deepened his understandings of Islam and nomads, and discovered new sources of pleasure in qat and local women.

Like Zeila, Berbera dated to ancient times. In the *Periplus* it was called Malao and described as a source of frankincense and myrrh. For half of the year a small town occupied by a few hundred inhabitants living in "a wretched clump of dirty mat-huts," during an annual trade fair from November to April, it witnessed its population swell to upward of twenty thousand, as caravans from the interior brought their products for sale to Arab and Indian merchants. Cruttenden had visited the fair at the peak of its activity. He described the scene "as a perfect Babel in confusion, as in languages: no chief is acknowledged, and the customs of by-gone years are the laws of the place. Disputes between the inland tribes daily arise, and are settled by the spear and dagger, the combatants retiring to the beach at a short distance from the town, in order that they may not disturb the trade."[65] By the second week of April, after the last caravans usually left, Berbera returned to its nearly deserted state of being.

On February 5, 1855, Burton sailed for Aden, leaving Stroyan and Herne to complete their survey work. Speke wasn't there. The rickety *El Kasab* moved slowly, making many stops along the way to take on or drop off passengers. Just before the party reached Aden, a storm blew up, nearly capsizing the boat. Burton took a kind of perverse pleasure in seeing the Somali on board suffering from seasickness. Nobody, though, was lost, and on February 9 the boat reached its destination.

In Aden, Burton set about writing a detailed report to Bombay about what had happened so far and sent it off on the February 22.[66] Included were recommendations for heightened British involvement in the area, with abolishing slavery a top priority because, in his words, where it "flourishes commerce declines. It is far more satisfactory for a barbarous people to fire a kraal and sell the fugitives than to sow cotton and grow coffee." Burton felt occupying Berbera would be the catalyst for change, and he didn't think the Somali would object because "they admire our rule, respect our power, [and] comprehend our forbearance." Once that rule was established, the Somali "ardour" for commerce would flourish and with it Berbera. He went on to say that while it would be natural to expect him to apply for the position of agent in charge, the original plan of geographical and commercial surveying must take precedence, and thus Burton asked the company for a second year of leave, promising not "to incur any immoderate risk." In a letter to Shaw he revealed his true intentions: "My plans (public) are now to march southward to the Webbe Shebayli and Garrana. Privately & *entre nous* I want to settle the question of Krapf and 'eternal' snows. There is little doubt of the White Nile being thereabouts."[67]

Burton wanted to leave Berbera in April in order to cross the vast, inhospitable Ogaden Plateau during the monsoon rains when ample water and forage for animals could be found. In order to discourage attacks by Somali and Oromo warriors, he'd earlier agreed to follow Outram's suggestion that for safety's sake the wisest course of action would be to travel with the last caravan from Berbera headed in that direction.

Speke arrived in Aden a week after Burton, not having found the Wadi Nogal and managing to secure only eight camels and five ponies. He did report hearing of an area called Nogal crossed by numerous wadis, and there is a Nugal Valley in the approximate area shown on Cruttenden's map. Although no watercourse by that name exists, the valley does contain numerous permanent wells, crucial to both humans and livestock. Actually, it's hard to tell exactly where Speke went. Only a few place names mentioned by him can be located today, and on two occasions he claimed being at altitudes several thousand feet higher than possible. About all that can be said with certainty is that he didn't go very far, nowhere near the six hundred miles the original plan called for.

Speke put the blame for the failed mission on the abban hired by Burton. Called Sumunter (Muhammad Sammatter was his true name), he was accused of causing numerous delays and of obstructing the course of the expedition by being much more interested in his own affairs than those of the expedition.[68] Furthermore, while in Dulbahante country, Speke claimed Sumunter did little or nothing to overcome the people's open hostility—they resented Speke's presence and couldn't understand why he was there, noting that even Arabs traders never bothered to come their way. At one point, Speke said he felt like shooting Sumunter in despair "of ever producing any good effect on his mind."[69] Burton insisted on a trial, at which Speke reluctantly agreed to serve as prosecutor. Sumunter was fined two hundred rupees, sent to prison for two months, and banned from Aden for life.

Speke desperately wished to redeem himself and volunteered to go back to the coast and at least complete the job of securing additional camels to take to Berbera. Burton concurred, since both the animals and an extra hand were needed for the long journey ahead. With a new abban secured by Aden's assistant political agent and twelve escorts he trained himself, Speke successfully accomplished his mission. It was during this trip that he claimed having been told about a great interior lake that had been "navigated by white men." At first blush the idea seemed implausible to him, but upon further reflection he figured some unrecorded travelers might have been on the lake.[70] In any event, Speke by now had added exploration to his reasons for being in Africa.

Burton returned to Berbera on April 7, 1855, aboard the gunboat *Mahi*. The expedition's camp rested on a ridge less than a mile outside town and contained forty-two men, including twenty Somali guards. Two days later storms in the distance signaled the onset of the monsoon rains and thus the end of the fair. The Ogaden caravan immediately packed up to leave, but instead of joining it, Burton decided to wait for mail and various instruments to arrive, feeling these more important than the extra security provided by the caravan. Days passed with still no ship in sight, and on April 17 three strangers rode into camp. Could they be advance scouts for an attack? Rumors were circulating about such a possibility because of fears that the Europeans were part of a plan to have Sharmarke take over Berbera and end the slave trade. Concern also existed over Burton's recommendation that abbanship be abandoned. Such talk worried him not a bit. After all, despite dire warnings he'd come back from Harar unscathed, Stroyan and Herne had gone about their jobs without opposition, and Speke's life was never in jeopardy during his stay among the Dulbahante. So, that night only the two usual sentries stood guard. Still, Burton must have had some concerns about security because earlier he'd requested more policemen and the stationing of the *Mahi* offshore until the expedition departed Berbera. Neither request was granted.

Events proved greater caution to have been the better bet, for around 2:00 a.m. on April 19 the camp came under attack by an untold number of men. In the darkness and chaos of fighting the four Europeans were separated. Burton thought he saw Stroyan on the ground and went toward him, all the while taking blows from clubs. On his approach to the fallen form, a spear pierced his left cheek, dividing the roof of his mouth and knocking out two molars, before exiting on the other side. After a night's wandering with the spearhead still in place, Burton reached a dry creek bed along the coast. Fortuitously, a small sailing ship had called the previous evening carrying some Somali looking to join the expedition for the trip home and was still offshore. Burton managed to struggle into view and was carried aboard. Herne, suffering only bruises and scratches from his attackers, had reached it on his own, and a search party was organized to look for the other two men. It quickly found Speke, who had miraculously escaped a capture that saw him beaten and stabbed several times. Stroyan met a less fortunate fate. He'd been clubbed and speared to death. Because of rapid decay under hot, humid conditions, they buried him at sea on the way back to Aden.

In a report of the incident sent to Outram's successor in Aden, Colonel William Coghlan, Burton praised the officers for how well they fought but castigated their Somali guards for exhibiting the "vilest cowardice." He blamed "brigands" from the Isa Musa clan of the Habr Awal for the attack and recommended that its members and two other clans "should at once be expelled from Aden with orders never to return until compensation be made & the murderers delivered." The sum he calculated to be exactly 1,390 pounds, 4 shillings. To guarantee compliance, a section of the coast should be blockaded. When handed over to authorities, it would be appropriate, he wrote, to hang the men "upon the very spot where the outrage took place & after burning their bodies, that the ashes should be thrown into the sea, otherwise, the felons will become mere martyrs."[71] He got a blockade, at least for a while, but not the murderers, although the following year the clan leaders of the Habr Awal claimed they caught and executed Stroyan's assailant and offered fifteen thousand dollars by way of compensation.[72] No money changed hands, and the three survivors never received a penny for their troubles.

Despite the ignominious ending at Berbera, Burton wasn't about to give up. He noted in his report that Speke and Herne had agreed to join him in another attempt to complete the proposed journey. This had to be done for reasons that went beyond exploration. Somali respect had to be won for the sake of future British expeditions: "Should we be deterred by the loss of a single life, however valuable, from prosecuting plans now made public we shall not rise in the estimation of the races around us. On the contrary, should we, after duly chastising them, carry out our original projects, we shall win the respect of the people & prevent the re-occurrence of these fatal scenes."[73] But, one suspects that the matter of respect didn't stop here. Burton's was on the line, both in the minds of others and, perhaps more importantly, in his own. A thorough physical exam showed Burton also suffered from second-stage venereal syphilis. Given that this usually appears within six to eight weeks after infection, the most likely source would have been a Somali prostitute, although earlier infection and then reinfection can't be ruled out.[74] Considering Burton's facial wounds and general fatigue, the doctor advised treatment and rest in Aden during the approaching hot season.[75] Burton took quarters at Steinhaeuser's comfortable home, where he regained enough strength to leave for London in mid-May. Speke was actually in worse shape, with death not out of the question. Confounding just about everyone, he healed rapidly and within three weeks was well enough to be sent home. Neither man ever returned to Somaliland, and the costs and dangers involved put off new exploring expeditions in the region until the 1880s.

Back in England, Burton quickly set about the task of writing up his account of the events, which he titled *First Footsteps in East Africa; Or, An Exploration of Harar*. Phrased as a letter to Lumsden, it's not so much about Harar as it is about getting there and back, with a liberal sprinkling of historical tidbits, poetry, sayings, attempts at humor, foreign words, advice, and, of course, opinions thrown in for good measure. In addition, Burton inserted 335 footnotes, some of them several paragraphs in length and often on arcane matters. He always found it hard to pass up opportunities to impress people with the depth and breadth of his knowledge. Nonetheless, despite its awkwardness, *First Footsteps* did inform about a part of Africa not previously known from firsthand accounts. Patient readers could learn about the Somali livestock economy, with camels the prized animals, and their highly segmented agnatic clan-based social-political organization in which conflicts over the critical resources of wells and grazing lands were endemic. They also could glean a wealth of information on such cultural matters as styles of dress, weapons, food, family, and religious practices, just as long as footnotes were read carefully. Because of the difficulties and dangers of working in the area, many of his ethnographic descriptions wouldn't be bettered until anthropologist I. M. Lewis began his study of the northern Somali nearly a century later.[76]

As for the Somali, Burton found them "by no means destitute of capabilities," meaning they understood the value of commerce. And in his scheme of things, the Somali stood somewhat higher on the scale of humanity than black Africans because of presumed mixing with white Semites from the north. The results he felt could be seen in both their physical attributes and character:

> The head is rather long than round, and generally of the amiable variety, it is gracefully put on the shoulders. . . . As far as the mouth, the face, with the exception of high cheek-bones, is good; the contour of the head ennobles it; the eyes are large and well-formed, and the upper features are frequently handsome and expressive. The jaw, however, is almost invariably prognathous and African; the broad, turned-out lips betray approximation to the Negro; and the chin projects to the detriment of the facial angle
> In mind the Somal are peculiar as in body. They are a people of most susceptible character, and withall uncommonly hard to please.
> They have all the levity and instability of the Negro character; lightminded as Abyssinians . . . soft, merry and affectionate souls, they pass without any apparent transition into a state of fury, when they are capable of terrible atrocities.[77]

Value judgments aside, no such mixing between the Somali and Semites ever took place. Burton was probably led to this view by Somali claims of Arab descent linking them to the Prophet. But the lineage is fictive and comes from their being devout Muslims. They are, in fact, indigenous to this part of Africa, as are the Oromo and Afar, all being Cushitic-speaking peoples. The notion of their Semitic origins would linger on until after the middle of the twentieth century.

On the policy front, perhaps the most significant revelation at the time concerned the city of Harar. It was hardly impressive and not a true center of learning, as Islam was the only subject taught. Ruled by a sickly emir, who had an army of no more than two hundred men, counting slaves, a small well-equipped force, Burton surmised, could take it without much difficulty.[78] The guardian-spell legend proclaimed that the city would fall shortly after successful entry by a Christian. That, in fact, soon happened, first to Egypt in 1875, and then even more ignominiously to Emperor Menelik's Christian Abyssinia in 1887. Harar didn't, however, disappear. Today it's the capital of an Ethiopian region of the same name, housing more than 120,000 people, with Harari predominant. And the wall (*Jugol*) still stands, now as a UNESCO World Heritage site.

Because Somaliland was mostly desert and scrubland, Burton saw no need to occupy the region. Besides, it could be controlled from Berbera, and Burton made even a stronger case for the port's occupation in the book than in his report. He called it "the true key of the Red Sea, the centre of East African traffic, and the only safe place for shipping upon the western Erythraen shore, from Suez to Guardafui." As such, it should be occupied, and if Britain turned down the opportunity, then "a rival nation will not be so blind." By now a staunch advocate of a "forward" imperial policy, Burton believed that if force was needed, then so be it.

"Peace," observes a modern sage, "is the dream of the wise, war is the history of man." To indulge in such dreams is but questionable wisdom. It was not a "peace-policy" which gave the Portuguese a seaboard extending from Cape Non to Macao. By no peace policy the Osmanlis of a past age pushed their victorious arms from the deserts of Tartary to Aden, to Delhi, to Algiers, and to the gates of Vienna. It was no peace policy which made the Russians seat themselves upon the shores of the Black, the Baltic, and the Caspian seas: gaining, in the space of 150 years, and, despite war, retaining, a territory greater than Britain and France united. No peace policy enabled the French to absorb region after region in Northern Africa, till the Mediterranean appears doomed to sink into a Gallic lake. The English of a former generation were celebrated for gaining ground in both hemispheres: their broad lands were not won by peace policy, which, however, in this our day, has on two distinct occasions well-nigh lost for them the "gem of the British Empire"— India. The philanthropist and the political economist may fondly hope, by outcry against "territorial aggrandisement," by advocating a compact frontier, by abandoning colonies, and by cultivating "equilibrium," to retain our rank among the great nations of the world. Never! The facts of history prove nothing more conclusively than this: a race either progresses or retrogrades, either increases or diminishes; the children of Time, like their sire, cannot stand still.[79]

As things turned out, the government did stand still when it came to Berbera, which wasn't occupied until 1884.

Burton added five appendices to *First Footsteps*, three of which are important in their own ways. Number I was a condensed version of Speke's diary of the attempt to find the Wadi Nogal. Its inclusion greatly offended Speke, and I'll return to this issue later on. Number II dealt with the Harari language. Although Burton lacked time to study it in detail, from word lists and some elements of grammar provided by an informant, he corrected prevailing opinion by proclaiming the language as more closely related to Amharic than Arabic, even though it was written in the latter script. He was right, and today Harari (Adar to the speakers themselves) is placed within the Ethio-Semitic family of the larger Afroasiatic grouping, which includes Arabic, Ancient Egyptian, Hebrew, and Amharic.

Number IV was about the Somali practices of female circumcision and infibulation, along with comments on their love-making habits. So as to sound clinical, Burton wrote in Latin. The publisher, however, wouldn't allow its inclusion, simply noting, "It has been found necessary to omit this Appendix." A few copies with it must have been released, for while doing research for her biography of Burton, Fawn Brodie came across a first edition containing two pages of the appendix. They were translated and published as Appendix 2 in the 1966 version of the book edited by Gordon Waterfield. The descriptions of the practices are quite vivid, as is that for intercourse after marriage. Burton then added, undoubtedly from experience, "There are no harlots in Somaliland: but there are plenty of wives who, because of the inactivity of their husbands, prostitute their bodies without scruple. The man makes his intentions clear by nods, smiles and shameless finger gestures. If the woman smiles, Venus rejoices. Then the fornicator indicates with his fingers the sum he is prepared to pay; the woman replies by a gesture, and both look forward to a suitable occasion. The adulterer always makes for the woman's house; to chat in public at the cross-roads is awkward in daylight, and dangerous at night."[80]

Burton returned to the subject of female genital mutilation in *The Book of the Thousand Nights and a Night*. He defended clitoral excision as the "proper compliment of male circumcision" and also noted that the Somali prostitutes in Aden "always had the labiae and clitoris excised and the skin showing the scars of coarse infibulation," indicating that Burton must have examined them in detail during his sexual escapades. He then remarked, "The moral of female circumcision is peculiar. While it diminishes the heat of passion it increases licentiousness, and breeds a debauchery of mind far worse than bodily unchastity, because accompanied by a peculiar cold cruelty and a taste for artificial stimulants to 'luxury.' It is the sexlessness of a spayed canine imitated by the suggestive brain of humanity."[81] Left unsaid were how he obtained such nonsensical information and the physical damages done to women by the practice.[82]

Despite all the hardships and disappointments endured, Burton's first footsteps in Africa had been taken largely in familiar and beloved circumstances —those of desert conditions occupied by nomads following the dictates of Islam. When he returned much had changed about the lands and peoples visited and, as we'll see, often not to his liking. But there would be an interlude before this happened, and it could have pointed him elsewhere.

3

INTERLUDES AND PREPARATIONS

Burton wearing his Jubah. (Reproduced with the permission of the London Borough of Richmond upon Thames Art Collection, Orleans House Gallery.)

BACK IN LONDON, BURTON'S facial wound healed quickly enough to allow him to read a paper on the journey to Harar before the RGS on June 11. He carried scars, though. The visible one on the left cheek accentuated the uniqueness of his appearance, which to some people now bordered on the sinister. In the late 1860s poet, diplomat, and social activist Wilfrid S. Blunt recalled him looking "dark, cruel, treacherous, with eyes like a wild beast's."[1] Nearly twenty years later Burton's eyes also caught the attention of writer and editor Frank Harris: "His face was bronzed and scarred, and when he wore a heavy mustache and no beard he looked like a prize-fighter; the naked dark eyes—imperious, aggressive eyes, by no means friendly; the heavy jaws and prominent hard chin gave him a desperate air."[2] Inside, the early boost to confidence provided by getting to Harar and back gave way to uncertainty. The RGS talk failed to make much of a stir, not because of its content, rather because of concerns about the direction of the Crimean War, which dominated the news. Harar and Somaliland seemed insignificant by comparison. Also weighing on Burton were accusations that he was responsible for the disaster at Berbera. Some in government and East India Company circles pointed fingers at him, citing poor judgment and planning. As the story went, he and the other officers should have been more cautious, given the unsettled conditions and rumors about the four Europeans being spies for an attempted territorial grab. Coghlan emphasized this in his official report of the incident:

> The reasons adduced by Lieut. Burton for the failure of the expedition are inconsistent; the surprise obviously occurred, less by the fault of his own raw recruits, than by the false security in which the Expedition indulged. To use Lieut. Burton's own words, "they felt no more need of watchfulness than if they had been living at Aden". . . . It may seem harsh to criticize the conduct of these officers, who, to the grief of their wounds and the loss of their property, must be added the total failure of their long-cherished scheme; but I cannot refrain from observing that their whole proceeding is marked by a want of caution and vigilance, which the character of the people amongst whom they dwell, ought to have suggested.[3]

Later interviews with key Somali members of the expedition convinced Coghlan of the rightness of his position on security.[4] He also felt that "plunder" was not the primary reason for the attack, as stressed by Burton. Although further inquiry did support the "plunder" thesis, the matter of lax security measures would not go away. That key people bought it probably explains why Burton's request for a second Somaliland expedition went begging.

Given available options, Burton decided that military service in Crimea offered the best prospects for career advancement. It also provided, he later explained, an "opportunity of recovering my spirits," and so once healthy enough Burton set about "the ungrateful task of volunteering."[5] British tactics and the ineptitude of commanders, most notably Lord Raglan, appalled him, and Burton figured he could help steer things right, although he never mentioned the nature of his plans. When attempts to get a posting from the War Office failed, he headed for Turkey to investigate prospects there.

Time allowed for a quick stop in Boulogne to visit his sister and brother before setting off for Istanbul, where Burton caught a ship headed to Balaklava in order to see about getting a commission in Ottoman forces under British command. He spent a week there talking with people and looking around. Overall, the situation appeared to have improved since his visit in October 1854, when he considered the siege then in progress absurd, since it couldn't be told who was besieging whom. At army headquarters Burton heard about Major-General W. F. Beatson's recent arrival from India. Burton had met Beatson, a soldier-of-fortune type with over thirty years of service in the Bengal army, in Boulogne in 1852. Among other activities, Beatson was forming some four thousand bashi-bazouk (a corruption of the Turkish *Başibozuk*) irregulars into a fighting force called "Beatson's Horse." Renegades and freebooters, mostly from the Balkans, they were currently stationed in the Dardanelles. Burton translated the appellation as *Têtes Pourries*, the equivalent of "Rotten Heads," and described them as "fierce enough and caring little for life." Beatson appointed Burton "chief of the staff" at the rank of captain, although Burton claimed the general recommended him for the position of lieutenant colonel.[6] If so, somewhere along the chain of command the recommendation was shelved, and he remained a captain for the rest of his military career. Beyond his enemies, Burton's lack of money meant that, unlike many others, he couldn't buy a promotion.

The war was actually winding down by this time, and consequently few prospects for advancement via combat existed. As a kind of last hope, Burton claimed he proposed using the bashi-bazouk to relieve the long beleaguered Ottoman fortress of Kars in Armenia. The added tolls taken by famine and cholera had weakened defenses to the point that its fall seemed imminent. Burton readied a force of 2,640 men, but the idea fell on deaf ears. The army wanted nothing to do with irregulars, and Beatson's bluntness on most matters meant he'd also made enemies in high places. More importantly, after considering several relief options, the army decided to abandon Kars to the Russians on November 23, 1855.

An incident involving the bashi-bazouk and Turkish army regulars that nearly resulted in bloodshed led to Beatson being relieved of command. Several appeals on his behalf went nowhere, and sensing Turkey offered little in the way of future prospects, Burton, who some accused of fomenting a mutiny among the bashi-bazouk, resigned. He remained an officer in the Indian army, though, and sailed for London on October 18. Day-by-day details of his time in Turkey are lacking. What we know comes largely from a chapter in *The Life* titled "With Beatson's Horse," but it's silent on such matters as the appalling medical care offered the troops and the Ottoman future, with little said about places visited and people met. McLynn has suggested "dumb horror" over the Sebastopol disaster as the likely cause.[7] Two other explanations that require less psychoanalysis come to mind for this departure from normal behavior: not enough time, given duties, and simple disinterest, since Burton hadn't really accomplished anything of note. The reason or reasons will likely remain a mystery.

Back in England, Burton wrote a strong letter to the *London Times* defending Beatson and the behavior of the bashi-bazouk, something that obviously didn't win him friends among higher-ups.[8] Later, Burton also testified for Beatson at a civil case the general brought against one of his slanderers. He lost on a technicality, although the evidence presented did vindicate him. A more pressing matter for Burton was what to do next, given Turkey's failure to yield anything of value. So, once again, he returned to thinking about a way to solve the Nile puzzle, this time by striking inland from Zanzibar. As Burton informed the RGS, he would make the journey alone—meaning without assistance from other Europeans—if necessary, in the guise of an Arab merchant.[9] The Expedition Committee reacted favorably to the idea and on April 12, 1856, issued a resolution, stipulating that

> not less on the ground of geographical discovery, than for the probable commercial and it may be, political advantages, and the establishment of amicable intercourse with the various tribes, it here be recommended

to the Council to invite the cooperation of Her Majesty's Government and that of the East India Company, in an Expedition from Zanzibar, or its neighborhood, to ascertain in the first instance, the limits of the Inland Sea or Lake known to exist, to record such geographical facts as may be desirable, to determine the exportable products of the country and the ethnography of the tribes. In addition to these advantages, the expedition may lead to the solution of that great geographical problem, the determination of the head source of the White Nile.

It added, "The Committee directs the secretary to write Captain Burton to say that his claims shall be duly considered."[10] The "Inland Sea" referenced came from a map drawn by missionary Jakob Erhardt in 1855 that showed a huge body of water identified as the Uniamesi Sea, or alternatively the Niassa.[11] Because of the sea's shape, it became popularly known as "slug map," while to Burton is was the "Mombas Mission Map." As matters stood, no one knew how many lakes existed in the interior, maybe one, maybe many, and although fantastical, Erhardt's sea raised quite a stir and helped to rekindle interest in discovering the source of the White Nile.

The good news set Burton to work finalizing plans, which he sent off to Shaw a week later.[12] In his usual, thorough way, Burton read everything available on the Nile, including works of classical authors in their original languages, and studied all available maps. However, as the committee resolution indicated, finding something was not sufficient in and of itself. The new empirical science that the RGS promoted required "facts," and this meant making careful measurements, which meant, in turn, carrying a whole array of instruments. This precluded the possibility of traveling incognito, and as a result, Burton could not be a participant-observer as he had been in India and Arabia. Instead, he would be looking at African culture from the outside, and much of the time he didn't try, as we shall see, to look very deeply.

In summarizing events in Africa during the previous year at the RGS Anniversary Meeting on May 26, the society's president, Rear-Admiral F. W. Beechey, told those assembled,

I must not conclude these brief remarks upon this continent without calling your attention to the limited extent of our knowledge of

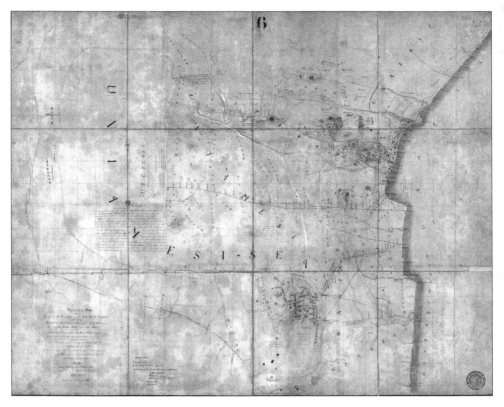

An original draft of Erhardt's "slug map." (Reproduced with permission of the Royal Geographical Society.)

that portion of it known as Equatorial Africa. This extensive region, occupying nearly twenty degrees of latitude and extending from coast to coast . . . still remains a terra incognita . . . and, yet by information from various sources, it seems to present a fruitful field for travellers. The thickly-inhabited towns and large rivers mentioned by the Arabs—the vast inland Sea of Niassa mentioned by Erhardt—alone would immortalize the discoverer who should undertake the task; while the existence of mines of copper and other precious metals in that direction, if true, would bid fair to repay the toil.

He went on to point out that the Nile's source resided within the region and that "the gallant Commander of the expedition from Zayla to Harar, Captain Burton, has volunteered to lead an expedition inland from Zanzibar."[13] The combination of the RGS and Burton illustrates well the "inquisitiveness" and "acquisitiveness" driving so much nineteenth-century exploration.[14]

The RGS agreed to commit a thousand pounds to the expedition to match the sum provided by the Foreign Office and forwarded Burton's proposal to the East India Company in hopes of obtaining an additional thousand.[15] When Bombay finally put its seal of approval on the project in September, it told Burton "you are permitted to be absent from your duties as a regimental officer whilst employed with an Expedition under patronage of Her Majesty's Government, to be dispatched to Equatorial Africa, for exploration of that country, for a period not exceeding two years . . . [and] you are permitted to draw the pay and allowances of your rank during the period of your absence, which will be calculated from the date of your departure from Bombay."[16] On October 1 the RGS gave its final go-ahead, noting, "The great object of the expedition is to penetrate inland from Kilwa, or some other place on the East Coast of Africa, and make the best of your way to the reputed Lake of Nyassa; to determine the position and limits of that lake; to ascertain the depth and nature of its waters and tributaries; to explore the country around it; to acquaint yourself with the tribes and towns on its borders; their minerals and other products of commerce."[17]

Nyassa, or Niassa, was a corruption of the widespread Bantu root *nyanza*, which means something like "large body of water." There would, of course, eventually be a Lake Nyasa, now Lake Malawi, but because of all the confusion that existed at the time about the lakes of eastern and central Africa, the above Nyassa shouldn't be considered one and the same. As for any additional funding, Burton was told, "It is to be most distinctly understood that the Royal Geographical Society will not consider itself responsible for any sums otherwise procured or drawn upon without its express authority, and that the parties drawing such bills will be themselves liable for them." The hoped for thousand pounds from the East India Company never materialized, and that, along with the RGS specifications, would lead to serious problems later on.

A more immediate problem needed resolution. Earlier, Burton had written Speke about joining the expedition. He claimed his sole motive rested with providing him "the opportunity of renewing an attempt to penetrate into Africa" in compensation for the losses, both financial (510 pounds) and personal, incurred at Berbera.[18] Burton's reasoning may have been more complex. He knew Speke was fearless, could do the necessary survey work, and had proved himself a good follower, thus unlikely to contest for leadership. Speke accepted the offer, even though this meant a last-minute cancellation of a hunting trip to the Caucasus Mountains. In addition to the lure of discovery, he still wanted to collect specimens of African animals, and it's likely the thought of finding the source of the Nile lurked in the back of his mind. Since the RGS had instructed Burton to obtain the assistance of someone to take astronomical and meteorological measurements, but the company had not yet given approval for Speke to be that someone, Burton proposed they both go to Bombay to see about getting him appointed.

During his time in London, Burton renewed acquaintances with Isabel Arundell, affectionately called "Puss" for the way she, as a little girl, cocked her head in kitten-like fashion when listening carefully. She was, however, no pussycat, being strong-willed and strong-minded. Burton and Isabel had met by chance six years earlier in Boulogne, and from that time on Isabel obsessed over Burton, hoping against hope to become his wife. She followed newspaper reports of his exploits religiously and later remarked, "I never lost an opportunity of seeing him, when I could not be seen."[19] The family's deep Catholicism and a mother who wanted more for her daughter than the likes of Richard Burton made any kind of relationship difficult. After a few weeks of secret meetings, Burton shocked Isabel by proposing marriage, and without hesitation she said yes, several times over. They set no date beyond it having to come after the expedition. Quite suddenly, without a word to her, Burton left to meet Speke for the trip to Bombay. He had a penchant for suddenly disappearing, and so this was not out of character.

In Cairo, Burton received orders to return to London in order to give testimony at a court-martial of Colonel A. Shirley on matters related to events in the Crimea. He decided not to comply, claiming "the missive was, as usual, so ineptly worded that I did not think proper to throw overboard the Royal Geographical Society—to whom my services had been made over—by obeying it."[20] A response, though, was required. Cleverly, Burton waited to send one from Aden through Steinhaeuser, knowing it would take many weeks to reach London. In the letter, he wrote that if he found an order waiting in Bombay requesting his return, it would, of course, "be instantly and implicitly obeyed." He hoped, though, that he'd taken the "proper course" of action and that if the letter demanding his return had not yet shown up in India upon arrival, he asked to "be permitted to proceed forthwith to Africa."[21] To the RGS, he wrote,

> Were I now to proceed directly from Bombay to England, it is evident that the Expedition which I am undertaking under your direction, must be deferred to a future and uncertain date. With a view to obviate this uncalled-for delay, I have the honour to request that you will use your interest to the effect that, as an officer virtually in your service, I may be permitted to carry out the views of your Society; and that my evidence, which can be of no importance to either prosecutor or defendant in the Court-Martial in question, may be dispensed with.[22]

The journey thus continued, and on November 23 the ship reached Bombay. No recall letter had yet arrived, and in fact, one didn't appear until more than a month later. It specified that for failure to respond to an order the Political Department had suspended authority for the expedition and wanted Burton detained pending further orders.[23] An official investigation into the matter might even be necessary.[24] But it was way too late because eight days after having reached Bombay, Burton and Speke, whose participation had been approved, boarded the Royal Navy sloop *Elphinstone* bound for Zanzibar. Steinhaeuser agreed to join them in Zanzibar later on and become part of the expedition. Two Goan boys, Valentine Rodriguez and Gaetano Andrade, were hired to be personal servants.

Eager anticipation of "to do or die" filled Burton.

> Of the gladdest moments in human life, methinks, is the departure upon a distant journey into unknown lands. Shaking off with one mighty effort the fetters of Habit, the leaden weight of Routine, the cloak of many Cares and the slavery of Home, man feels once more happy. The blood flows with the fast circulation of childhood. Excitement lends unwonted vigour to the muscles, and the sudden sense of freedom adds a cubit to the mental stature. Afresh dawns the morn of

life; again the bright world is beautiful to the eye, and the glorious face of nature gladdens the soul. A journey, in fact, appeals to Imagination, to Memory, to Hope,—the three sister Graces of our moral being.[25]

The chance to sail aboard a spic-and-span man-of-war (such a ship was meant to be a show of force) devoid of annoying passengers added to Burton's pleasure. With time on his hands and nothing to distract attention beyond seabirds, he wrote a long letter to the Royal Geographical Society about conditions in the Red Sea, asking that it be forwarded to the East India Company's Court of Directors or the Foreign Office for private inspection. Two things concerned him most: protecting British interests, most notably lives, and interrupting the slave trade. Toward these ends he advised where and how to best intervene in the region. "With little increase of present expenditure," he observed, "the Red Sea might be effectually commanded."[26]

Fueled by favorable winds and calm waters, the *Elphinstone* moved swiftly, and on December 18 it passed Pemba Island. A sudden drop in the wind required making a landfall on the small island of Tumbatu, where Burton got his first look at one of the many peoples within Zanzibar's jurisdiction. Referred to as Makhádim (serviles) by the ruling Omani Arabs, they depended on fishing for their livelihood and, although Muslims, retained many pre-Islamic practices such as divination. When the ship dropped anchor just offshore of Zanzibar City the next day, the harbor seemed strangely quiet. Once on land the reason why became apparent—Sultan Seyyid Said had unexpectedly died during a voyage from Muscat to Zanzibar. Their arrival coincided with the last day of the required forty for mourning.

Zanzibar was in the midst of an economic boom brought on largely by Said's decision to relocate his headquarters to there from Muscat in 1832. Omani Arabs, profiting from ever-increasing demands for ivory and slaves, had been active along the eastern coast for many decades beforehand. It, thus, made good sense for the sultan to move closer to the sources of supply. According to an Arab saying, "If you play on the flute at Zanzibar, everybody as far as the lakes dances."[27] In time, revenues from clove plantations on nearby Pemba Island and those producing gum copal along the adjacent mainland coast made the decision to move look even wiser.

ZANZIBAR TOWN FROM THE SEA.

Zanzibar town in 1858 as portrayed in The Lake Regions of Central Africa. *(Reproduced with permission of the Special Collections Research Center, Syracuse University Library.)*

Burton's first order of business was to call on the British consul, Lieutenant-Colonel Atkins Hamerton, who'd arrived in May 1841 in the capacity of the East India Company's agent at Muscat. Just fifty-three years old, Hamerton looked to be on his last legs—a "once fair and ruddy" complexion having given way to one "bleached ghastly pale by ennui and sickness."[28] Heavy drinking, a common behavior among the British in Africa, undoubtedly took its toll on the consul's health. Nonetheless, Hamerton refused to leave his post. He planned to endure to the very end and die on the job. Although leery of the expedition's prospects, the colonel took a liking to the two men and offered to help as best he could, once he was convinced that they might succeed. In fact, he wrote a quite positive letter to the authorities in Bombay, saying, "I have every hope of the Mission being able to overcome all difficulties and with the blessing of God to obtain the object in view. I have well prepared the Arabs and the principal men of this place for their reception of the mission and I am very glad to say that I have every reason to believe that I have succeeded in overcoming old prejudices and fears which the people of this country have long entertained of foreigners penetrating into Africa. And as yet all promises well."[29]

At the moment, though, conditions argued against the expedition leaving any time soon. Said had split the sultanate and designated his son Said bin Majid as successor in Zanzibar. Factions, however, gathered around each of the two other surviving sons, and the politics were getting dicey, with war a possibility. If fighting broke out, any hopes of travel would be dashed for quite some time to come. On top of this, smallpox had visited the coast. Majid, himself, was suffering from a mild case, and a serious drought raged in the interior. Porters would thus be hard to find, and with no navigable rivers to follow, they were the primary bearers of commodities in this part of Africa. Although the wiser course of action dictated returning to Bombay, Burton would have none of it, preferring a trip to "Hades" instead.[30]

Still, a wait would be necessary, especially since the onset of the *masika*, or great rains, was imminent. While the masika was likely to break the drought, traveling during it would mean long waits at flooded rivers and wading through large stretches of deep, glue-like mud, along with enduring damp, chilly nights. All things considered, sometime in mid- to late May looked to be the earliest that the journey to the interior could begin. Time therefore existed to explore a place often visited but little known to the outside world. Burton's book on Zanzibar didn't come out until 1872. The package containing the complete manuscript was supposed to be delivered to the Royal Geographical Society but wound up instead in a strongbox at the Bombay branch of the Royal Asiatic Society, where it remained hidden from view for eight years. The alterations Burton subsequently made to the text are fairly easy to discern. The most important concern matters related to Speke and their journey to and from Lake Tanganyika. Also included are comments on some other subsequent events, often inserted for comparative purposes. Then, too, Burton wrote more immediate articles for *Blackwood's Magazine* and the *Journal of the Royal Geographical Society*, and thus, it's possible to reconstruct Burton's observations and views at the time with a reasonable degree of certainty.

His most immediate impression of Zanzibar was that it "seemed wrapped in a soft and sensuous repose," with "no trace of mountain or crag."[31] The island's fertility looked to be so "prodigious " that he believed one could almost see things growing. But such fertility had a downside as well. It produced miasma, a noxious effluvium linked to organic decay, the breathing of which since time immemorial had been thought to cause numerous fatal diseases. Among them was malaria, literally "bad air," here especially common after the rains. It would be a while yet before *plasmodia* and its *anopheles* mosquito vector were discovered as the real culprits in malaria transmission. In addition, syphilis afflicted many of Zanzibar's Africans, with gonorrhea even more prevalent. Ulcers, scabies, and yaws plagued limbs, as did elephantiasis, which also attacked the scrotum. Virtually everyone seemed to suffer from hemorrhoids. Bronchitis became a problem during colder months, and drinking the polluted water brought on attacks of dysentery. As in India Burton recommended port as a precaution, opining that in lands like this one, "a drunkard outlives a water drinker."[32]

As for the city, Burton found it dirty and unkempt. He called the harbor front, "a mere 'dicky,' a clean show concealing uncleanness. . . . Corpses float at times upon the heavy water; the shore is a cess-pool, and the younger blacks of both sexes disport themselves in an absence of costume which would startle even Margate."[33] The corpses he saw were those of slaves who because of illness or physical infirmity were jettisoned at sea in order to avoid paying duty on them. Customary practice also led slave owners to use the beaches as slave burial grounds. Hungry dogs did much of the cleaning up. The native, or African, part of town struck Burton as a "filthy labyrinth, a capricious arabesque of disorderly lanes, and alleys, and impasses, here broad, there narrow; now heaped with offal, then choked with ruins." The poorest lived in "mere sheds," the worst made of palm and without walls, "hardly less wretched than the west Ireland shanty."[34] Ireland often served as a yardstick against which to measure poverty elsewhere, and Burton invoked it often, usually in negative terms, despite the family connection. Even the more prosperous Arab quarter had little to recommend it. "The masonry shows not a single straight line; the floors may have a foot of depression between the middle and corners of the room; whilst no two apartments are on the same level, and they seldom open into each other. Joiner's work and iron-work must be brought in from India."[35]

The above remarks illustrate Burton the critical, but mostly objective, observer at work. He described what he saw and heard, and by all measures beyond its tropical luxuriousness, mid-nineteenth-century Zanzibar hardly qualified as a paradise, even for the rich. This side of Burton can also be seen in overviews of Zanzibar's resources and economy, the workings of government, and general history that filled in knowledge blanks and corrected past misinformation. It was when Burton turned attention to his most favored subject, people, that his other side, a man mired in prejudices, emerged. The roles played by notions of racial/cultural superiority linked to elements of environmental determinism ring loud and clear. For example, he saw the Arabs of Zanzibar as having degenerated owing to the tropical climate and involvement in slavery. The combination made them indolent and "constant" only in their "procrastination." Lying had become a way of life, and when wealthy they displayed "unbridled licentiousness" in which "the sexual requirements of the passive exceed those of the active sex." He claimed the women preferred "Banyans [Hindu Indians] to those of the True Faith, whilst the warmest passions abandon themselves to African slaves."[36] Here Burton contributed to an enduring myth of the tropics— that it was a place where sexual passions run rampant, especially among women. It became an obsession among European men during colonial times to protect their wives and daughters from too close contact with African men. They assumed neither could be trusted to control their desires.

Burton's views of Zanzibar's Arabs were mild compared to his characterizations of the Waswahili, whom he called Sawahili. They appeared to him "the 'foumarts [polecats], not civets,' of the human race" for the "rank foetor" supposedly derived from their black African heritage.[37] Body odor and skin color were widely viewed as correlated, with white milder than black or yellow, this despite the fact that Europeans at the time bathed infrequently, if at all. Color also made the Waswahili an "ugly race," in which even a certain "prettiness" of young girls qualified as *beauté du diable.* Burton proceeded to comment on their facial features: "The national peculiarity is the division of the face into two distinct types, and the contrast appears not a little singular. The upper, or intellectual part, though capped by wooly hair, is distinctly Semitic—with the suspicion of a caricature—as far as the nose-bridge, and the more ancient the family, the more evident is the mixture. The lower, or animal half, especially the nostrils, lip, jaws, and chin is unmistakably African."

He also saw a dual heritage in the people's character. "From the Arab they derive shrewd thinking and practice in concealing thought: they will welcome a man with the determination to murder him; they have unusual confidence, self-esteem, and complacency; fondness for praise, honours, and distinctions; keenness together with short-sightedness in matters of business, and a nameless horror of responsibility and regular occupation." The Africa side supposedly contributed a "comparative freedom from bigotry," a languor that "prevents their becoming fanatics, and proselytizers," and "a sluggish imagination and small powers of concentration." Africa also, in his mind, bequeathed to them "negro duplicity" and lack of honesty. "When they assert they probably lie, when they swear they certainly lie."[38] Burton hadn't had much contact with black Africans at this time, so these comments likely reflect later views.

Characterizations aside, Burton erred in portraying the Waswahili as a mixture of Africans and Arabs. While they imbibe considerable cultural influence, including the adoption of Islam, from the latter, the Waswahili are of African origin, having derived from Bantu-speaking peoples who reached the Kenya coast some 2,500 years ago from western sources. In the centuries afterward, they created a series of coastal trade centers based on the monsoon winds that allowed dhows to ply the waters between this part of Africa and India. The Arab biological contribution was and is minimal. Burton did get the language right, however, calling it "distinctly African" and related to those dialects stretching southward from the equator. Today, it is put within Northeast Coastal Bantu of the wider Niger-Kordofanian grouping.

Burton didn't stop here. The average Mswahili, he said, was "an inveterate beggar" lacking in common sense and forethought.

> When his mind is set upon an acquisition, he becomes a monomaniac, like that child-man, the savage. His nonchalance, carelessness, and improvidence pass all bounds. He will light his pipe under a dozen leaky kegs of gunpowder; he will set a house on fire, as it were, to roast his eggs; he will wreck his ship because anchoring her to the beach saves trouble in loading; he might make his coast a mine of wealth, but he will not work till hunger compels him, and his pure insouciance has allowed his valuable commerce to be wrested from him by Europeans, Hindus, and Arabs.

Furthermore, "In disposition the Msawahili is at once cowardly and destructive: his quarrelsome temper leads him into trouble, but he fights only by being brought to bay. Sensual and degraded, his self-indulgence is that of the brutes. He drinks and always to excess. He would stake and lose his mother at play. Chastity is unknown in this land of hot temperaments—the man places paradise in the pleasures of the sixth sense, and the woman yields herself to the first advances." Burton undoubtedly could speak from experience about women yielding. As for the Waswahili's good points, he could only find "careless merriment, an abundance of animal spirits; strong attachments and devoted family affection" as worthy of note.[39]

The wait for the westward journey to begin also led Burton to plan a "preparatory visit" to the mainland coast to survey the main ports. In addition, some useful information about the difficulties of the journey ahead might be picked up.[40] The Europeans in Zanzibar knew nothing about the mainland, and after getting an earful from the Arabs and Waswahili, Burton labeled the information "worse than none."[41] As he later commented, the trip did show them that when traveling by caravan in East Africa, one "must ever be prepared for three distinct departures—the little start, the great start, and the start."[42] That Africans lacked a concept of time would become mantra among Europeans who worked with them. Of course, what they lacked was a linear sense of time based on the clock.

Burton also wanted to visit Rebmann. Leaders of the Church Missionary Society in London had granted him permission to join the expedition, but so far no word one way or the other had been forthcoming. Through the intercession of Hamerton, Majid willingly provided a *firman* to guarantee safe passage among his subjects. In general, the sultan approved of Burton and Speke's plans, in spite of concerns among some of his subjects about Europeans cutting into their trade monopoly. Majid also lent thirteen Baluchi *askari* (soldiers) for purposes of protection and supplied ten slaves to serve as carriers. Originally immigrants to Muscat from Baluchistan, the Baluchi, whom Burton knew from India, dabbled in a number of activities, thievery being a prominent one. They then became soldiers of a sort in the service of the sultan and added Arabs, Afghans, and other renegades to their ranks, which brought their numbers under Zanzibar authority to upward of a thousand. Placed at strategic locations here and there, they mostly lived off what they could extort. The Arabs along the coast held them in contempt. Burton concurred, calling them a "rabble rout," no more than a "tame copy of the Turkish Bashi Buzuk," who "live the life of the Anglo-Indian soldier of the past generation, drinking beer when they can 'come by it,' smoking, chatting, and arguing; the younger wrestle, shoot, and exchange kit; and the silly babbling patriarchs, with white beards and venerable brows, tell wondrous tales of scenes long gone by, and describe to unbelieving ears the ice and snow, the luscious fruits and sweet waters of the mountains and valleys of far Balochistan."[43]

In return for the favors, Burton promised not to try to convert anyone to Christianity, hardly a concession on his part. Earlier, Omani Said bin Salim el Lamki had been appointed by Majid to serve as *kirangozi*, or guide, both for this trip and the longer one to come. Although Said did not appear to be the strongest of men, Burton felt someone like him would provide the expedition an air of "respectability," as he reputedly knew many people in important positions. Said, for his part, didn't want the job but could hardly refuse an order from the sultan. The two Goan boys rounded out the party.

During the evening of January 4, 1857, they all boarded the rickety, vermin-infested *Riámi*, manned by a crew of misfits picked up in the bazaar. Towed behind was an ironclad boat called *Louisa*, named after Isabel's cousin Louisa Segrave (née Buckley), whom Burton had fallen for in Boulogne. Twenty feet long and divided into seven sections of forty pounds each, she was intended to be of use on rivers and lakes. A review of supplies revealed that neither water nor wood had been loaded, and thus they had to wait for deliveries the next morning before sailing away. Various delays cost a further day and night. Another interruption quickly followed when strong headwinds from the northeast monsoon forced taking refuge for several days in a safe cove only a few miles from Zanzibar City. During the interlude, Burton visited a nearby village. He found it "mostly tenanted by women who hid themselves, by children who ran away, and by slave-girls who squatted, combing and plaiting one another's locks; these grinned merrily enough, having nought to fear. The faces were hideous to look upon, with black, coarse skins, scarred and seamed by small-pox; huge mouths, and rolling eyes. Not a few were lame and toothless."[44]

Ignoring still rough seas, they set off and reached Pemba Island on January 10. Local legend proclaimed it to be where William "Captain" Kidd buried his gold and jewels in 1698. People have from time to time found pots filled with gold lumps, most likely formed from naval coat buttons. The real treasure has never been unearthed here or in any of the many others places it's been thought to be. The "wondrous fertility of the land" impressed Burton even more than Zanzibar's. Everything seemed to grow in abundance. But, as on Zanzibar, diseases ran rampant: "hydrocele is a plague, and the population is decimated by small-pox, dumb agues, and bilious fevers."[45]

Once again when at sea, inclement weather slowed progress to a crawl, and they didn't reach their destination of Mombasa until January 16. Burton described the voyage as a miserable one aboard "a cranky old tub half manned by a useless, careless crew, beating against and often taken aback by half a gale, with a strong current setting the wrong way."[46]

Situated on a small coral island just a stone's throw from the mainland and with safe harborage, Mombasa had developed into an important Indian Ocean trade center. Ibn Batuta paid a visit in 1330 and had only good things to say about the town, noting that "the inhabitants are pious, honorable, and upright, and they have well-built wooden mosques."[47] Vasco da Gama sailed into the harbor in 1498 and found a city with beautiful gardens, well-constructed buildings, and a wealthy ruling class. A century later the Portuguese built Fort Jesus as part of their effort to control the East African coast from Somaliland to Mozambique. All that they really managed to do with their violent, heavy-handed approach, which involved burning Mombasa three times, was disrupt commerce, and in 1729 Portugal lost the fort for good. Today its ruins house a museum. When Seyyid Said came to power, he sought to control Mombasa, and this set off years of conflict with the city's longtime Mazrui rulers, who'd profited mightily from the slave trade. In 1823 the British intervened and hoisted the Union Jack, but took it down three years later. This provided Burton with another opportunity to criticize government policy. According to him, had it not been withdrawn, "the whole interior would now be open to us. But such is the history of Britain the Great: hard won by blood and gold, her conquests are parted with for a song."[48] In any event, by the time he and Speke appeared on the scene, Mombasa had been brought within Zanzibar's sphere of influence, and peace more or less prevailed.

Still, it looked more like a village than emporium to Burton, and he found the inhabitants, estimated at about eight thousand, less than welcoming. "These people are taxed by other Arabs with overweening pride, insolence of manner, bigotry and evil-speaking, turbulence and treachery. The habits of pilfering are inveterate; few travellers have failed to miss some valuable. All seemed to regard us as rivals and enemies. They devoted energy to the task of spoiling us, and failing that, they tried insolence."[49] At one point, Burton said he had to draw his sword to get down a flight of stairs jammed with hostiles.[50]

He and Speke didn't tarry long, boarding canoes early the next morning for the trip across the channel that separated the island from the mainland. Once on the other side, they followed a twisting stream to reach the trail leading to the Mombasa mission station in the nearby Rabai Hills. They spent seven hours journeying ten miles on water and then walked five more miles before they reached their destination. The Rebmanns greeted them warmly, and during conversation the reverend mentioned that the letter from the Church Missionary Society had yet to reach him. While at first he was enthusiastic about joining the expedition, health reasons caused him to decline participating, much to Burton's relief. As he informed Shaw,

> I have been strongly advised by Colonel Atkins Hamerton, H.B.
> M.'s Consul, by whose long experiences and friendly council I have
> been and shall be guided in all points, on no account to associate this
> missionary with the expedition. He suffers from enlarged spleen, he is
> unfit for walking and hard work. He has never used a gun and he is
> ignorant of the language and localities beyond Mombas. Finally, though
> I have the highest respect for Mr. Rebmann, his presence would give
> a missionary semblance to the Expedition and prove a real calamity.
> Certain unwarrantable political interferences on the part of Revd. Dr.
> Krapf have rendered the estimable body to which he belongs particularly
> unpopular at Zanzibar.[51]

The route from Mombasa to the interior looked to be the most direct one to the supposed location of the Mountains of Moon and the great sea. Rebmann urged the party not to go this way because it passed through country under Maasai control. Their *moran* (warriors) would almost certainly attack a small, lightly armed caravan. For protection, some that crossed their lands numbered up to a thousand men. In fact, moran were currently in the vicinity raiding for cattle, and the two travelers got a close-up look at what they would be facing. Speke, though, felt they could get through and later considered the failure to strike across Maasailand a mistake. As events transpired, he was probably right.

Drought and concomitant lack of provisions scotched plans to visit Mt. Kilimanjaro, which had yet to be scaled and thus remained a mystery. For example, a then-current legend proclaimed the existence of a Portuguese-made image of a woman with long hair holding a child in her arms somewhere on the slopes.[52] No such image has ever been found, and it's unlikely that the Portuguese ever made it to Kilimanjaro. In any event, Burton told the RGS that going there was out of the question. "Indeed it is to be feared that the entrance to Chaga, Kilimanjaro, and the hill country around, will now be closed for many years. Caravans dare not face a contest of professed plunderers, and a successful raid hereabouts always leads to divers repetitions. Such is the normal state of East Africa, from the Red Sea to the Cape. The traveller never can be sure of finding any particular road open to him—a few deaths will shut it for years and stop the explorer at the threshold of his explorations."[53]

Traders had recently found a new route to the interior through Ukambani to the fertile highlands of the Wakikuyu. Burton, however, didn't see its prospects as all that great. "But let not geographers indulge in golden visions of the future! Some day the Arabs of Mombas will seize and sell a caravan, or the fierce Galla will prevail against it. Briefly, no spirit of prophecy is needed to predict that the Kikuyu line will share the fate of many others."[54]

A hundred men with matchlocks and five thousand pounds in cash would probably provide for a secure journey, but Burton's party had neither. Besides, provisions had to be spared for the exploration awaiting them. Later Burton would be criticized by mapmaker Augustus Petermann for failing to go where missionaries went without weapons. Burton responded in a humorous vein: "This gentleman from Germany had visited England, and had created for himself the title of 'Physical Geographer to the Crown': when, however, no salary was the result, he returned to his native land, declaring that the Crown must take its geography without physic."[55]

The small party left the mission on January 22 for a quick return to Mombasa. As a result, Burton had only passing contact with the Wanyika, a name encompassing nine small, closely affiliated Bantu-speaking groups on the mainland adjacent to Mombasa. *Nyika* means something like barren land or even desert, which is what the Waswahili perceived the countryside to be. Most of Burton's information about the Wanyika came from Rebmann, and while reasonably accurate on matters like dress and age grade organization, in other instances the "facts" presented were either wrong and/or wrapped in prejudice. For example, after remarking on the Wanyika's physical appearance he concluded that the man's "figure is, like his features, Semitic above and Negritic below." To him the contrast was especially noticeable among the women, whose "haunches" appeared as those of the "Medician Venus," whereas the face was "hideous" and "wrinkled."[56] Of course, people with diverse genetic backgrounds don't come out neatly divided into parts, and whatever non-negroid characteristics the Wanyika showed came from intermixture with people like the Somali and Oromo, whom, as seen earlier, Burton misjudged as Semitic, which is a language not a genetic grouping, in any case. As for character, he summed them up as "a futile race of degraded men, drunken, destructive, cowardly, boisterous, immoral, indolent, and improvident."[57] Did Rebmann really tell him that?

The return to Zanzibar began on January 24, the winds and currents this time favoring passage. The first stop was Wasin Island, which Burton described as being populated by a "bigoted and evil-minded race, a collection of lymphatic Arabs, hideous Sawahili, ignoble half-castes, and thievish slaves."[58] After a few more quick calls that yielded little of interest, they reached Tanga, an important trade center of four to five thousand inhabitants. The town put on a cordial reception, topped off by an *ngomakhu*, or grand celebration of music and dance. Various delays kept them in place for six days, and during the interlude, Burton visited the nearby ruins of an old Arab settlement, then used by the locals for penning their livestock. Reverting to previous practice, he dressed as an Arab to wander inconspicuously through the market at Amboni, where people from far and wide came to trade livestock, grains, ghee, blue cottons, fish, spices, and metal wares.

Early in the morning of February 2 the party slowly coasted southward. Numerous villages lined the shore, as did abandoned settlements with the remains of houses, cemeteries, and inscribed tombs, a paradise for archaeologists. The next day they reached Pangani, the starting point for a journey to Fuga, the royal capital of the Washambaa Kingdom in the Usambara Mountains, another place said to be forbidden to strangers, this time supposedly because the king's wives lived there. Visiting Fuga would have to do as an adventure for now, as they simply didn't have the resources to engage in any real exploration. Nonetheless, Burton's mood seems to have improved after he left Wasin Island, for he rhapsodized over the scene that graced his eyes early the next morning. Of course, in this instance he was commenting on the landscape, not people.

> The vista of the river—with low coco-groves to the north, tall yellow cliffs to the southern side, a distance of blue hill, the broad stream bounded by walls of verdure, and the azure sea, dotted with diobolites, or little black rocks—wanted nothing but the finish and polish of art to bring out the infinitude and rude magnificence of nature. A few donjon-ruins upon the hills would enable it to compare with the most admired prospects of the Rhine, and with a half-a-dozen white kiosks, minarets, and latticed summer-houses, it would almost rival that gem of creation, the Bosphorus.[59]

Pangani with three surrounding villages housed about four thousand people, many of them slaves, the majority being women serving various domestic needs. Its Indian residents profited greatly from caravans bringing ivory, rhinoceros horns, and hippopotamus teeth from the interior. More dangerous game lurked nearby, as demonstrated during the party's short stay when a leopard took a slave girl and a crocodile made off with a young boy. Another problem involved attacks in the hinterland by the Wazigula, whom Burton called a "violent and turbulent race."[60] Locals advised him and Speke to take a circuitous route to Fuga, rather than the direct one following the Pangani River, which went through Wazigula territory. But wanting to explore the river, he and Speke, with a small party, set off secretly on February 6.

Crocodiles and hippopotamuses infested the waters, and silence reigned as Burton and Speke slowly made their way upstream. After a little more than thirteen miles the party left the river to visit the Baluchi garrison at Chogwe. Why one existed here puzzled Burton, given the poor soils, endemic sickness, and lack of a nearby source of freshwater. Furthermore, the Wazigula hardly

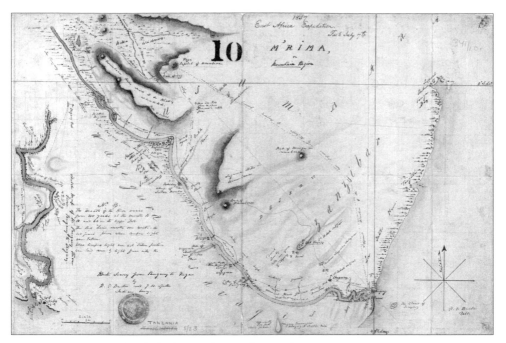

Speke's draft of a map showing the route from Pangani to Fuga.
(Reproduced with permission of the Royal Geographical Society.)

appreciated the garrison's presence and launched occasional attacks to show their feelings. The Baluchi themselves didn't bother to fight, handing that task over to slaves. Burton felt that "a few stout fellows, with a competent leader and a little money for good arms and ammunition, might easily establish an absolute monarchy" over the area.[61]

From Chogwe the track went through difficult country marked by a succession of ridges, dense thickets, and hordes of biting ants. At night, swarms of mosquitoes did their best to make life miserable. Disputes with the men arose, and every so often a carrier dropped out. At one point Burton and Speke got separated from the rest of the party. Shots and shouts brought no response, and as night fell it became obvious that they couldn't wander around hoping to be reunited. A decision to retrace their steps early the next morning produced success. Burton remarked that "after shaking hands all around, and settling sundry small disputes about the right and the wrong, we spread our mats in the grateful shade and made up for the past with tea and tobacco."[62]

The farther they went, the more populous the countryside became. The path was crowded at times with market women. When on one occasion a Baluchi asked several of them if they would like white men for husbands, the women adamantly replied no.[63] In addition to being strange looking, Burton and Speke had nothing of real value to offer them.

On February 15 the party began an arduous climb up the steep eastern face of the Usambaras, and before the end of the day, Fuga, an unwalled town of some five hundred huts, came into view. No entrance could take place without royal permission, and thus they settled down to wait. Late in the afternoon three ministers arrived to find out why the men had come. Once the ministers were satisfied that they harbored no ill intent, Burton and Speke, accompanied by three Baluchi, were allowed to enter Fuga. King Kimwere, known as Simba wa Mwene, literally "the Lion Himself," welcomed them personally. Older than old, he hardly looked lionlike with an "emaciated frame, shaven head, beardless wrinkled face, somewhat like an elderly lady, red eyes, toothless jaws, and hands and feet stained with leprous spots."[64] Judging by his proclaimed three hundred wives and ninety sons (daughters weren't counted), he must have been quite vigorous in his younger days. With a substantial musket-armed bodyguard at his disposal, Kimwere firmly held the reins of power. As a sign of friendship, he arranged a feast, including a bullock that quickly turned into steaks for the party's men. They ate with such gusto, according to Burton, "that unpleasant symptoms presently declared themselves in camp."[65]

Fuga was as far as they would go. Rain poured down barring further travel into the mountains, and so after just two nights the coastward return began. According to Burton, Kimwere was devastated by their departure. He said that he had expected a white *mganga* (doctor) to bring him a life-extending potion. Now two white men had come but would leave without giving him one. His case, Burton remarked, went "far beyond" what skills they had.[66] As it turned out, Kimwere was still around more than a decade later.

The way down the Usambaras proved harder than the way up, mostly because it rained in torrents. Moving as quickly as possible, they reached Chogwe on February 20 with everyone famished and fatigued to the bone. Since Krapf had previously followed the same basic trail, there were no new discoveries to report. Burton, though, did add more details about the countryside and its inhabitants

Looking toward Fuga as portrayed in Zanzibar: City, Island, and Coast. *(Reproduced with permission of the Special Collections Research Center, Syracuse University Library.)*

and corrected some errors, mostly of distances, in his report to the RGS. As regards the Usambaras, he deemed it bountiful country, suitable for European settlers. They did come during colonial times, but not in great numbers. The Washambaa struck Burton as industrious for Africans, which he attributed to the bracing effects of a cool mountain climate. Still, he called them a "moody, melancholy brood, a timid, dismal and ignoble race, as indeed are for the most part those barbarians who have exchanged pastoral for agricultural life."[67] Once again, Burton let physical features, like somewhat lighter skin color and white hair in the elders, lead him astray, feeling these indicated the Washambaa being "abundantly leavened with Arab blood."[68]

Burton's writings also fed a European theme that romanticized African cattle herders like the Maasai. Tall and proud behind spears and shields, they represented the mythical noble savages who disdained the softness of villagers, much like his beloved Bedouin Arabs. This allowed them, in the prevailing view, to dominate presumed lesser folk. While the Maasai did raid settled communities for cattle and women, they fought mostly among themselves for control of prime grazing lands. They were not overlords, as they lacked institutions that would allow them to govern others.

Earlier, good fortune led to the hiring of Seedi Mubarak, more commonly called "Bombay," as a gun bearer.[69] A Yao from near Lake Malawi, he'd been enslaved when a teenager. Sold at Kilwa and taken to India, Bombay later gained freedom, went to Zanzibar, and joined a Baluchi unit near Tanga. Burton paid off Bombay's debts so that he could join the expedition. With a modicum of Hindustani at his command, he served as Speke's primary assistant. Bombay would become a fixture on exploring expeditions in East Africa, working in years to come for the likes of Henry Morton Stanley and Verney Lovett Cameron, among others.

The boat for Zanzibar wasn't due for a while, and so Speke organized a hippo hunt that turned into what might better be called a killing frenzy. The Baluchi and Wasegeju did, though, appreciate the bounty of meat from the many carcasses left behind. With nothing more to amuse them at Chogwe, Burton and Speke headed for Pangani on February 26 to wait for the boat. Within a few days both suffered attacks of malaria, a seasoning according to the prevailing view that would make subsequent attacks less severe. This turned out to be another myth. Burton left a fairly graphic account of the symptoms he experienced:

> Our attacks commenced with general languor and heaviness, a lassitude in the limbs, a weight in the head, nausea, a frigid sensation creeping up the extremities, and dull pains in the shoulders. Then came a mild, cold fit, succeeded by a splitting headache, flushed face, full veins, vomiting, and an inability to stand upright. . . . The eyes become hot, heavy, and painful when turned upwards; the skin is dry and burning, the pulse full and frequent, and the tongued furred; appetite is wholly wanting (for a whole week I ate nothing), but a perpetual craving thirst afflicts the patient, and nothing that he drinks will remain in his stomach. During the day extreme weakness causes anxiety and depression; the nights are worse, for by want of sleep the restlessness is aggravated. Delirium is common in the nervous and

bilious temperament, and if the lancet be used, certain death ensues; the action of the heart cannot be restored.[70]

Malaria wasn't all they suffered from. According to Burton, "Repose was out of the question. During the day, flies and gnats added another sting to the horrors of fever. At night rats nibbled at our feet, mosquitoes sang their song of triumph, and torturing thirst made the terrible sleeplessness yet more terrible."[71]

By the time the boat showed up early on March 6, Speke could walk to it by himself, whereas Burton "was obliged to be supported like a bedridden old woman."[72] Their conditions put an end to further surveying work along the coast, and later that day they were back in Zanzibar. Rest there and heavy doses of quinine (only recently discovered as a palliative for malaria) helped each recover his health. Burton's favorite concoction was Warburg's Drops, which added opium to the quinine. Continuing rains actually proved a godsend, as they allowed preparations for the expedition to move at a leisurely pace. The interlude also gave Burton time to further his study of Kiswahili. They would need it along trade routes. Speke didn't make an effort and remained essentially monolingual. Burton also spent much time writing, most of it devoted to the Zanzibar book manuscript.

During the wait Burton paid another visit to the mainland, this time at the behest of the Bombay Geographical Society. Members were particularly interested in gum copal, an important component of varnishes and lacquers. Lately production had fallen off, making prices dear. To see what might be done about this, Burton left with Bombay and Said bin Salim for Sadani, a village on the mainland directly across from Zanzibar on May 11. Said had once been its mayor, and they thus received a warm welcome. The fossilized resins from the tree *Trachylobium verrucosum* that form East Africa's version of gum copal are mined from coastal sands, and after surveying the situation, Burton concluded production increases would require major changes, including an infusion of workers from elsewhere, something the sultan would not permit at this time. Maybe later, Burton thought. Although that never happened, the industry did develop, and today Tanzania is an important exporter of gum copal.

As he would often do, Burton sent his friend and confidant Richard Monckton Milnes, later Lord Houghton, a letter designed both to amuse and to make a point. This time he noted, "One of the tribes through which we pass I am delighted to say are real bona fide cannibals. It is one of my pet ambitions to see a man eaten: next to that a tribe of bona fide naked humans. The eating we may see; the nakedness I fear not. Curse American loin cloths!"[73]

Rain finally stopped falling the first week of June. The time for the journey inland had come, which set in motion a fury of last-minute activities. But the expedition wouldn't have the services of Steinhaeuser. A bout of illness set him back, and then an outbreak of cholera in Aden further delayed his departure. With no boat scheduled any time soon from there to Zanzibar, he went to Berbera intent on marching along the coast. By then it was too late to reach Burton and Speke in time, so Steinhaeuser reluctantly decided to turn back. This meant no doctor along to treat injuries and illnesses and the two men having to foot the responsibilities of overseeing the expedition themselves. In the end, it all proved to be too much and, as a result, changed the course of each man's life in ways never anticipated. For Burton, at least, the change turned out to be mostly for the worst.

4

A TALE OF TWO LAKES

BURTON AND SPEKE DEPARTED Zanzibar for the short trip to the mainland aboard Majid's slow but steady corvette *Artémise* at midday on June 16, 1857. The sultan saw them off and provided three letters of introduction to subjects in the interior in order to ensure their full cooperation. Two African gun bearers, Bombay for Speke and Muinyi Mabruki for Burton, eight Baluchi guards, and the two Goan boys rounded out the party.

Hamerton warned against using Kilwa as the point of departure because the town was only nominally under the sultan's jurisdiction and he had no authority over the Wayao, who controlled the hinterland. Safety, therefore, could not be guaranteed. Better, therefore, to start from the coast immediately west of Zanzibar, and so the *Artémise* anchored off Wale Point to allow for final arrangements to be made at the small village of Kaole, a few miles south of the main caravan depot at Bagamoyo.

The plan called for following the well-trodden route to the trade center of Unyanyembe, one of several chiefdoms comprising Unyamwezi, meaning "land of the moon." How it got that name is a mystery. There's certainly nothing lunar about a landscape composed mainly of homes, agricultural fields, and woodlands. Building upon earlier experiences in regional long-distance trade, the Wanyamwezi had formed the bulk of the porters working the route since the 1840s. For young men the job provided a way to earn bride price, and many stayed at it longer in order to supplement household wealth. Some eventually ran their own caravans, and it's highly unlikely that significant trade to the coast would have been possible without the labors of the Wanyamwezi.[1]

Mnyamwezi ivory porter as portrayed in The Lake Regions of Central Africa. *(Reproduced with permission of the Special Collections Research Center, Syracuse University Library.)*

Said bin Salim had arrived earlier to round up the 170 porters Burton judged the expedition required, but there weren't many takers when word spread that a *mzungu* ("white person," in Kiswahili) would be in charge. In some African cultures a white skin signified ghost, in others an unwelcome creature from the sea, a natural enough conclusion given how Europeans reached the continent. In the end, only thirty-six Wanyamwezi signed on. With so few bodies, many of the goods, including ammunition and the boat, were placed in the hands of Indian merchants for a later shipment to be carried by twenty-two additional porters. The boat never did make it, and months passed before the remaining supplies were forwarded on. To haul everyday needs, and for riding when necessary, Burton managed, by hook or crook, to come up with thirty donkeys.

Despite being on death's door, Hamerton accompanied them to Wale Point and kept the *Artémise* at anchor for two weeks so that Burton and Speke might have more comfortable quarters during preparations. He also said the boat would remain there for a few days after the expedition departed to make sure it got off to a safe start. Hamerton unfortunately died shortly after the party's departure. Burton said the venture would never have been possible without all the support and assistance the colonel provided. He'd treated the two travelers almost like sons, and upon hearing the news of his death, Burton eulogized, "He was a loss to his country, an excellent linguist, a ripe oriental scholar, and a valuable public servant of the old Anglo-Indian school; he was a man whose influence over Easterns, based upon their respect for his honour and honesty, his gallantry and determination, knew no bounds; and at heart a 'sad good Christian,'—the Heavens be his bed!"[2]

In East Africa, people often received the names they became known by from others. The Waswahili called those occupying the maritime region opposite Zanzibar Wamrima, which basically means coastal inhabitants. They weren't so much one as a congeries of groups that had come under Waswahili and Arab influences. Burton wasn't impressed. He called them "an ill-conditioned race" that "spend life in eating, drinking, and smoking, drinking and dancing, visits, intrigue, and low debauchery." Furthermore,

> With them the lie is no mental exertion, no exercise of ingenuity, no concealment, nor mere perversion of the truth: it is apparently a local instinctive peculiarity in the complicated madness of poor human nature. The most solemn and religious oaths are with them empty words; they breathe an atmosphere of falsehood, manoeuvre, and contrivance, wasting about the mere nothings of life—upon a pound of grain or a yard of cloth—ingenuity of iniquity enough to win a crown. And they are treacherous as false; with them the salt has no signification, and gratitude is unknown even by name.[3]

True to form, the distaff side of the population caught Burton's eye. "Many girls," he noted, "have a pretty piquancy, a little minois chiffonné, a coquettishness, a natural grace, and a caressing look, which might become by habit exceedingly prepossessing." However, "in later life, their charms assume that peculiar solidity which is said to characterise the beauties of Mullingar, as a rule they are shockingly ugly." To make his point stronger, Burton went on to modify a Castilian proverb—"the English woman should be seen at the window,

the French woman on the promenade, and the Spanish woman everywhere"—
to include "the African woman should be seen nowhere, or in the dark."[4]

Uncooperative Indian merchants made every transaction difficult. They
feared Europeans might become competitors and thereby cut into their profits,
and hoping to scare off Burton and Speke, told them stories about the horrors
that awaited in the interior.

> We were warned that for three days we must pass through savages,
> who sat on the trees, and discharged poison arrows into the air with
> extraordinary dexterity (meaning the Amazons); that they [the men]
> must avoid trees (which was not easy in a land all forest); that the
> Wazaramo had sent . . . several letters forbidding the white man to enter
> their country, and that they buried their provisions in the jungle, that
> travellers might starve; that one rhinoceros kills two hundred men; that
> armies of elephants attack camps by night; that the craven hyaena is
> more dangerous than a Bengal tiger.[5]

One certain danger, malaria, awaited, and with the rains having just ended,
they were setting out when the risk of exposure was greatest. As usual, Burton
dismissed warnings about this and other dangers, and furthermore, both he and
Speke had had their "seasoning." The threat, thus, seemed minimal.

Burton left Kaole on June 27 for Kingani to rendezvous with Speke,
who'd gone ahead with a contingent of porters. Only about ninety minutes
away, it would be the final staging point before the caravan began its journey
to Unyanyembe, where they could resupply for the march to the Sea of Ujiji, as
the Nyassa was now generally called. By this point in time Burton and Speke
were quite confident that more than one lake existed in the interior. Ludha
Ramji, a Banyan who served as Zanzibar's customs master, provided ten slaves
to the expedition. He called them his "sons," and so they became "sons of
Ramji" to Burton. In point of fact, they weren't true slaves, rather individuals
who'd been pawned by kinsmen to pay debts. Each of the "sons" received six
months' salary in advance, with the balance to come at the end of the journey
or when their services were no longer needed. Ramji took half-shares for debt
payments. Burton was sensitive to the fact that slaves would form part of the
caravan. As he explained it,

I had no power to prevent Said bin Salim, the Baloch escort, and the "sons of Ramji," purchasing whomever they pleased; all objections on my part were overruled by, "we are allowed by our law to do so," and by declaring that they had the permission of the consul. I was fain to content myself with seeing that their slaves were well fed and not injured, and indeed I had little trouble in so doing, as no man was foolish enough to spoil his own property. I never neglected to inform the wild people that Englishmen were pledged to the suppression of slavery, and I invariably refused all slaves offered as return presents.[6]

The hiring of five additional guards, a tailor boy, and five donkey tenders brought the final party to nearly a hundred members, which also included women to provide for the men's domestic and sexual needs. In a pinch, they also helped carry loads and proved useful at gaining information during stops. The thirty-six Wanyamwezi porters with two of the "sons" had been sent on ahead. The rendezvous would occur at a place called Zungomero, where up and down caravans reprovisioned owing to the bounty of grain available.[7] As noted previously, plans called for an ethnographic survey of the lake region and identifying products for export. Should they find the source of the Nile in the process, the return might be downriver. If not, crossing Africa to the western coast before returning to England remained a possibility.

Sweltering heat and hordes of mosquitoes made for an unpleasant stay at Kingani. It took most of the day on the thirtieth to get under way, and so they spent only an hour and a half on the road before stopping. The Baluchi proved to be a major headache. They didn't want to move and resented working for infidel Europeans. (Unbeknownst to them, Burton could understand their conversations.) Then as soon as they got under way again, men began deserting. Dense stands of grass over ten feet high and jungle-like tangles of bushes served as effective hideaways for those stealing off. "The fickle and inconsequent negro slave must," Burton later said, "run away once in his life." As for the free porters, "they disappear en masse if commons wax short, if loads be too heavy, if a fight be threatened, or if wasting ammunition be forbidden."[8] All told, Burton described overseeing the caravan something akin to "driving a herd of wild cattle."[9]

The main trunk road went southwestward following the Ruvu River Valley, also at the time called the Kingani. It led into Uzaramo and the beginning of *honga*, the price demanded for passage. Depending on preferences, the products could be cotton cloth, beads, copper wire, or some combination, and each change of territorial control required new negotiations. Burton considered the African desire for such articles childlike. As he put it,

> The African preserves the instincts of infancy in the higher races. He astonished the enlightened De Gama some centuries ago by rejecting with disdain jewels, gold, and silver, whilst he caught greedily at beads and other baubles, as a child snatches at a new plaything. To the present day he is the same. There is something painfully ludicrous in the expression of countenance, the intense and all-absorbing admiration and the greedy wistfulness with which he contemplates the rubbish. Yet he uses it as a toy . . . and then, child-like, weary of the acquisition, he will do his best to exchange it for another.[10]

As noted, the image of Africans as children would become a standard of imperial/colonial discourse and the need to raise them to adulthood integral to the "white man's burden."

The appearance of so-called fetish houses indicated entry into non-Muslim Africa, the land of the Washenzi, meaning "barbarians" or the "uncivilized," according to "the Faithful." The area teemed with malaria, and Speke, despite "seasoning," came down with a bad case. Because of the fever few people lived along the lower reaches of the river. Their places had been taken by lions and hyenas, the latter of which feasted on the donkeys, especially those from Zanzibar, when tethered for the night. The less tame donkeys from Unyamwezi had better luck fending off attacks with potentially skull-shattering kicks. Their feistiness also made them difficult to manage. "The asses, shy, stumble, rear, run away, fight, plunge and pirouette when mounted; they hog and buck till they burst their girths; they love to get into holes and hallows; they rush about like pigs when the wind blows; they bolt under tree-shade when the sun shines; so they have to be led, and if the least thing happens the slave drops the halter and runs away."[11]

On July 6 they stopped for two nights to take on provisions, as reports indicated none might be available for the coming week. To the Arabs it was "the

Valley of Death and the Home of Hunger."[12] On the ninth, a large contingent of Wazaramo warriors suddenly appeared along the path. Contrary to what Indians had said, the men did no more than silently gaze at the passing strangers. Burton found them almost noble looking. "I could not but admire," he said, "the athletic and statuesque figures of the young warriors and their martial attitude, grasping in one hand their full-sized bows, and in the other sheaths of grinded arrows, whose black barbs and necks showed a fresh layer of poison."[13] The Wazaramo also appeared rich compared to their neighbors: Men and women dressed well in cottons, and the houses reminded Burton of Anglo-English bungalows or a "humbler sort of English cow-house." Despite this, he called the Wazaramo "an ill-conditioned, noisy, boisterous, violent, and impracticable race."[14] Such a characterization and much of what Burton told readers about their culture could have come only from informants, as he had no more than a passing acquaintance with them.

Wearily they trudged on, with both Burton and Said bin Salim joining Speke on the malaria rolls. Donkeys had to be used for carrying the three of them, which meant burdening the others with heavier loads. A cloud of despair hovered over Burton. "The new life, the alternations of damp heat and wet cold, the useless fatigue of walking, the sorry labour of waiting and re-loading the asses, the exposure to sun and dew, and last, but not least, the wear and tear of mind at the prospect of imminent failure, all were beginning to tell heavily on me."[15]

The trail passed near the spot where French navy officer M. Maizan lost his life in 1845. On a personal quest to be the first European to explore the interior lake or lakes, Maizan stayed eight months in Zanzibar to study Kiswahili before joining up with a large caravan at Bagamoyo for the westward journey. After traveling a short distance, one of his servants fell ill, and Maizan decided to wait with only a couple of unarmed porters until the man recovered before moving on. During a robbery attempt, Maizan was seized, bound to a pole, tied to a tree, tortured—which included the severing of limbs—and finally beheaded. His killer was never apprehended, although investigators did find an accomplice who reportedly beat a drum during the affair. He spent two years chained in front of the French embassy in Zanzibar before he was confined to prison. Hamerton had taken Burton to see him in order to demonstrate the dangers associated with interior travel.

On July 14 the caravan entered Ukutu, a land rich in produce and known as a safe haven for merchants. Nature, however, didn't cooperate as heavy rains broke, soaking everyone to the bone and creating bogs of knee-high mud a hundred or more yards across. Exhaustion plus continuing fevers forced a nearly weeklong stop at Dutumi, where an Arab merchant resided. Delirious much of the time, Burton recalled having had "a queer conviction of divided identity, never ceasing to be two persons that generally thwarted and opposed each other." In addition, "the sleepless nights brought with them horrid visions, animals of grisliest form, hag-like women and men with heads protruding from their breasts." According to Burton, Speke was even worse off, suffering from a "fainting fit which strongly resembled a sun-stroke, and which seemed permanently to affect his brain."[16]

In more lucid moments, Burton, despite a "swimming head and trembling hands," drafted a letter to the RGS recapping their route to this point. Speke did the same, and these were sent back to the coast along with a request for medical supplies.[17] According to Burton, the exploration of Africa had changed considerably over the years:

> The African Traveller, in this section of the nineteenth century, is an animal overworked. Formerly, the reading public was satisfied with dry details of mere discovery; was delighted with a few latitudes and longitudes. Of late, in this, as in other pursuits, the standard has been raised. Whilst marching so many miles *per diem*, and watching a certain number of hours *per noctem*, the traveller, who is in fact his own general, adjutant, quarter-master, and executive, is expected to survey and observe—to record meteorology, hygrometry, and hypsometry— to shoot and stuff birds and beasts, to collect geological specimens, to gather political and commercial information, to advance the infant study ethnology, to keep accounts, to sketch, to indite a copious legible journal, to collect grammar and vocabularies, and frequently to forward long reports which shall prevent the Royal Geographical Society napping through evening meetings. It is right, I own, to establish a high standard which insures some work being done; but explorations should be distinguished from railway journeys, and a broad line drawn between the feasible and impossible.[18]

To repay the kindness extended by the villagers, Burton helped them recover several of their own who had been captured after an altercation a few days earlier. He also dismissed the two remaining guards from Kaole for stealing supplies and general unruliness. The three others had already deserted.

Miserable conditions continued to be the norm as the journey resumed on July 24. The ground was soaked and the path "crossed by llianas, creepers and climbers, thick as coir-cables." Burton found it a hellish place.

> The earth, ever rain-drenched, emits the odour of sulphuretted hydrogen, and in some parts the traveler might fancy a corpse to be hidden behind every bush. To this sad picture of miasma the firmament is a fitting frame: a wild sky, whose heavy purple nimbi, chased by raffales and chilling gusts, dissolve in large-dropped showers; or a dull grey expanse, which lies like a pall over the world. In the finer weather the atmosphere is pale and sickly; its mists and vapours seem to concentrate the rays of the oppressive "rain-sun." The sensation experienced at once explains the apathy and indolence, the physical debility, and the mental prostration, that are the gifts of climates which moist heat and damp cold render equally unsalubrious and uncomfortable. That no feature of miasma might be wanting to complete the picture, filthy heaps of the rudest hovels, built in holes in the jungle, sheltered their few miserable inhabitants, whose frames are lean with constant intoxication, and whose limbs, distorted by ulcerous sores, attest the hostility of Nature to mankind.[19]

Finally, after four excruciating weeks on the road, they reached Zungomero. In addition to grain, another desired commodity grown in abundance here was bhang, the name for Indian hemp (*Cannabis sativa*) smoked in quantities by Arabs and Africans alike. Burton didn't mention joining them, but it's hard to imagine him abstaining.

Located beyond Zanzibar's control, Zungomero harbored numerous touters, mostly escaped slaves and criminals, who pillaged the countryside while waiting for ivory. Heavily armed, they'd overrun the area's Wakhutu inhabitants, whom Burton described as inferior to the Wazaramo, being "very dark, and [bearing] other marks of a degradation effected by pernicious climatory conditions," like eyes red with "perpetual intoxication" and villages "slovenly" in a manner similar to character.[20] By this time he'd come to view tropical climates as inimical to human physical and cultural development, thus lending an authoritative voice to a widely held mantra. Burton, though, saw the slave trade as the real culprit for the Wakhutu's condition. It had, in fact, reduced the population to a state beneath pity, for according to him, the traveler

> is ever in the dilemma of maltreating or being maltreated. Were he to deal civilly and liberally with this people he would starve: it is vain to offer a price for even the necessaries of life; it would certainly be refused because more is wanted, and so on beyond the bounds of possibility. Thus, if the touter did not seize a house he would never be allowed to take shelter in it from the storm; if he did not enforce a "corvée," he must labour beyond his strength with his own hands; and if he did not fire a village and sell the villagers, he might die of hunger in the midst of plenty. Such in this province are the action and reaction of the evil.[21]

The Wakhutu kept losing ground, and few can be found today.

Each day at Zungomero proved more excruciating than the previous one. Either rain pelted down or the sun burned like fire. The Baluchi quarreled with their slaves and stole from villagers, while sickness laid many of the party low. Only five new porters had been added, instead of the hoped for twenty-two supposedly on their way from the coast. Weary and dispirited, the expedition pulled up stakes on August 7 after a fortnight's stay, with both Burton and Speke so weak from malaria they could barely sit atop their donkeys. Two routes led west. Although the southernmost was shorter and went through fairly well-provisioned country, Burton chose the northern one because of less onerous honga demands. The first day proved especially taxing. Deep mud covered the many fords of the Mgeta River, while local feuds and the "slave trade had made a howling desert of the land."[22] Leaving the river valley, the trail led into the hill country along the western foothills of the Uluguru Mountains, which Burton mistakenly called part of the Usagaras. Suddenly the sun broke through the clouds, the air sweetened, and great solitary trees replaced "dull mangrove, dismal jungle, and monotonous grass." Burton's spirits revived.

By night, the soothing murmurs of the stream at the hill's base rose mingled with the faint rustling of the breeze, which at times broken by the scream of the night-heron, the bellow of the bull-frog in his swampy home, the cynhyaena's whimper, and the fox's whining bark sounded through the silence most musical, most melancholy. Instead of the cold night rain, and the soughing of the blast, the view disclosed a peaceful scene, the moonbeams lying like sheets of snow upon ruddy highlands, and the stars hanging like lamps of gold from the dome of infinite blue.[23]

He even praised the men, noting that they'd so far behaved "tolerably well," and went on to recommend that the consul at Zanzibar should "reward them liberally in case of good conduct" because "this will greatly facilitate the ingress of future travelers."[24] This was substantially at odds with what he would say about them later.

Burton's state of relative euphoria didn't last for long, as the up-and-down trail through the hills took its toll on men and donkeys alike. Loads had to be adjusted, sometimes every fifteen minutes or so, and one by one the animals fell by the wayside as a result of predation by hyenas and just plain fatigue. Cases of smallpox thinned the ranks, its horrors made more evident by a passing caravan that had lost fifty members, with many others desperately ill. Other than this, the first days brought no signs of people, and thus food began to run short.

At one point the Baluchi threatened to turn back, and the sons of Ramji considered joining them. Burton and Speke agreed to rely on the Wanyamwezi porters and go on as planned, no matter what. But they didn't have to, as the threats proved to be just that and nothing more.

During a halt at Muhama to reprovision, two more men came down with smallpox, and Burton experienced a relapse of malaria that lasted a week. Speke was also ill. Even so, August 21 saw them on the road again as the trail led from the hills to the plains below. Evidence of the slave trade now presented itself. One village revealed a scene in which "the huts were torn and half burnt, and the ground was strewed with nets and drums, pestles and mortars, cots and fragments of rude furniture." Two "wretched villagers . . . lurking in the jungle, not daring to revisit the wreck of their homes," provided the only visible sign of life. A common Arab slaver tactic of pretending to cook and eat those killed in a raid was enough to make survivors secret themselves from anyone following in their wake. The sight of the devastation caused Burton to ponder human character. "Can it be," he wrote, "that, by some inexplicable law, where Nature has done her best for the happiness of mankind, man, doomed to misery, must work out his own unhappiness?"[25]

Hordes of red and black biting ants attacked with ferocity, as did tsetse. Rather presciently Burton noted that if something like an insect-eating bird came along to eliminate the fly, it "will be the greatest benefactor that Central Africa ever knew."[26] Its link to sleeping sickness had yet to be demonstrated, and so Burton singled out the stinging bite as the hazard posed to humans and beasts.

On August 25 they began following the Ngerengere River (Burton's Mukondokwa) toward the Nguru Mountains and Usagara proper. Although many more people lived here, the violence of the slave trade had made them suspicious of strangers. Higher up the situation improved, with ample supplies available at the caravan rest stop of Rumuma. Still, the two days spent to stock up hardly qualified as pleasant, what with hot and windy afternoons, cool and damp nights, and various diseases continuing to flare up. The march from Rumuma took place under a scorching sun, with little water to quench thirsts. Good fortune, though, led to a village with milk, butter, and honey for purchase. In addition, a down caravan provided several donkeys, the originals by this time having been reduced by half, and three Wanyamwezi agreed to sign on to help fill the void for six porters lost along the way.

The grueling final phase of the trip through Usagara now faced them. First they would have to ascend to a point 5,700 feet above sea level and then descend some 3,000 feet. By this time, Speke lay in a virtual coma and spent two nights wildly delirious. According to Burton, they removed his weapons in order to avoid a catastrophe. He didn't say who was most at risk. In all, the trek took eight days to complete, and although hungry and exhausted, they made it to Ugogi on the plain below without major incident. It was September 18, in all forty-three days out from Zungomero, twice the usual amount of time taken by caravans.

While traversing the Ulugurus, Burton saw no Waluguru. In fact, he wasn't even sure they actually existed. And since he had little contact with the Wasagara, his observations were mostly limited to matters of dress and general appearance.

Repeating the racial-environmental correlation made for the Washambaa, he labeled the men living at higher elevations as "fine, tall, and sturdy," while the women appeared "remarkable for a splendid development of limb."[27]

Instrument breakage and malfunction made Speke's job of taking accurate measurements of latitude, longitude, and elevation next to impossible, even when he was well enough to do so. For distances and directions he was forced to rely on the stars, a pedometer, and compass. Burton's sharp eye, though, did produce a wealth of information about the natural environment. Compared to the lowlands, the mountains had a sanatorium-like quality. He felt the area would be suitable for acclimatizing settlers and missionaries for life in East Africa. Although Europeans did eventually come in these and other guises, the Uluguru and Nguru mountains never served in this capacity.

Ugogi marked the halfway point to Unyanyembe, and three days were spent there stocking rations, as uninhabited country lay immediately ahead. By this time, all but the Goan boys felt much better, and Speke had recovered sufficiently to do some hunting. The braces of partridges and guinea fowl he brought back made for the best eating in quite a while. Only nine donkeys remained, but fifteen Wanyamwezi porters seeking to go home signed on.

The countryside immediately west of Ugogi seemed like a desert to Burton, but not an open one as the trail was lined with thorns that ripped even the most durable clothing. "Hot, tired, and testy," he said, the men "who had wives beat them, those who had not 'let off the steam' by quarreling with one another."[28] A swarm of attacking bees didn't help their dispositions. One porter deserted, taking with him an almanac, surveying books, and writing materials.

On September 26 they reached a large *ziwa*, or water hole, on the eastern border of Ugogo, a land the caravans dreaded crossing, not so much because of the hostile physical environment as because of the hefty honga demands levied by the Wagogo. Rather than engage in slave raiding, they took advantage of their location along the main east-west route to extort what they could from passing caravans. And the demands had force behind them, as each headman, or sultan, according to the Arabs, could muster a sizeable group of warriors when needed. They resembled Maasai moran and on more than one occasion had bested them in battle. Burton, though, didn't see honga as unjust; he called it a kind of "customs-dues of the government" that the headman must redistribute among

An explorer on the road in East Africa as portrayed in The Lake Regions of Central Africa. *(Reproduced with permission of the Special Collections Research Center, Syracuse University Library.)*

his followers.[29] Because fights would benefit no one, negotiations were often long and difficult. Burton, though, worried that there might be trouble awaiting them.

> Some half-caste Arabs had gone forward and spread evil reports of us. They said we had each one eye and four arms; we were full of magic; we caused rain to fall in advance, and left droughts in our rear; we cooked water-melons, and threw away the seeds, thus generating small-pox; we heated and hardened milk, thus breeding a murrain amongst cattle; our wire cloth, and beads caused a variety of misfortunes; we were Kings of the Sea, and therefore white-skinned and straight-haired, as are all men who live in salt water, and next year we would seize their land.[30]

True to form the four days at the ziwa were spent haggling with several headmen, mostly about rights to water. But the wait wasn't entirely in vain, as an Arab-led up caravan arrived with good news—the items that went missing with the porter had been found. The leader also proposed the two caravans travel together, bringing the total to nearly two hundred men. Numerous wives accompanied them, and according to Burton, the entourage also included "female slaves, negroid beauties, tall, bulky . . . attired in tulip-hues, cochineal and gamboges, who walked the whole way, and who when we passed them displayed an exotic modesty by drawing their head-cloths over cheeks which were little ambitious to profane."[31]

Kanyenye required another four-day honga stop, and this time a down caravan made an appearance. Its Arab leader provided rice and a goat, gave Burton a riding donkey, helped round up some deserters, and agreed to take reports and letters to the coast. The one sent to the consul in Zanzibar (he didn't know who'd replaced Hamerton) included a complaint about the twenty-two men with the stored loads having yet to show up and another about the lack of communication, even the forwarding of letters, from the coast. Constant fevers in the ranks, Burton wrote, required an immediate shipment of quinine. Banking on patriotism and duty obligation to produce results, he went on to write, "I have the honour to express my conviction that you will not allow 2 officers esp. employed under the patronage of H. B. M.'s Foreign Office, to suffer any longer from such undeserved & disgraceful neglect."[32] They would be neglected for quite a while longer.

The most vexing halt occurred at Khokho. It consumed five days of discussions with the most powerful of the Wagogo headmen Maguru Mafupi (Short-shanks), whom Burton wrote "becomes man, idiot, and beast with clockwork-regularity every day; when not disguised in liquor he is surly and unreasonable, and when made merry by his cup he refuses to do business."[33] In addition, cold and damp weather made for uncomfortable nights, while during the day tsetse bit with impunity and swarms of bees and gadflies pestered man and beast alike. An attack of *siafu*, biting ants that march in columns of thousands, drove Burton from his tent, after which the insects turned their jaws on the donkeys. Then, to top things off, the fifteen recently acquired Wanyamwezi porters suddenly absconded.

While happy to get going again on October 17, Burton had to walk so that his donkey could carry a load of clothes and shoes. It turned out to be a brutal walk under a burning sun across country that alternated between "a rough, thorny, and waterless jungle" and "a grassy plain of black and sun-cracked earth."[34] Still weakened, he needed to rest every thirty minutes or so.

Poor health didn't keep Burton from making observations of Ugogo's geology, climate, flora, and fauna. Despite it being a semiarid land with no permanent rivers, a comparative lack of diseases other than malaria made Ugogo "eminently wholesome," so long as, he said, one had proper housing, water, and a good diet. The Wagogo struck him as standing above their neighbors. They appeared "fine, stout, and light-complexioned," possessed superior dress, were hospitable, and showed via their curiosity the prospect of "improvability,— of power to progress."[35] Still, Burton railed against their demands, bullying style, and a "semi-nude barbarity" that produced "truly unseemly spectacles." In addition, he called the Wagogo thieves, beggars, ill mannered, and almost always in a drunken state, men and women alike. Matters of sex naturally caught his attention. According to him, Wagogo women were "well disposed towards strangers of fair complexion," although he never mentioned how he came by this bit of information.[36] It could have been just an attempt to prick Mrs. Grundy.

Between Ugogo and Unyamwezi lay the *mgunda mkali,* or fierce field, a name derived from the area's lack of surface water during the dry season. The crossing took eight tedious days, with little of note happening and thus reported on. Once across they entered Itura, a borderland where Wakimbu colonists were busy establishing new settlements. Since the sixteenth century, the interior of East Africa had been in a highly volatile state: peoples on the move created new polities, while in other instances previous ones disappeared. Expanding trade networks from the coast served only to heighten the forces bringing change as groups vied for favorable locations. For some it was a matter of seeking greater profits, for others the search for safety took precedence.

Compared to what they had just been through, the cool rolling hills lined with many villages surrounded by richly laden fields of grain and other crops made Itura appear to be paradise. On a negative note, the last of the thirty original donkeys expired, leaving the caravan with only four obtained en route. A few new porters were engaged to help with the loads.

Only one obstacle now stood between Burton and Speke and Unyanyembe: the Kigwa Forest, labeled the "place of terror" owing to many incidents of robbery and murder. Using darkness as cover, the expedition reached a place called Kazeh on November 7, 1857. Only a little more than 350 miles in straight-line distance from the coast, they'd traveled some 600 miles over the course of 134 days, including halts. The "heart-wearing work," Burton later noted, was "cheered only by two stimulants, the traveller's delight in seeing new scenes unfold themselves before his eyes and the sense of doing something lastingly useful to geographers."[37] When Henry Morton Stanley arrived in 1871, Kazeh had disappeared, most likely having become part of what became and still is Tabora.

Although hardly in tip-top shape, the two travelers were at least alive, and they received a warm welcome from the Arabs, their "open-handed hospitality and hearty goodwill of this noble race," a marked contrast, Burton said, to the "niggardness of the savage and selfish African—it was heart of flesh after heart of stone."[38] He was back "home" among familiar and respected people. For their part, the Arabs took to Burton. As in Harar, he could play the role of haji and regale them in their own language with stories from *The Arabian Nights*. They could also share feelings of mutual superiority over "savage" Africans, and do so in quite pleasant conditions, everything considered. "The Arabs live comfortably, and even splendidly. . . . The houses, though single-storied, are large, substantial, and capable of defense. Their gardens are extensive and well planted; they receive regular supplies of merchandise, comforts, and luxuries from the coast; they are surrounded by troops of concubines and slaves, whom they train to divers crafts and callings; rich men have riding asses from Zanzibar and even the poorest keep flocks and herds."[39] Burton's dwelling place, however, wasn't so sumptuous. A flat-topped, mud-walled house called a *tembe*, its other inhabitants included hens, pigeons, rats, scorpions, earwigs, crickets, cockroaches, lizards, spiders, flies, and ticks.

The downtime allowed Burton to do some reflecting on events so far. Two statements are particularly interesting. One speaks to how the men felt about him and his interpretation of what it meant. "Sometimes," he said, "they compose songs in honour of me. I understand them, and the singers know that I do. They sing about Muzungú Mbáya, 'the wicked white man;' to have called me a '*good white man*' would mean that one was a natural, an innocent, who would be plucked and flayed without flinching."[40] This implies they feared him in some way, which was doubtful, given his and Speke's invalided states during much of

A view of Unyamwezi as portrayed in The Lake Regions of Central Africa. *(Reproduced with permission of the Special Collections Research Center, Syracuse University Library.)*

the journey. Both could easily have been stripped naked and left to their own devices or even killed. A more likely explanation is the common practice among East Africans of giving strangers nicknames, often with jest implied.

The other describing nightfall at the end of a long day's journey shows Burton in a more contemplative mood.

At this time, especially when in the jungle-bivouac, the scene often becomes truly impressive. The dull red fires flickering and forming a circle of ruddy light in the depths of the black forest, flaming against the tall trunks and defining the foliage of the nearer trees, illuminate lurid groups of savage men, in every variety of shape and posture. Above, the dark purple sky, studded with golden points, domes the earth with bounds narrowed by the gloom of night. And, behold! in the western horizon, a resplendent crescent, with a dim, ash-coloured globe in its arms, and crowned by Hesperus, sparkling like a diamond, sinks through the vast of space, in all the glory and gorgeousness of Eternal

Nature's sublimest works. From such a night, methinks, the Byzantine man took his device, the Crescent and the Star.[41]

Snay bin Amir, one of the first Arabs to settle in Unyanyembe, proved to be an especially valuable contact. Burton described him as "of a quixotic appearance, high featured, tall, gaunt, and large limbed. He was well read, had a wonderful memory, fine perceptions, and passing power of language. He was the stuff of which I could make a friend, brave as all his race, prudent, ready to perish for honour, and as honest as he was honourable."[42] Most of what Burton seems to have learned about the area and its peoples during the time spent in Kazeh came from conversations with Snay bin Amir, who did his utmost to help reorganize the expedition and make sure that reports and letters were sent to the coast.

Plans called for a fortnight's stay, not the usual six weeks to two months, in order to prepare for the next leg of the journey. Some uncertainty existed about just where to go. Reports proclaimed another large lake, variously called Ukerewe, or simply Nyanza, was located north of Kazeh. If true, then Erhardt had combined at least three lakes to form the "slug." Speke favored having a go at it. Burton, however, decided to stick with the original plan of heading for the lake to the west, as he deemed it a more likely part of the Nile drainage system. Furthermore, the Arab trade center of Ujiji was said to be only about twenty marches away. As usual, an array of problems lengthened the stay in Kazeh. First, in line with the norm for up caravans, most of the Wanyamwezi porters decided to call it quits and go home to tend to farms and be with families. Finding replacements for them proved next to impossible. Then rain started to fall in veritable torrents, and while waiting for it to stop, some of those who remained with the expedition became ill. Burton himself suffered a malaria relapse that produced a month of "distressing weakness, hepatic derangements, burning palms, and tingling soles, aching eyes, and alternate thrills of heat and cold."[43] Thusly impaired, he wasn't able to observe much or do his usual interrogating.

On December 5 Speke left for Zimbili, some two hours away, to prepare for the next leg of the journey. Burton followed a few days later and, feeling "more dead than alive," had to be carried in a litter. One by one the rest of the party drifted in, and on December 15 Burton moved to the next stop at Yombo, where he found some pleasure in watching "the softer part of the population." Among them stood three women who "would be deemed beautiful in any part of the world. Their faces were purely Grecian; they had laughing eyes, their figures were models for an artist." That they were basically naked made the scene even more enjoyable for him, as evidenced by his proclaiming, "These 'beautiful domestic animals' graciously smiled when in my best Kinyamwezi I did my devoir to the sex; and the present of a little tobacco always secured for me a seat in the undress circle."[44] Although physically incapacitated, he could still look.

The expedition started up again on December 18. Speke, who'd returned to Kazeh to fetch the porters and loads that had finally arrived from the coast, caught up a few days later. Burton fumed at the poor-quality cloth and beads so useless that some had to be discarded. Furthermore, there were no letters, nor requested medical supplies. The two men then separated again. Speke wanted to do some hunting, and Burton's weakness required extra-slow going. They planned to reunite in the district of Msene, a center in this part of Unyamwezi for coastal Arabs and Waswahili. Although it required deviating from the direct route to Ujiji, most caravans went there to recruit porters and to trade. The halt lasted twelve days, largely because the men were reluctant to leave. It was hard to pull them away from the all the drinking, dancing, and sex that Msene offered, and the country beyond had a reputation for being unhealthy and unfriendly. Nonetheless, they were finally cajoled into going on, and during a stop at the Gombe River, the sons of Ramji were discharged. Their term of service was up, and moreover, according to Speke, they did little valuable work and the expedition could use their rations.[45]

On the other side of the Gombe, Burton once again fell ill.

I was obliged to lay aside the ephemeris by an unusual sensation of nervous irritability, which was followed by a general shudder as in the cold paroxysm of fevers. Presently the extremities began to weigh and to burn as if exposed to a glowing fire, and a pair of jack-boots, the companions of many a day and night, became too tight and heavy to wear. At sunset, the attack had reached its height. I saw yawning wide to receive me

"those dark gates across the wild
That no man knows."

The whole body was palsied, powerless, motionless, and the limbs appeared to wither and die; the feet had lost all sensation, except a throbbing and tingling, as if pricked by a number of needle points; the arms refused to be directed by will, and to the hands the touch of cloth and stone was the same. Gradually the attack seemed to spread upwards till it compressed the ribs; there, however, it stopped short.[46]

None of the usual remedies worked, and Burton felt the die part of "to do or die" near at hand. It might remain to Speke to bring the expedition to fruition. One of the guards had suffered a similar attack after eating wild mushrooms and predicted the worst would be over in ten days. Whether Burton ate the mushrooms can't be determined. Anyway, he did recover. Walking, though, was out of the question, and six additional porters were hired to carry him by litter. Indeed, almost a full year would pass before Burton could walk very far without help or frequent rest.

A few days later Speke took a turn for the worse, this time from a painful eye infection that produced a state of near blindness. Since childhood he'd been plagued by a recurrence of vision problems. The Goan Valentine also had difficulty seeing. Still, on they went, slogging at times through thick jungle and paying honga.

On February 3 the trail brought them to the Malagarasi River. Since the Wavinza on the left bank refused travelers right of passage, it was necessary to be ferried to the other side. Once across, Burton said they entered a "howling wilderness" that was the product of Wangoni (then often called Watutu) raids. Originally from southern Africa, Wangoni warriors had recently entered this part of Africa, destroying villages and taking what they could. Instead of people, the area now housed mainly swarms of mosquitoes, which Burton said, "feasted right royally upon our life, even during the day time."[47] Then suddenly, on February 13, a thin wisp of water came into view. When told they were looking at the Sea of Ujiji, or Tanganyika Nyanza, as locals called it, Burton felt cheated that so much had been risked for so little, and he seriously considered turning back to explore the other lake. A few yards farther on the scene changed dramatically and so did Burton's mood. He now felt that "nothing could be more picturesque than this first view of the Tanganyika Lake, as it lay in the lap of the mountains, basking in the gorgeous tropical sunshine. . . . Truly it was a revel for soul and

sight! Forgetting toils, dangers, and the doubtfulness of return, I felt willing
to endure double what I had endured; and all the party seemed to join with
me in joy."[48] Speke, though, couldn't share in the moment and recorded later,
"Here you may picture to yourself my bitter disappointment when, after toiling
through so many miles of savage life, all the time emaciated by divers sicknesses
and weakened by great privations of food, I found, on approaching the zenith
of my ambition, the Great Lake in question nothing but mist and glare before
my eyes."[49] Still, his name would be forever linked to the discovery of the lake
and the revelation that more than one large one existed in eastern Central Africa.

The next morning saw them coasting in canoes for three hours to Ujiji.
By now they had traveled some 950 statute miles over the course of seven and a
half months, two-thirds of the days spent in halts. Ujiji turned out to be something less than Burton had imagined, certainly nothing to compare to Zanzibar
as some Arabs claimed. In fact, like virtually all the other such settlements seen
thus far, it was a cluster of small villages, the largest being Kawele, where Burton
and Speke set up residence in a rundown tembe. The Arabs lumped the villages
under the regional name of Ujiji, and so it became to European mapmakers. On
a positive note, there was a well-provisioned bazaar, thanks to the countryside's
productivity.

The depiction of the Wajiji reveals Burton's evolving views of Africans,
both physically and behaviorally. To him they appeared to be

> a burly race of barbarians, far stronger than the tribes hitherto traversed,
> with dark skins, plain features, and straight, sturdy limbs: they are larger
> and heavier men than the Wanyamwezi, and the type, as it approaches
> Central Africa, becomes rather negro than negroid. Their feet and
> hands are large and flat, their voices harsh and strident, and their looks
> as well as their manners are independent even to insolence. The women,
> who are held in high repute, resemble, and often excel, their masters
> in rudeness and violence; they think little in their cups of entering a
> stranger's hut, and of snatching up and carrying away an article which
> excites their admiration.[50]

He also claimed the Wajiji used spears and daggers on guests "with little
hesitation," something that likely came secondhand from Arabs. Burton found

little to recommend their chiefs and elders, claiming, "Their intellects, never of the brightest, are invariably fuddled with toddy."[51] The "toddy" in this case would have been sorghum-based brews and much stronger palm wine. Burton wasn't the first and wouldn't be the last European traveler to be struck by what seemed like daily drunkenness among African rulers.

Kawele's headman, Kannena, proved to be especially difficult. Burton, though, didn't help get their relationship off to a good start when he rejected the gift of a large elephant tusk, saying trade in slaves and ivory wasn't among his interests. Such a response puzzled Kannena, as what other reason would prompt a stranger to travel such a great distance. The incident caused Burton to wish he had adopted the guise of a trader. "In the first place it explains the traveller's motives to the people, who otherwise lose themselves in a waste of wild conjecture. Secondly, under this plea, the explorer can push forward into unknown countries; he will be civilly received, and lightly fined, because the hosts expect to see him or his semblables again; whereas, appearing without ostensible motive amongst them, he would be stripped of his last cloth by recurring confiscations, fines, and annoyance which greed of gain can suggest."[52] On top of this, came a serious faux pas. The next time Kannena stopped by he was turned away. No one recognized him because of a change in clothing. His anger would cost the expedition both money and time.

An indeterminate stay in Ujiji loomed ahead. How long would depend on securing porters to replace the Wanyamwezi, who'd used their cloth and beads to buy ivory or slaves to take home and sell for profit. Finding replacements wouldn't be easy because the Wajiji refused such work. The days dragged on unpleasantly. They were chilly and damp, and the roof of the tembe leaked like a colander. Thieves broke into the storerooms at night, and soon milk became too expensive to buy. A diet rich in fish and vegetables caused stomach problems, and no one had much energy. Burton recorded that he "lay for a fortnight upon the earth, too blind [his conjunctivitis had flared up] to read or write, except with long intervals, too weak to ride, and too ill to converse." Speke could still barely see, and he developed a facial muscular problem that caused him to "chew sideways, like a ruminant."[53] Both Goan boys fell ill, as did many of the Baluchi. Still, Burton and Speke worked when they could, determined to explore the northern end of the lake.

As in Kazeh, Arabs provided much of the information. Sailing times showed the lake to be long and linear, although Burton's calculations from them underestimated its length by about 150 miles. Malfunctioning thermometers also produced a seven-hundred-foot lower elevation than is the case, a crucial error with regard to later controversy about Lake Tanganyika's role in the Nile equation. And, contrary to Livingstone's assumptions, Burton learned that it did not drain to the east. The Arabs were also the source of the lake country's ethnographic accounts. Burton said he offered these accounts "without any guarantee of correctness," noting, "It is the explorer's unpleasant duty throughout these lands to doubt everything that has not been subjected to his own eyes."[54] As seen, he didn't always follow this maxim.

After several further delays over supplies, Speke set off across Lake Tanganyika with Bombay and a contingent of Baluchi to see about renting a dhow said to be in the possession of Sheikh Hamid bin Sulayim. With the *Louisa* having been left behind, they needed some kind of craft to explore along the lake. After Speke departed, Burton settled into a routine he described as "chiefly spent in eating and drinking, smoking and dozing."[55]

Twenty-seven days after his departure, Speke returned without the dhow, looking, according to Burton, "thoroughly moist and mildewed."[56] Speke's accounts didn't mention the wet part. After initially promising to make the boat available, Hamid told Speke the wait would be three months and the price five hundred dollars in goods, both deemed unacceptable. Besides having to suffer the mortification of another failure, he was in intense pain from an attempt to extract a beetle that had crawled into his ear. When several remedies resulted only in the beetle burrowing deeper, Speke resorted to using a penknife, the point of which caused a badly infected wound. He couldn't open his mouth for several days and a tumor developed that produced temporary deafness and ate a hole, which, when he blew his nose, produced a whistle-like sound from the ear, a condition that persisted for nearly seven months.[57]

In somewhat better health, although still hardly able to walk, Burton decided to join the party going in search of the river known to be at the northern end of the lake. Burton said he "was resolved at all costs, even if we were reduced to actual want, to visit the mysterious stream."[58] Speke later claimed he questioned his decision. "I was sorry for it," he wrote, "as my companion was still suffering so severely, that anyone seeing him attempt to go would have despaired of his ever returning. Yet he could not endure being left behind."[59] If the stream turned out to be an effluent, as Hamid reportedly told Speke (although he probably misunderstood him), then they might find the long sought after source of the White Nile. Negotiations with Kannena eventually produced a captain and crew of fifty-five men to carry them and seven other members of the expedition in two roughly fashioned, lopsided canoes that required constant bailing to keep afloat. Kannena decided to come along, bringing along a substantial retinue in tow. The journey began April 10, moving in fits and starts owing to weather and the whims of the crew, who made frequent halts to smoke bhang and visit with friends and relatives. According to Burton, "Obeying only impulse, and wholly deficient in order and purpose, they make the voyage as uncomfortable as possible; they have no regular stages and no fixed halting-places; they waste a fine cool morning, and pull through the heat of the day, or after dozing through-out the evening, at the loud cry of 'Pakírá Bábá!'—pack up hearties!—they scramble into their canoes about midnight."[60]

On April 15 they halted for several days at a place called Wafanya, where Barundi opposition forced them to cross the lake and follow the western shore. Further delays caused by weather and a minor rebellion among the men delayed reaching it until April 23. They first touched land at a point controlled by the Wabembe, who were feared as cannibals by others. Burton found no reason to doubt the "fact" and told readers, "The practice arises from the savage and apathetic nature of the people, who devour, besides man, all kinds of carrion and vermin, grubs and insects, whilst they abandon to wild growths a land of the richest soil and of the most prolific climate. They prefer man raw, whereas the Wadoe of the coast eat him roasted."[61] Needless to say, they weren't eaten, and a hard day of paddling brought them to the border of Uvira, the northernmost outpost of the Arabs. All that remained to complete the mission was to find the stream. Disappointing news came almost immediately. Locals said the stream, known as the Rusizi, flowed into the lake, not out of it. Burton's heart sank.

They stayed in Uvira for nine days. Although uncomfortable weather-wise, provisions were more than ample and everyone caught up on much-needed rest. Burton, though, had developed a tongue ulcer that required living off of milk and water sucked through a straw. He could hardly utter a word. Out of fear of

Journeying on Lake Tanganyika as portrayed in The Lake
Regions of Central Africa. *(Reproduced with permission of the
Special Collections Research Center, Syracuse University Library.)*

the Barundi, Kannena refused to go any farther, and a brewing storm clinched
the decision to return to Ujiji, leaving it to Stanley and Livingstone to show in
1871 that the Rusizi did indeed flow into the lake. On May 13 shouts from
an enthusiastic crowd greeted their return to Ujiji. They could have arrived the
night before, but Burton decided to wait until morning because "we were too
proud to sneak home in the dark; we had done something deserving a Certain
Cross, we were heroes, braves of braves; we wanted to be looked at by the fair, to
be howled at by the valiant."[62] It was, at best, a consolation prize.

Despite everything, Burton was on the mend. His tongue problem cleared
up, and feeling came back to hands and fingers, enough so that he could once
again write. As for Speke, while still almost deaf, his vision slowly improved.
Helping matters, at least psychologically, the rains ended. They were, however,
in desperate need of supplies. "'Wealth,' say the Arabs, 'hath one devil, poverty
a dozen,' and nowhere might a caravan more easily starve than in rich and fertile
Central Africa. Travellers are agreed that in these countries 'baggage is life:' the

heartless and inhospitable race will not give a handful of grain without return, and to use the Moslem phrase, 'Allah pity him who must beg of a beggar!'"[63]

Unexpectedly, a large caravan arrived, bringing the first letters and newspapers in eleven months, along with much-needed goods, although most of the loads contained useless ammunition and poor-quality merchandise. What remained would be enough to cover their return to Kazeh but hardly sufficient for further exploration, such as the planned survey of the southern shores of Lake Tanganyika. So, on May 26 they prepared to leave in the company of a caravan led by Said bin Majid.

In all, the return consumed twenty-six days of delays, confusions, discomforts, desertions, and honga demands. They avoided the detour to Msene this time, the usual practice for down caravans wanting to get their valuable cargoes of ivory and/or slaves to Unyanyembe as quickly as possible. Indeed, the desire for speed caused Majid to set off on his own at about the halfway point. Near the end of the journey, Burton learned from a letter that his father had died on September 6, 1857. "Such tidings," he noted, "are severely felt by the wanderer, who, living long behind the world, is unable to mark its gradual changes, lulls (by dwelling upon the past) apprehension into a belief that *his* home has known no loss, and who expects again to meet each old familiar face ready to smile upon his return, as it was to weep at his departure."[64] Burton had heard of his mother's death on December 18, 1854, also at a distance. Another bit of information involved the Indian Mutiny, something he feared would one day happen.

Sickness returned in spades. By the time they reached Kazeh on June 20, Burton suffered from swollen, numb limbs; Speke was nearly deaf and his vision had again worsened; and the two Goan boys were bedridden with fever, rheumatism, and liver pains. But with the help of an array of substances, including narcotics, they slowly convalesced. Burton wrote Shaw saying that with five thousand pounds "we might I believe without difficulty have spanned Africa from East to West," a rather doubtful boast.[65] Still, having gotten this far provided Burton some solace. "I felt the proud consciousness," he said, "of having done my best, under conditions, from beginning to end, the worst and most unpromising, and that whatever future evils Fate might have in store for me, it could not rob me of the meed won by the hardships and sufferings of the past."[66] As it turned out, he would be robbed in a way never envisioned.

Several Arab merchants were about to leave for the coast, but instead of accompanying them, Burton and Speke decided to stay in Kazeh a little longer. A return via Kilwa remained a possibility, and the northern lake, said to be grander even than Tanganyika and only some fifteen or so marches distant, beckoned. According to Burton, Speke volunteered to go once he felt able to, and it seemed like a good idea; later, on several occasions, he would claim having "dispatched" Speke to the lake.[67] With him out of the way, Burton could attend to other important matters, like gathering ethnographic information, working on his report to the RGS, and readying the caravan for departure to the coast. Besides, a respite from his traveling companion would be welcomed. As for Speke, he was only too happy to be rid of Burton for a while.

What caused such ill feelings? Speke's dislike of Burton seems to have begun with the attack at Berbera. During the initial rush, he moved a few paces backward in the tent to get a better line of sight for firing. Burton reportedly called out, "Don't step back, or they'll think we are running!"[68] Speke apparently interpreted this as a criticism of his manhood, instead of as tactical advice. Afterward Burton did two things to make matters worse: He sent the animal skins Speke had collected to the Bombay Museum and published, without asking permission, a completely rewritten version of Speke's diary about events in Somaliland as appendices in both the *Journal of the Asiatic Society of Bombay* and *First Footsteps in East Africa*. According to Burton the editing was necessary because the original was "unfit for publication" owing to its style and certain "geographical assertions."[69] The depth of Speke's animosity for Burton can be seen in a letter he wrote to his mother in June 1857: "I have now had ample analogous proof that B. never went to Mecca & Harar in the common acceptation of that word but got artful natives to take him to those places. . . . Wishing I could find something more amusing to communicate than such rot about a rotten person."[70]

Many years later a council member of the RGS named A. H. Layard reported having received a letter in 1862 in which Speke accused Burton of having put poison in one of his medications, which Bombay then refused to give to him. Speke's sister supposedly verified the fact, noting "it caused her brother great distress for some time."[71] The incident is not mentioned in any other surviving source and seems highly implausible. Despite once joking about having killed someone during the Mecca pilgrimage, there's no evidence that Burton ever did anything of the sort on purpose. And he could have poisoned Speke himself, with no one knowing. Why let Bombay in on it? In fact, Burton was more annoyed than angry with Speke, largely over his lack of language skills and general disinterest in matters of African culture. Speke's tendency to treat Arabs as inferiors who owed him deference didn't help matters, nor did his penchant for slaughtering animals for no particular reason other than sport.

Personality differences undoubtedly also contributed to their falling out. Francis Galton termed the two men "naturally unsympathetic": Burton was "a man of eccentric genius and tastes, orientalised in character and thoroughly Bohemian. Speke, on the other hand, was a thorough Briton, conventional, solid, and resolute."[72] Whatever the case, by now a mutual antipathy had developed that would only deepen with the passage of time.

At some point—it's unclear just when—Burton received a letter stating that the government in Bombay viewed with "displeasure" his "want of dis-cretion, and due respect for the authorities to whom you are subordinate" as expressed in the Red Sea report.[73] He wrote back immediately: "I beg to express my regret that it should have contained any passages offensive to the authorities to whom I am subordinate; and to insure the Right Honourable the Governor in Council that nothing was farther from my intentions than to displease a government to whose kind consideration I have been, and am still, so much indebted."[74] Burton then penned a letter to Shaw at the RGS, telling him, "The document in question was forwarded, not for publication, but as expressly stated, for the infor., C. of Drs. of the F. Off. I have expressed my regret for having offended a Govt. to which I am much indebted, at the same time, I am at a loss to understand how I have offended."[75] The whole ordeal rankled enough that he felt the need to defend his actions in *The Lake Regions of Central Africa.*

> I have perhaps been Quixotic enough to attempt a suggestion that, though the Mediterranean is fast becoming a French lake, by timely measures the Red Sea may be prevented from being converted into a Franco-Russo-Austrian lake. But an Englishman in these days must be proud, very proud, of his nation, and withal somewhat regretful that

he was not born of some mighty mother of men—such as Russia and America—who has not become old and careless enough to leave her bairns unprotected, or cold and crusty enough to reward a little word of wisdom from her babes and sucklings with a scolding or a buffet.[76]

In another context Burton would later write, "All that my political views aimed at was to secure supremacy of my country in the Red Sea."[77]

Assembling a party for the journey to the lake took longer than expected because none of the men wanted to go. But eventually a contingent of thirty-three, including Bombay, was put together, and on July 10 they set off, anticipating a round-trip of about six weeks. During Speke's absence, Burton attempted to learn all he could from the Arabs about the lands and peoples near the lake. The two most important were reported to be the kingdoms of Karagwe and Buganda. Informants told him that they were "superior in civilisation and social constitution to the other tribes of Eastern and Central Africa. . . . [T]hey have built extensive and regular settlements, and the reverence even to worship a single despot, who rules with a rigour which in Europe would be called barbarity. Having thrown off the rude equality of their neighbors, they recognize ranks in society; there is order amongst men, and some idea of honour in women; they add to commerce credit, without which commerce can hardly exist; and they hospitably entertain strangers and guests."[78] This fit Burton's racial view of the world, according to captives he'd seen in Unyanyembe. "Their heads are of a superior cast: the regions where the reflective faculties and the moral sentiments, especially, benevolence, are placed, rise high; the nose is more of the Caucasian type; the immoderate masticating apparatus which gives the negro and the lower negroid his peculiar aspect of animality, is greatly modified, and the expression of the countenance is soft, kindly, and not deficient in intelligence."[79]

Burton spent much of his time studying the languages encountered from the coast to Unyamwezi. He started with Kiswahili, Snay bin Amir being his primary tutor. For the other languages he relied mostly on slaves as informants. With nothing much written to go by, Burton had to establish the rules of grammar and syntax by himself. Fluency wasn't his goal, rather he sought to work out their relationships, one to another. Eventually they would all be placed together within the Bantu family, which covers nearly half the continent from the equator to the Cape of Good Hope. As a side note, Burton is often credited with having spoken or known anywhere from twenty-nine to forty languages. Closer to the truth is the statement by Arthur Symons that he was "acquainted with twenty-nine languages."[80]

Readying the caravan for the road was Burton's other main task. With this completed, he became bored. Most of the Arabs had left either for the coast or joined an expedition to revenge a killing. As a diversion he decided, despite a still weakened condition, to do some exploring south of Kazeh. Before this could happen shouts and gunfire echoed through the camp announcing Speke's early return. Excitedly, he reported having reached the northern lake on August 3. Burton reacted with delight. Speke had, after all, gone through some two hundred miles of unmapped country and found what he'd set out to find. Based on Speke's past failings, Burton may have doubted success possible, but succeed he had. The mood changed when Speke proclaimed the lake to be the source of the White Nile. He based his conclusion on previous speculations, what locals told him, and the gestures of a so-called great traveler who repeatedly thrust his right hand northward to indicate "something immeasurable."[81]

The thinness of the evidence flabbergasted Burton. Speke had spent less than three days at the shore where the current city of Mwanza is located and never ventured on the water because negotiating for canoes would, he said, have taken up too much time. The local chief also hemmed and hawed over allowing him to go farther. Furthermore, Burton thought there must have been translation problems because neither Speke nor Bombay spoke Arabic or any of the local languages. As a result, any information obtained would necessarily have had to come via several translations and thus likely be in error. The best course of action, clearly, would have been for both of them to go and have a look, which they contemplated doing. But meager supplies, likely hostility en route, and being near the end of their leave time made this impossible. Many years later Isabel said Richard told her that he recommended to Speke that they should return home in order to "recruit our health, report what we have done, get some more money, return together and finish our whole journey."[82] Had this happened, both men's futures would likely have turned out better. After a couple of days filled with arguments about the Nile connection, they agreed for the good of the expedition to end discussion of the matter.

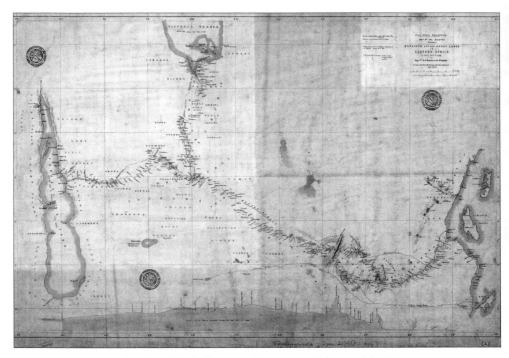

An original draft of the map that accompanied Burton's 1859 article of the exploration of East Africa. (Reproduced with permission of the Royal Geographical Society.)

There is more, however, to the tale about Speke's journey of discovery than is usually told. In a 1964 publication about maps of the sources of the Nile drawn during the latter half of the nineteenth century, G. R. Crone, librarian and map curator at the RGS, contended that such a mission was part of the expedition's duty. "It is sometimes said that Speke set out from Kazeh (Tabora) to find the northern lake on the strength of personal inspiration. It is perfectly clear, however, that Burton and Speke had been instructed by the Royal Geographical Society to look for that lake after Lake Tanganyika had been reached. Had they returned without making the attempt, they could have been censored for neglecting an important part of their orders. Perhaps it was consciousness of this that helped inflame Burton's animosity toward Speke."[83]

Those instructions were contained in the October 1, 1856, letter sent to Burton about the terms of the expedition. After spelling out the expectations for Lake Tanganyika it went on to say, "Having obtained all the information you require in this quarter, you are to proceed northward towards the range of mountains marked upon our maps as containing the probable source of the 'Bahr al Abia,' [White Nile] which it will be your next great object to discover." Interestingly, neither Burton nor Speke ever mentioned having received such instructions. No matter, Burton made a grave error by not accompanying Speke. As historian Robert O. Collins put it, "At one decisive moment, he lost the opportunity to become one of the great names of African exploration rather than simply an erudite but eccentric traveler."[84]

The sons of Ramji had decided to stay in Unyanyembe, which hardly pleased the locals. When they were asked to leave because of troublesome behavior, Burton allowed them to rejoin the caravan as long as they obeyed and agreed to carry the lighter loads of valuables. To make his point about obeying, he flogged several of them. As usual, the first start proved to be a false one, and for the next three weeks they hardly moved. Finally, in anticipation of the real start, they settled accounts with Snay bin Amir and exchanged fond adieus on August 27. Snay died shortly thereafter in one of the periodic wars besetting this part of Africa.

The down journey was slated to begin on September 6, which meant traveling during the "dead season," when provisions were hard to come by, if they were come by at all. If all went well, they could reach the coast by December. It wouldn't happen. For one, problems with the porters surfaced almost immediately. Many wouldn't agree to long hauls, which meant a sequence of short haul contracts, a time-consuming and expensive proposition. Desertions occurred almost immediately, and some of the men shuttled back and forth between camp and Unyanyembe when it was still within reach. As before, days of halts outnumbered those of marches. Speke suddenly became quite ill again. Still suffering from deafness, an eye inflammation, and facial swelling, he now experienced severe burning pains called "little irons" that coursed through his body, accompanied by hallucinations. After one spasm, Burton noted, "He began to utter a barking noise, and a peculiar chopping motion of the mouth and tongue with lips protruding—the effect of difficulty of breathing—which so altered his appearance that he was hardly recognizable."[85] Fearing the worst, Speke tried writing a farewell letter to his family. It was illegible. Then as quickly as the pain came on it let up, enough, at least, to allow him to rest, although he had to do this in a half upright position for several weeks. Jon Godsall has suggested trichinosis as the disease.[86] The symptoms make this highly unlikely, as does the fact that no one else in the party suffered from the "little irons." Their cause thus remains a mystery.

This episode revealed to Burton the full depth of Speke's dislike for him. During one attack of the "little irons" he reportedly raged about how Burton had no right to publish a redacted version of his diary in *First Footsteps*, and in another he uttered something about Burton having accused him of cowardice during the attack at Berbera.

On October 13 the coastward journey finally began in earnest. The going was still slow, although more as a result of concerns about being attacked than problems with the porters. All told the caravan numbered 152 members, and after two weeks a six-day-long halt was needed to take on provisions. The crossing of Ugogo took from November 14 to December 5, although this time few difficulties were encountered beyond the usual honga demands. During the transit they joined up with a large Wanyamwezi down caravan and once on the other side came upon one heading to Unyanyembe that carried a packet of mail. The news wasn't good for Burton. Friends had been murdered, and a press cutting told of the massacre of nearly all Christians in the Red Sea coast city of Jeddah on June 30, 1858, another event Burton predicted as likely to happen one day. In addition, he learned his old nemesis from language competitions in India, Captain Christopher Rigby, had succeeded Hamerton in Zanzibar.

At Ugogi they decided to take the more direct route to Zungomero and thus endure the likelihood of incessant honga demands. As matters turned out, arduous passes and numerous muddy fords were more annoying. Furthermore, it rained virtually every day. On the plus side, food and freshwater were plentiful. December 29 saw them at Zungomero, where Burton brought up the prospect of going to Kilwa. A number of the Wanyamwezi refused, saying they hadn't contracted for such a journey. Burton responded by withholding their rations, hoping to "starve them into compliance."[87] That didn't work, as they were able to forage for themselves. In the end, many decided to leave the expedition and head straight for Kaole or Bagamoyo.

Two options now faced Burton and Speke: either send to the coast for replacements or wait to join another caravan. They chose the latter, and during the wait nine porters from an up caravan agreed to join them. Much-needed medical supplies also arrived. The first down caravan proved to be one from Ubena. A flash flood along the Ruaha River had swept away 150 or so slaves and much of the ivory collected. Having lost provisions as well, the survivors had to scavenge for food. Joining them was thus not an option.

Finally, on January 19, 1859, a large Wanyamwezi caravan made an appearance, and two days later Burton's party departed Zungomero with it along a mostly familiar path. One weary day followed another. "In places, after toiling under a sickly sun, we crept under the tunnels of thick jungle-growth veiling the Mgazi and other streams; the dank and fetid cold caused a deadly sensation of faintness, which was only relieved by a glass of aether-sherbet, a pipe or two of the strongest tobacco, and a half hour's repose."[88] Many of the loads had to be abandoned as the Wanyamwezi and the "sons" became less controllable the closer they came to the coast. An attack by Wazaramo said to be imminent never transpired, and on February 3 the journey thankfully ended at the small coastal village of Konduchi.

Everything seemed in utter chaos. Smallpox had raised its ugly head once again, to be joined by an outbreak of cholera that destroyed many villages along the Indian Ocean. On top of this, war looked to be imminent between Sultan Said bin Majid and his brother Said bin Thuwani (Thwain), ruler of Muscat. Thuwani considered Zanzibar his and, with French backing, was headed there with four gunboats. As word spread so did panic, bringing trade to a virtual stand-still. Nonetheless, Burton and Speke decided to visit Kilwa and asked Zanzibar to send medical and other supplies. These arrived at Konduchi in the hands of an unexpected guest, Dr. Albrecht Roscher, a Prussian engaged in exploring the coast and its hinterland. Burton couldn't believe the man's foolishness. He claimed to be immune to malaria and went unarmed. In November 1859 Roscher was slain near Lake Nyasa (now Malawi) by two of his own men.

On February 10 Burton and Speke sailed southward on a decrepit old tub, their cabin steaming hot and vermin infested. Almost immediately two of the crew of seven succumbed to cholera, and then three more came down with it. Only one of them survived. The bodies were committed to the sea. Nonetheless, Burton and Speke forged on, stopping at Mafia Island before an intended survey of the Rufiji River, thought to be a highway to the interior like the Zambezi River. Inundation caused by heavy rains precluded entering the Rufiji, and so they sailed away, passing by the small offshore island of Kilwa Kisiwani on February 15. A little over twelve miles south on the mainland lay the trade center of Kilwa Kivinje, which at the time was "nearly depopulated by cholera."[89] The horror surpassed anything Burton had witnessed in India.

> There were hideous sights about Kilwa at the time. Corpses lay in the ravines, and a dead negro rested against the walls of the Custom House. The poorer victims were dragged by the leg along the sand, to be thrown into the ebbing waters of the bay; those better off were sown up in matting, and were carried down like hammocks to the same general depôt. The smooth oily water was dotted with remnants and fragments of humanity, black and brown when freshly thrown in, patched, mottled, and parti-coloured when in a state of half pickle, and ghastly white, like scalded pig, when the pigmentum nigrum had become thoroughly macerated. The males lay prone upon the surface, diving as it were, head downwards, when the retiring swell left them in shallow water; the women floated prostrate with puffed and swollen breasts. . . . Limbs were scattered in all directions, and heads lay like pebbles upon the beach.[90]

Amid the carnage, Burton collected twenty-four skulls and sent them to the Royal College of Surgeons for examination.

Bad weather kept them in the town until February 20, when they crossed the channel to examine the ruins on Kisiwani. Here, too, cholera had taken its toll, although the worst of the epidemic seemed to have passed. Upon returning to Kivinje, Burton asked about the feasibility of marching to Lake Nyasa. He was told this might be possible in June when the first caravans would arrive from the interior, but certainly not now. Since waiting that long was out of the question, they set about for Zanzibar on February 24. More bad weather stretched the return into nine days.

Exhausted, unwell, and depressed, the thirty-eight-year-old Burton hoped to secret himself in quarters at the British consulate. He'd written to both the RGS and Bombay government asking for additional funds and extended leave time in order to make plans for a new expedition. There were reports to finish, and Majid wanted him to stay until the political crisis passed, which it shortly did, at least for a while, when the captain of HMS *Punjaub* convinced Thuwani to return to Muscat. The news set off a raucous week of celebrations on Zanzibar. Life at the consulate, however, proved to be uncomfortable, and Burton remarked that he felt himself "too conversant with local politics, and too well aware of what was going on to be a pleasant companion to its new tenant."[91] He thus decided to head for home as soon as possible, which didn't disturb Rigby, who'd become chummy with Speke. As he relayed in a letter to a friend in London, "Speke is a right good, jolly, resolute fellow. Burton is not fit to hold a candle to him and has done nothing in comparison with what Speke has, but Speke is a modest unassuming man, not very ready with his pen. But Burton will blow his trumpet very loud and get all the credit of the discoveries. Speke works. Burton lies on his back all day and picks other people's brains."[92]

The issue of paying the men their due came up. As early as June 24, 1858, Burton wrote to Shaw saying the sums promised by Hamerton couldn't be afforded, especially since he'd already dipped into his own pocket to the tune of some five thousand pounds to cover expenses over and above the amount provided by the RGS. Burton felt a "disagreeable position at Zanzibar" could be expected unless the current resident made good on the promise.[93] There was also the matter of pay for the Wanyamwezi who'd signed on in Unyanyembe. When things did indeed become "disagreeable," Burton claimed the men undeserving of anything because of poor behavior. The Baluchi, in particular, drew his ire. They had no stamina, were hardly brave, and were "always an encumbrance."

> Like the lower races of Orientals, they were ever attempting to intrude, to thrust themselves forwards, to take an ell when an inch was offered; they considered all but themselves fools, ready to be imposed upon by the flimsiest lie, by the shallowest of artifices. Gratitude they ignored; with them a favour granted was but an earnest of favours to come, and one refusal obliterated the trace of a hundred largesses. Their objects in life seemed to be eating, and buying slaves; their pleasures, drinking and intrigue. Insatiable beggars were they; noisy, boisterous, foul-mouthed knaves, swearers "with voices like cannons;" rude and forward in manner, low and abusive in language, so slanderous that for want

of other objects they would culminate one another, and requiring a periodical check to their presumption. I might have spent the whole of my day in superintending the food of these thirteen "great eaters and little runners."[94]

It's likely Burton exaggerated the situation in order to avoid going further into debt, but whatever the reasons, he stuck to his guns, something that would come back to haunt him.

After bidding a fond farewell to his good friend Majid, Burton joined Speke aboard the American clipper *Dragon of Salem* on March 22 for the first leg of the voyage home to Aden. Calm winds delayed the arrival until April 16, and after disembarking they went to stay with Steinhaeuser. Two days later Speke hurried off to join HMS *Furious* bound for England. For health reasons (he'd relapsed with malaria), Burton waited for the next ship home scheduled to leave on the twenty-eighth. He said he remembered Speke's words to him being, "Good-bye old fellow; you may be quite sure I shall not go up to the Royal Geographical Society until you come to the fore and we appear together. Make your mind quite easy about that."[95]

Burton also mentioned Speke sent a letter from Cairo reaffirming his intention and telling him "to take all the time and rest that broken health required."[96] Or was this all something he made up later? The oft-quoted remark was not included in *The Lake Regions of Central Africa.* In fact, it first appeared in Isabel's *The Life.* Shedding a somewhat different light on expectations is a letter Burton wrote to Shaw while he was still in Aden. "Capt. Speke . . . will lay before you his maps & observations & two papers, one a diary of his passage of the Tanganyika between Ujiji & Kasenge, and the other his exploration of the Nyanza, Ukerewe or Northern Lake. To which I would respectfully direct serious attention of the Committee, as there are grave reasons for believing it to be the source of the principal feeder of the White Nile."[97]

Speke's only words on the matter are recorded in a recent discovery of an eight-page addition to *What Led to the Discovery of the Nile* that was never published, although apparently it was attached to at least three private copies.[98] The gist of it is that Speke didn't expect to see Burton in London any time soon, that he'd indicated a desire to go to Jerusalem first, and that afterward who knew where else.

5

REGROUPING

ON MAY 21 THE SHIP CARRYING Burton reached England. Because the hour was late, he waited until the next morning before hurrying off to London. Whatever may have been said in Aden, Burton learned that Speke had told Shaw upon his return two weeks earlier about having discovered the source, or at least one source, of the White Nile. Immediately afterward, he hustled off to see Sir Roderick Murchison. Impressed by the evidence presented to him, Speke said the RGS president told him, "we must send you there again," meaning, of course, another journey to the Nyanza.[1] Something of the sort is confirmed by Murchison's address at the May 23 anniversary meeting of the RGS when he said, "Let us hope that when re-invigorated by a year's rest, the undaunted Speke may receive every encouragement to proceed from Zanzibar to his old station, and thence carry out to demonstration the view which he now maintains, that the Lake Nyanza is the main source of the Nile."[2] The lake hadn't yet received the name Victoria. Speke's original sketch map showed it as Lake Nyanza, and Burton called it the Nyanza or Ukerewe Lake.[3] According to Speke, the idea to make the change came when the queen graciously asked him about his health.[4] In any event, suddenly Speke had become London's latest "lion," and the RGS Exploration Committee approved in principle a plan to make him commander of a new expedition. Burton later told Isabel that this made him feel as though the ground had been cut from beneath his feet.[5] Here we encounter Burton the victim speaking, for nothing would be finalized for more than a month. And for the second time he'd allowed Speke go off without him. Naiveté? Indifference? No matter, Burton had set himself up for a fall.

An enduring question is, Why were Murchison and the RGS so quick to jump on the Speke bandwagon? He was pretty much an unknown to them, whereas Burton, in the realm of African exploration at the time, ranked behind only David Livingstone. With no hard evidence to draw upon, one can only speculate about what happened. It could have had something to do with the controversies surrounding Burton. His sharp tongue certainly wasn't an asset. Plus, the disaster at Berbera still lingered in the background, and he, not Speke, had been in command. As Donald Young put it, an opportunity now existed to put aside a liability in favor of "God's own Englishman: a blue-eyed, fair-haired, sun-burned explorer claiming to have just discovered the source of the Nile."[6] Dorothy Middleton summed up the situation as a match between the "*enfant terrible*" and the "*bon enfant*."[7] Or perhaps, as she also suggested, "The Society was concerned with getting the land mapped, the distances assessed, the relations between hill to valley, of stream to lake, correctly laid down" and thus saw Speke as "better fitted" for such tasks.[8] It certainly didn't hurt to have Rigby in his camp. For example, Rigby had told the Indian government, "From his tact in conciliating the natives, his resolution and scientific acquirements, I am confident that he [Speke] has proved himself eminently qualified for any future African explorations."[9]

Burton hurried off to RGS headquarters to give his report. A quickly assembled ad hoc committee of three listened attentively and suggested he apply for funds to support another Nile expedition after regaining his strength. They also told Burton he would receive the Founders Gold Medal at a special meeting the following day and that Murchison would make the presentation. The president's words at that event stopped well short of heaping praise on Burton, noting simply the "geographers of England have watched your various and most adventurous explorations with deepest interest" and that he, himself, rejoiced in the society's members having "it in their power to recompense your highly distinguished services." Murchison then referred to Speke's discovery of "the vast interior Lake of Nyanza," saying it qualified as "well worthy of the highest honour this society can bestow," namely its gold medal. Burton gave only a brief, but highly pointed, response designed to get back at Murchison and diminish Speke:

> I thank you, Sir, most sincerely for this honour, and for the kind and
> flattering expressions by which you have enhanced its value. . . . Justice

compels me to state the circumstances under which it attained that success. To Captain J. H. Speke are due those geographical results to which you have alluded in such flattering terms. Whilst I undertook the history and ethnography, the languages, and peculiarities of the people, to Captain Speke fell the arduous task of delineating an exact topography, and of laying down our position by astronomical observations—a labour to which at times even the undaunted Livingstone found himself unequal.[10]

On June 13 both men addressed the RGS. Burton spoke mostly about economic and ethnographic conditions in East Africa, while Speke focused on Lake Victoria, often reading from his notebooks. Neither communicated directly with the other. Speke's argument failed to impress the highly regarded "arm-chair geographer" James MacQueen. In particular, he pointed to a timing problem— the rains at Lake Victoria started in September–October, whereas the flood in Egypt occurred in June. Speke could only reply that his visit to the lake took place during the dry season. MacQueen also doubted the measurements of latitude. George Robinson, First Marquess of Ripon, summed up the current situation: "The arguments adduced by Captain Speke, I think we all will admit, are of a very great weight, although probably some gentlemen here may be inclined to question them. No doubt his conclusion cannot be absolutely established until farther explorations have been made, which I hope will be carried on under the same excellent explorers: and I trust such fresh discoveries will bring forward complete evidence of the fact, or rather support that which is now only a matter of opinion."[11]

On June 21 the Expedition Committee formally agreed to send Speke's plan to the council for approval. Burton's plan to proceed up the Nile toward the Victoria Nyanza was forwarded as well, and on the twenty-seventh of the month the council gave its seal of approval to both.[12] Further evidence that Burton was still in the society's good graces was the unprecedented act of devoting the entire 1859 edition of its journal to his 454-page-long account of the expedition.

Another difficult issue for Burton involved his brother, Edward. He'd suffered multiple traumas while serving as a regimental surgeon with the British Army in Ceylon and was currently invalided in a mental asylum in Surrey. Release came only via Edward's death in 1895.

Burton's thoughts also included Isabel. She'd spent a lot of time during his absence traveling throughout Europe. Men sought her out, and several proposed marriage. But they didn't have a chance. Only Richard mattered, and so she waited, even though she was uncertain when, if ever, he'd return. Isabel had received just four letters from him, and none in a year, in contrast to her output of two per month. Then, out of the blue, a short poem from Richard with no accompanying letter arrived in the mail:

To Isabel
That brow which rose before my sight,
As on the palmer's holy shrine;
Those eyes—my life was in their light;
Those lips—my sacramental wine;
That voice whose flow was wont to seem
The music of an exile's dream[13]

Hope surged, and according to Isabel—and hers is the only account we have—upon leaving the RGS on May 22, Richard went directly to a mutual friend's house to inquire into Isabel's whereabouts. By chance she happened to be there. They embraced, and each said how much the other had been missed. Richard's appearance provided a shock. Isabel remembered him looking like "a mere skeleton, with brown-yellow skin hanging in bags, his eyes protruding, and his lips drawn from his teeth."[14] He immediately ordered a cab, and the leisurely ride about town allowed them to get reacquainted. Afterward, Isabel returned home and told her mother they still intended to marry. It elicited the same adamant opposition: He was not a Catholic and had little money. Isabel's long letter stating everything she felt made no difference whatsoever.[15] Her father, on the other hand, didn't object. Still, the better course of action dictated the two should meet on the sly for now, so as to avoid any chance of nasty scenes taking place. At the outset, Richard's weakness restricted them to garden walks and visits to friends' houses nearby, with Isabel often holding him by the arm to make sure he didn't fall.

At the same time, the acrimony between Burton and Speke surfaced. It began with an exchange of letters regarding Speke's responsibility to compensate

Burton for using out-of-pocket money to cover expedition expenses. Speke admitted he'd agreed to be "answerable for the half of any sums that might be legitimately expended in prosecution before us" and felt it his "duty-in-honor" to pay up should reimbursement from the government not be forthcoming. Burton's demand, though, shocked Speke in light of the "Somali affair." "Then I spent *everything*; ready money, and, received *nothing* in return. You in virtue of your position as Commandant took my diaries from me, published them and never offered me even half returns for your book in which they were contained. My specimens also which I had industriously collected, together with my notices of their habits etc, etc, you took from me, and, presented them to the Bengal Museum, recording the appended 'remarks' as originating from yourself, when, very well knowing that I alone had collected everything."[16]

The two men kept at it into the coming year. Speke accused Burton of "shunning" him, and Burton responded by saying the whole matter of financial transactions was "distasteful" to him.[17] At one point Speke said he agreed to go to Africa in the first place under a "proviso" that he "not be called upon to pay any money whatever."[18] When it became clear that no compensation from Bombay would be forthcoming any time soon, if at all, Speke agreed to make good on the six hundred pounds owed.[19] His brother Benjamin handled the transaction, noting that he hoped this would end discussion of the matter.[20] It did, at least publicly.

Before the settlement another battle erupted over Burton's refusal to pay the men of the expedition. While en route home from Zanzibar, Speke wrote two letters to Rigby supporting their claims. After hearing pleas from both Ramji and Said bin Salim, Rigby sent an official letter to H. L. Anderson of the Bombay government spelling out the requirements for compensation. In an attached personal note he said that "these poor people really have been very badly treated, and instead of the rewards they expected for their twenty months' wanderings through unexplored countries they have not even received what was justly due them."[21] The government more or less concurred and gave Rigby authorization to pay the men what he felt they deserved, adding, "Captain Burton should be required to explain why he neither paid these men nor brought their services and his debt to them to the notice of Government."[22]

Speke received support from other quarters as well. The influential Lord

John Russell met with and took a liking to him, and the Blackwood Brothers, publish-ers of *Blackwood's Magazine*, signed Speke up for a series of three articles based on his journals of the trips to Lake Tanganyika and the Victoria Nyanza. In the process they became advocates of his cause. Burton later pointed to the public-ation of the articles as the real turning point in his feelings about Speke.[23] Although Burton did have friends and supporters, most tended to be among literary and intellectual types who had far less influence with people that mattered. Milnes was the major exception. The two shared an interest in erotica, and Milnes's library was known for its huge collection.

In the *Blackwood's* articles Speke defended his claim about the Victoria Nyanza being the source of the White Nile. "Here we see," he said, "how singularly all the different informers' statements blend together, in substantiating my opinion that the Nyanza is the great reservoir or fountain-head of that mighty stream that floated Father Moses on his first adventurous sail—the Nile." With more time and goods, he felt he could have "settled every question we had to ascertain."[24] Interestingly, Speke refrained from saying anything negative about Burton. Indeed, he painted a quite cordial picture of his return from the lake, noting, "Captain Burton greeted me on arrival at the old house, where I had the satisfaction of finding him greatly restored in health, and having everything about him in a high state of preparation for the journey homewards."[25]

Burton, meanwhile, challenged the validity of Speke's geographic claims at every opportunity. He didn't see how the Victoria Nyanza could possibly extend to four or five degrees north latitude, since this would put the town of Gondokoro underwater. From 1839 to 1842 Egypt under Muhammad Ali Pasha launched three exploratory expeditions up the Nile. The second managed to reach just beyond Gondokoro before being turned back by rapids. Knowledge of the river thus ceased at this point.[26] Burton also claimed that Speke got the direction of the Kivira River (no such river actually exists and it's impossible to tell which one they meant) wrong—it flowed into the lake from the north instead of out. Furthermore, the hills to the north of Lake Tanganyika couldn't possibly be the Mountains of the Moon, as Speke insisted. He'd only conjectured about them from a distance, and they were neither high enough nor in the right location.[27]

When they next met at the RGS on November 25, Burton chose to avoid Speke and put his letters to and from the government on tables for all to see. In the future, he preferred that direct communication between the two cease. Speke reported this to Rigby and also said that he loathed Burton and would have brought the payment issue to attention "long before," except for concerns about Burton's response and being able to prove his case.[28]

In the end, Rigby's intervention brought results, and at the India Office's request, Burton wrote a long letter disputing each point made against him and laid out the various misconducts of the men in question that he felt disqualified them from receiving payment.[29] In his interpretation of the events, Speke supported several of the claimants, most notably Ramji.[30] In mid-January 1860 the India Office informed Burton that it was his "duty" to have settled this matter before leaving Zanzibar, adding, "The adjustment of the dispute would, in all probability, have been effected at a comparatively small outlay." His and Speke's letters would be forwarded to the Bombay government, "with whom it will rest to determine whether you shall be held pecuniarily responsible for the amount which has been paid in liquidation of the claims against you."[31]

Burton shot back, "I did not know that demands for wages existed against me on the part of those persons, and that I believed I had satisfactorily explained the circumstances of their dismissal without payment in my official letter of the 11th November, 1859." He went on to observe, "I represented the whole question to Captain Rigby, who, had he then—at that time—deemed it his duty to interfere, might have insisted upon adjudicating the affair with me, or with Captain Speke, before we left Zanzibar." Hurt and indignant, Burton concluded by writing, "I venture to express my surprise, that all my labours and long services in the cause of African exploration should have won me no other reward than the prospect of being mulcted in a pecuniary liability incurred by my late lamented friend, Lieut.-Colonel Hamerton, and settled without reference to me by his successor, Captain Rigby."[32] As things turned out, Burton didn't get "mulcted" financially, but clearly the psychological price paid was a steep one. Furthermore, another black mark had been added to his record. He didn't help his cause by also noting in the letter, "I have the honour to remark that the character of the British Government has *not*, and cannot (in my humble opinion) have suffered in any way by my withholding a purely conditional reward when forfeited by gross neglect and misconduct; and I venture to suggest that by encouraging such abuses serious obstacles will be thrown in the way of future exploration, and that the liberality of the British Government will be more esteemed by the native than its character for sound sense."

As January ticked down, Burton decided to leave England for Boulogne in order to work on the book about the journey to Lake Tanganyika. It turned out to be a wise decision, for on April 10 a completed manuscript of *The Lake Regions of Central Africa* was on its way to the publishers. During this time, Burton abandoned the idea of leading a new Nile expedition and instead turned his thoughts on other places to visit. The matter came up over dinner one night with Steinhaeuser, who, feeling no pain from all the alcohol consumed, shouted out, "I'll go to America."[33] Burton jumped at the idea. He wanted to see the reputed Wild West and visit yet another "holy" place, the Mormons' Salt Lake City. An added inducement was being able to eat and drink his way across the continent with a longtime friend (whom he referred to as Stiggins), sampling such new delights as "Smilers and Mint Juleps, Brandy-smashes, Whiskey-skies, Gin-slings, Sherry-cobblers, Rum-salads, Streaks of lightening, Morning Glory." The trip wouldn't be cheap, and where the money came from is unclear. Burton didn't have much of his own, so perhaps Steinhaeuser provided most of it.[34] On April 21 the two boarded the SS *Canada* for the transatlantic crossing. Isabel learned by note that she would once again have to endure an indeterminate period of loneliness. Richard had kept the trip from her, claiming he "could not bear the pain of saying goodbye" in person.[35] This, however, doesn't ring true, particularly since he also informed Isabel that during his absence she should decide between him and her mother. A better interpretation is that Burton just wanted to avoid an awkward situation.

At the same time, Speke was about ready to leave for East Africa, having chosen Captain James A. Grant, an affable friend from Bombay days, to be second in command. Funding delays had pushed back the departure well beyond that initially intended. Interestingly, in mid-April Burton and Speke exchanged their last direct communications. Speke said he couldn't leave England with such cold feelings between the two. Burton remarked that "any other tone would be extremely distasteful" to him.[36]

The surviving, though mostly unreadable, documents portray a playful Atlantic crossing in which Burton enjoyed spoofing and making fun of people and events in a make-believe young woman's diary.[37] After disembarking at Halifax,

Nova Scotia, on May 2 Burton and Steinhaeuser journeyed to Boston, New York City, and Washington, D.C., and paid a visit to George Washington's tomb at Mt. Vernon. A southern excursion followed, but the next surviving words came from St. Joseph, Missouri, where Burton went to catch a stagecoach destined for Salt Lake City. Earlier, likely at some point during the southern swing, Steinhaeuser had left for England. The two men would never carouse together again, as some five years later the good doctor died unexpectedly in Berne, Switzerland, from a heart attack. Burton dedicated his book on Zanzibar "To The Memory of My Old and Lamented Friend, John Frederick Steinhaeuser," and went on to write,

> The absence of Dr. Steinhaeuser cost the East African Expedition more than can be succinctly told. A favorite with "natives" wherever he went, a tried traveler, a man of literary tastes and extensive reading, and better still, a spirit staunch and determined as ever attempted desperate enterprise,—he would doubtless have materially furthered our views, and in all human probability Lieut. Speke would have escaped deafness and fever-blight, I paralysis and its consequent invalidism. We afterwards wandered together over the United States, and it is my comfort, now that he is also gone, to think that no unkind thought, much less and unfriendly word, ever broke our fair companionship. His memory is doubly dear to me. He was one of the very few who, through evil as well as through good report, disdained to abate an iota of his friendship, and whose regard was never warmer than when all the little world looked its coldest. After long years of service in pestilential Aden, the "Coal-hole of the East," he died suddenly. . . . At that time I was wandering about the Brazil, and I well remember dreaming, on what proved to be the day of his death, that a tooth suddenly fell to the ground, followed by a crash of blood. Such a friend, indeed, becomes part of oneself. I still feel a pang as my hand traces these lines.[38]

Meanwhile, *The Lake Regions of Central Africa* finally made it into print. Publication had been delayed, Burton said, by "impaired health, the depression of spirits, and worse still the annoyance of official correspondence."[39] In retrospect, it can be seen as ushering in a new era of travel narrative, one combining science and discovery with tales of adventure. Later travelers to the region, such as Cameron and Stanley, found the geographic information packed in the pages invaluable to their efforts, and Stanley followed its format in *How I Found Livingstone*. Unsurprisingly, Burton used the book as a platform. In the preface he took a potshot at Speke, noting, "During the exploration he acted in a subordinate capacity; and as may be imagined amongst a party of Arabs, Baloch, and Africans, whose languages he ignored, he was unfit for any other but a subordinate capacity."[40] To show his disdain, Burton never once referenced Speke by name. He simply became "my companion." As Burton informed the RGS prior to publication, the book contained an appendix with all of the correspondence related to the salary issue. This was necessary, he said, in order "to avoid the possibility of a charge being concealed in the pigeon-holes of the India House, to be produced, according to custom, with all the effect of surprise whenever its presence is convenient."[41] This outraged Rigby. In a long letter to Anderson he called the book full of "gross calumnies," listing twenty-four points to prove his case.[42] Rigby sent a similar letter to Shaw, who showed it to Burton, and he immediately fired off a missive to Rigby, noting, "A person who could act as you have acted must be held by everyone to be beneath notice of any honourable man." Burton felt that any contest over "personal veracity" would favor him.[43] In fact, it turned out to be the other way around.

Near the end of volume 2 of *The Lake Regions of Central Africa*, Burton presented a two-chapter summary of East Africans. The chapter titled "Village Life in East Africa" is, for the most part, a fairly straightforward account of such matters as the daily rhythm of life, foods and their preparations, weapons and hunting, pottery, weaving, music, dancing, and the treatment of diseases. Still, temptation to render caustic opinions overtook Burton from time to time. For example, upon completing a meal, he claimed the "East African invariably indulges in a long fit of torpidity, from which he awakes to pass the afternoon as he did the forenoon, chatting, playing, smoking, and chewing." As regards what Burton called "brain-work," it applied only to the "simple wants of life" and to gambling.[44] But it's in the chapter dealing with so-called character traits that Burton's racist leanings can be seen in full light. The long paragraph at the beginning pretty much said it all:

> The study of psychology in Eastern Africa is the study of man's rudimental mind, when, subject to the agency of material culture, he

neither progresses nor retrogrades. He would appear rather a degeneracy from the civilised man than a savage rising to the first step, were it not for his apparent incapacity for improvement. He has not the ring of true metal; there is no rich nature, as in the New Zealander, for education to cultivate. He seems to belong to one of those childish races which, never rising to man's estate, fall like worn-out links from the great chain of animated nature. He unites the incapacity of infancy with the unpliancy of age; the futility of childhood, and the credulity of youth, with the scepticism of the adult and the stubbornness and bigotry of the old. He has "beaten lands" and seas. For centuries he has been in direct intercourse with the more advanced people of the eastern coast, and though few have seen an European, there are not many who have not cast eyes on an Arab. Still he has stopped short at the threshold of progress; he shows no signs of development; no higher and more varied orders of intellect are called into being. Even the simple truths of El Islam have failed to fix the thoughts of men who can think, but who, absorbed in providing for their bodily wants, hate the trouble of thinking. His mind, limited to the objects seen, heard, and felt, will not, and apparently cannot, escape from the circle of sense, nor will it occupy itself with aught but the present. Thus he is cut off from the pleasures of memory, and the world of fancy is altogether unknown to him.[45]

Burton also added a long descriptive appendix on the region's primary commodities, and, as with Somaliland, he saw free trade as the way forward to future prosperity. Nowhere, however, did he urge territorial acquisitions to encourage it. Rather, free trade needed merchants, and they, not missionaries, would, in his view, put an end to the slave trade. And only merchants, he later wrote, could make the ivory trade profitable by building better roads to the source. At the low returns current caravans received, it wasn't worth the investment.[46]

Nothing of real excitement occurred as the mule-drawn stagecoach bumped westward for nineteen days. That Burton hoped otherwise is revealed by his packing two Colt six-shooters, along with a Bowie knife. He did manage to see a few Indians but not long enough to learn anything of substance from them, and thus for accounts he was forced to rely mostly on what he'd read and heard. To him they ranked higher on the racial scale than blacks, and their plight did elicit a bit of sympathy: "The chiefs are still bribed, and the people cheated, by white traders, and poverty, disease, and debauchery."[47] Later on, however, he would refer to them as the "human wild beast which is happily being extirpated."[48] The sight of "half-breeds" brought out Burton's usual disdain for white-nonwhite intermixture. He called them "short-lived, peculiarly subject to infectious diseases, untrustworthy, and disposed to every villainy."[49] Given the limited contact, such an evaluation could have come only from informants, and hardly unbiased ones at that.

Besides seeing new lands and peoples and drinking various whiskeys on a regular basis, Burton enjoyed the company of Lieutenant James J. Dana, who was on his way to a Utah posting with his wife and young daughter. Burton referred to him as my "*compagnon de voyage*" for providing good conversation and introductions to military personnel along the way.[50] Burton was somewhat less pleased with a young woman wearing bloomers who boarded at Fort Laramie:

> It is only fair to state that it was the only hermaphrodite of the kind that ever met my eyes in the United States: the great founder of the order has long since subsided into her original obscurity, and her acolytes having relapsed into the weakness of petticoats. The Bloomer was an uncouth being, her hair cut level with her eyes, depended with a graceful curl of a drake's tail around a flat Turanian countenance, whose only expression was sullen insolence. The body-dress, glazed brown calico, fitted her somewhat like a soldier's tunic, developing haunches which would be admired only in venison.[51]

The ride ended at Salt Lake City on August 25. Outbreaks of violence between Mormons and non-Mormons had been ongoing since the Saints reached the Great Salt Lake in 1847, and the recent arrival of federal troops put talk of war in the air. That, of course, didn't deter Burton, who quickly set about making ethnographic and other observations. As events transpired, he stayed only twenty-four days, which prompted him to write in an unusual display of humility, "But there is in Mormondom, as in all other exclusive faiths, whether Jewish, Hindu, or other, an inner life into which I cannot flatter myself or deceive the reader with the idea of my having penetrated."[52] He met with Brigham Young and came away impressed, although not with *The Book of Mormon*: "Surely there never was a book so thoroughly dull and boring: it is monotonous as a sageprairie."[53] His renderings of Mormons in *The City of the Saints* were far different from those of Africans in *The Lake Regions of Central Africa*. He made few negative or disparaging remarks and overall provided a quite sympathetic take on Mormonism. No savages or barbarians here, for sure. Some of this can be credited to his not suffering as in Africa, but of equal, if not greater, significance was that the people in question were white instead of black or brown. Indeed, most of them had roots in Great Britain, where the Mormons had been busy recruiting members for more than a decade.

Naturally enough, Burton looked favorably on Mormon polygyny, and he devoted a substantial portion of *The City of the Saints* to their and his own justifications for the practice. While Mormons stressed the theological—in other words, polygyny coming from God—he emphasized demographic, physiologic, and economic rationales. In each instance, Burton spoke without much evidence to support his positions. For example, he thought polygyny led to more children than monogamy in less-populated lands. As later data have shown, if any correlation exists, it's the other way around. The confusion came from measuring fertility by number of children per family instead of per woman. Polygyny in Burton's mind also supposedly produced superior physiques because it was associated with a ban on women having intercourse while breastfeeding. While this practice does serve as a form of birth control, evidence hardly supports the physique contention, as many other factors come into play. And his economic connection rested on the view that an Anglo-American woman couldn't shoulder the workload by herself. The many pioneer women who worked daily before sunup till after sundown would surely have found such thinking nonsense.

On September 19 the westward journey resumed, passing through Carson City, crossing the Sierra Nevada Mountains to Sacramento, and ending up in San Francisco. Cold and snow in the mountains and the site of a station recently attacked and burned by Ute Indians made for a more adventurous trip than the one to Salt Lake City. Still, as before, the guns went unused. Socializing took up the ten days Burton spent in the city by the bay. Although other interesting places beckoned, he'd run out of steam. "But in sooth I was weary of the way; for eight months I had lived on board steamers and railroad cars, coaches, and mules; my eyes were full of sight-seeing, my pockets empty, and my brain stuffed with all manner of useful knowledge. It was far more grateful to flaner about the stirring streets, to admire the charming faces, to enjoy the delicious climate, and to pay quiet visits like a 'ladies' man,' than to front wind and rain, muddy roads, *arrieros*, and rough teamsters, fit only for Rembrandt and the solitude of out-stations."[54] Burton failed to mention the heavy drinking he'd done at every opportunity as a likely cause. On November 15 the homeward journey began, first via ship to Panama, then across the isthmus by train to catch the *Seine* bound for Southampton, where it docked New Year's Eve.

The separation tore at Isabel. She took to bed with various illnesses for six weeks and lived in a constant state of apprehension, heightened by an unconfirmed report that Richard had been murdered. The person in question turned out to be another Captain Burton. Isabel didn't know otherwise until the January 1, 1861, edition of the *Times* listed Richard as one of the passengers who had disembarked from the *Seine*. She was at a party in Yorkshire and immediately made plans to leave for the city, where she met Richard the following day. Upon their meeting he brought up the matter of having to choose between her mother and him, threatening to do further exploring or go back to India if she didn't. Isabel responded, "Quite. I marry you this day three weeks, let who will say nay."[55] Following a brief discussion over propitious and unpropitious days (both were highly superstitious), they set Tuesday, January 22, for the wedding. As expected, her mother once again objected. She refused to attend the wedding and wouldn't allow Isabel's sisters to either. Mr. Arundell and her brothers could decide for themselves. Earlier, in attempt to appease, Burton signed in front of Roman Catholic Cardinal Wiseman a promise to allow Isabel to practice her faith, raise any children Catholic, and be married in the Church.[56]

In the end, not a single relative from either side appeared at the ceremony held in the Church of Our Lady of the Assumption, also called the Bavarian Catholic Church. Indeed, the wedding party totaled only eight, including a registrar, a requirement for mixed marriages. To forestall any unpleasantness occurring, a decision was made to keep the news from Mrs. Arundell until some future date. The cover story had Isabel staying at a friend's country house.

Richard and Isabel at the time of their wedding. (Reproduced with permission of the London Borough of Richmond upon Thames Art Collection, Orleans House Gallery.)

No honeymoon followed. Instead, after a post-wedding meal at the home of friends, Richard and Isabel went straight to their small apartment on Bury Street. There the first weeks passed with Richard working on *The City of the Saints* during the morning and spending nights in conversations with an array of friends at several favored drinking establishments. The time in between he devoted to Isabel. There's no evidence of extramarital dalliances while they were together in Britain and elsewhere, and everything points to him having cared deeply for Isabel. Later Burton dedicated *Abeokuta and the Camaroons Mountains* to her with the words, "To My Best Friend, My Wife." Whether he remained faithful when out of the country on his own is arguable. There is absolutely no doubt about Isabel's devotion and faithfulness to him. Henceforth, she would serve as his book agent and advocate in just about everything. An outstanding question is the degree of their sexual intimacy. Nothing survives to say anything with certainty one way or the other. All that biographers who've addressed the issue have been able to offer are their own speculations.

It took only a few weeks before news reached Mrs. Arundell of Isabel's whereabouts. She quickly wrote her husband who was away at the time; he telegraphed back, "She is married to Dick Burton and thank God for it."[57] According to Isabel, a family meal ensued shortly afterward, and peace was established when Mrs. Arundell accepted the fact of the marriage and even asked to be pardoned for her opposition. Georgiana Stisted claimed she never did accept Burton as a son-in-law.

Isabel had many important social contacts and was even received by Queen Victoria. In addition to everything else, she served as Richard's liaison with high society and was instrumental in getting Lord John Russell, the secretary of state for foreign affairs, to recommend Burton to the consular service. He desperately wanted the Damascus posting, but it was not to be, at least just now. Instead, they offered him the open consulship overseeing the coastal area of West Africa abutting the Bights of Benin and Biafra, part of the so-called Slave Coast, with its headquarters, rather ironically, in Santa Isabel (now Malabo) on the island of Fernando Po (now Bioko). A Spanish possession, the harbor was used by the British navy as a base of operations for their antislavery patrols. Although a bottom-rung position with a salary of only five hundred pounds, plus two hundred for expenses, per annum, Burton said yes. As he told Milnes, who'd become Lord Houghton, "Needless to say that I have accepted it. The dog that refuses the Governmental crumb shall never be allowed by a retributive destiny to pound with his mollars the Governmental loaf."[58] He was in no hurry to leave, however, and on July 7 the Foreign Office sent a note telling him "to make arrangements for proceeding at once to your post at Fernando Po." Burton responded by asking that the start be delayed until August 24, as this would allow him to arrive after the unhealthiest time of year and thus avoid a "bad beginning." The Foreign Office agreed to the delay.[59]

Before the year was out Burton's name was removed from the list of Indian army officers owing to his long absences from duty, and with that went rank, half-pay, and pension rights.[60] This time, Isabel's contacts could do nothing to alter the decision. This came on top of the warehouse fire that destroyed most of his belongings, including manuscripts, books, journals, costumes, and souvenirs, mostly pertaining to India. Much was irreplaceable, and though insured, the owners refused to pay a cent by way of compensation.

The rest of the spring and summer brought a round of social engagements, in between which Burton put the final touches to *The City of the Saints*. The day of leaving for Fernando Po came on August 24. Despite her pleadings, Isabel would not be going along. The Foreign Office considered the site too dangerous for dependents because of disease, and Burton concurred. Deaths from fevers, dysentery, and lately cholera had produced a series of appellations: "White Man's Grave" for the coast of West Africa in general; "Coffin Squadron" for the antislavery patrol; "Foreign Office Grave" for Fernando Po itself. Later Burton wrote, "There is no place where a wife is so much wanted as in the Tropics; but then comes the rub—how to keep the wife alive."[61] The best Isabel could do was to see him off and make sure he had needed creature comforts for the long voyage. Thus ended what she termed seven months of "uninterrupted bliss."[62]

6

PORTS OF CALL

BURTON SAILED OFF IN A SOUR MOOD. He was headed for a "back-of-beyond" part of the world aboard the African Steam Ship Line's *Blackland*, a mail packet with a top speed of only eight knots and destined for numerous ports of call along the way. Furthermore, unlike the journeys to Harar and Lake Tanganyika, this trip would follow a well-trodden path. Since the mid-fifteenth-century arrival of the Portuguese, Europeans, including the British, had been active along Africa's West Coast, looking mostly for gold, slaves, and malaguetta peppers. At key locations, they built and staffed forts and factories, leading to the establishment of settlements and several small colonies. Thus, with no new geographic discoveries on the horizon, Burton decided to write a travel handbook, one designed to "lay down what a tolerably active voyager can see and do during the few hours allowed by the halts of a mail packet."[1] He sought to obviate criticism about the short time spent at each port hardly being adequate to make valid observations by claiming,

> I am convinced . . . that if a sharp, well-defined outline is to be drawn,
> it must be done immediately after arrival at a place; when the sense of
> contrast is still fresh upon the mind, and before second and third have
> ousted first thoughts. . . . Except in a New World, where the mind is
> stunned, observation will, a few days after arrival, lose all its distinctness.
> The man who has dwelt a score of years in a place, has forgotten every
> feeling with which he first sighted it; and if he writes about it, he writes
> for himself and for his fellow-oldsters, not for the public.[2]

Wanderings in West Africa was published in 1863. It's an inapt title because Burton couldn't wander very far from the ports. And, contrary to the "first thoughts" claim, he edited his journal notes, usually by adding new information derived from later readings and experiences. Burton made the author out to be F. R. G. S. (Fellow of the Royal Geographical Society), something he did on other occasions, and often wrote in the third person. In this case, Burton didn't use a pseudonym to maintain his anonymity, as, given style and subject matter, there was no way to hide the true identity of the writer. Sarcasm is a more plausible reason. It's certainly there in the dedication, which took a potshot at Britain's philanthropic organizations and overseas policies.

TO

THE TRUE FRIENDS OF AFRICA

—NOT TO THE "PHILANTHROPIST" OR TO EXETER HALL —

These Pages are Inscribed,

BY

A HUMBLE MEMBER OF THEIR FRATERNITY

And it abounds in the text as well, which included pages full of opinions, designed, Burton openly admitted, "To relieve the dryness of details."[3] Some are nothing more than prejudicial rants, but also scattered about are observations that reveal a scholar and astute observer at work. Among his most prescient insights was recognizing the affinities between many of the languages spoken in West Africa and those spanning the continent to the east and south. It took nearly a hundred years of research to confirm this in the form of the Niger-Kordofanian family of languages. Burton also accurately challenged David Livingstone's assertion that "no African tribe has ever been destroyed," contending, "Nothing but the profoundest ignorance could have dictated such a declaration."[4] The whole coast from Liberia to Gabon, he correctly argued, was a scene of displacement, with many former groups having gone the route of extinction. Although peace currently prevailed, in the sense that no major wars were being fought, Burton didn't expect it to last. This proved to be true as well.

In the rest of this chapter we'll follow the itinerary Burton described in *Wanderings* in order to examine the evolution of his thoughts about Africans, plus the place of Europeans in West Africa. He considered health maintenance as the main issue facing the latter and thus decided to make it a focus of concern while stationed at Fernando Po. But, as we shall see, an array of other matters occupied his mind and time.

Rain and mist accompanied the *Blackland* as it sailed from Liverpool harbor. This seemed appropriate to Burton: "Who ever landed at Southampton in other but the worst of weather? Who ever left Dover on a fine clear morning?" he asked.[5] The first leg of the voyage to Funchal, Madeira, covered over fifteen hundred miles, and along the way Burton found many things besides bad weather to complain about. Quarters were cramped and luxuries mostly nonexistent. He considered stewardesses necessary for passenger comfort, and the only one on the *Blackland* was scheduled to depart at Funchal. "Even a black woman would be better than nothing," he quipped.[6] Screw noise and deck washing at 4:00 a.m. became irritants, although nothing bothered Burton more than the lack of something decent to drink.

> The beer and stout are tolerable, but at this rate will not last; and the ice may possibly endure to Lagos, the soda water to the Bonny. But the wine is dear, and, what is worse, execrable: The African Steam Ship Company makes little by it, so we have to pay dear for simple carelessness touching our comforts. The claret is black strap, the hock is sourish, the champagne all syrup, the Burgundy is like the house of Burgundy of the Reform Club—meat as well as drink; the Moselle *sent son perruquier*; the sherry is a mine of bile; and of the port—the less said the better of such "strong military ditto." The coffee and tea are not bad naturally, but artificially; and to distinguish between them requires a very superior nose.[7]

At around 10:00 p.m. on August 30 the *Blackland* slipped into Funchal Harbor. Burton considered Madeira, which translates as "wood," part of Africa and its inhabitants Africans, something he noted they didn't like hearing. That's understandable. The chain lies nearly four hundred miles off the coast of Morocco, and the original settlers (there were no indigenous inhabitants) of the two habitable islands, Madeira and Porto Santo, came mainly from the Algarve and Minho regions of Portugal shortly after the islands were discovered in 1418–20. The Purple Islands mentioned by Roman mariners are likely the same, although the Romans appear not to have made landfall on the chain. Africans were brought over to work sugar plantations, but few of them existed by Burton's time. Intermixing had, however, created a small mulatto population.

Before sunrise the next day, Burton went ashore to see the sights. He spent the first few hours wandering about the city, making observations and chatting with locals. Rugged topography limited how far he could go into the interior. Unusually, Burton had little to say about the women. His only comment of note was about "lower orders," which he characterized as having "swarthy skins, flat faces, round, stout contours bons-sens expression, and a wondrous waddle."[8]

Burton paid more attention to the British residents. England did hold the islands briefly in the early eighteenth century, but the three to five hundred there at the moment had come mostly for health reasons. General consensus held Madeira's climate to be the finest in the northern hemisphere, one especially well suited to those suffering from lung diseases, especially tuberculosis. Burton wasn't so sure because of the high humidity. Many of the residents looked "thin, pale, sub-green tinted like East Indians," and he jested "that the English constitution cannot thrive without a winter."[9] The biggest problem to him, though, was that of ennui: "Little islands are all large prisons: one cannot look at the sea without wishing for the wings of a swallow. This, with the usual sense of confinement, combines the feeling of an hospital, or a sick-bay, and one soon sighs to escape from its dreary volcanic rocks."[10]

Next came a stop at Santa Cruz de Tenerife in the Canary Islands. The name for the archipelago comes from the Latin *canaria*, which means land of dogs, although the connection remains mysterious. The bird derived its name from the islands. Here one does enter Africa because of the presumed relationship of the aboriginal inhabitants, the Guanche, to the mainland Berbers. The evidence, though, is tenuous, and how they reached the islands is a particular puzzle. The fifty-mile crossing would have required seaworthy vessels, which the Guanche don't seem to have had. No land bridge spanned the distance, so the only plausible conclusion is that they lost boat-building technology sometime after settlement. Unfortunately, none of the Guanche survived the Spanish conquest that started in 1402. By the end of the fifteenth century, wars, disease, and intermixture had all taken their respective tolls on the population. Although mummified remains were discovered in some caves, most of these wound up being ground into medicines for an array of conditions, such as fractures, nausea, epilepsy, and liver ailments, long ago. The few specimens in museums have yet to be studied in detail.

At 9:00 p.m. on Sunday, September 1, the *Blackland* dropped anchor off Santa Cruz. Since he had only the next morning to see things by light of day, Burton went ashore as soon as the health officer cleared passengers to leave ship. Despite looking barren when compared with Madeira, Tenerife was preferred by Burton because of its inhabitants. He called the men "a fine race, tall and sinewy," whose "manly aspect contrasts strongly with the half-starved Madeirans."[11] Women also constituted "a most distinct improvement," with their "fine eyes, luxuriant hair, clear olive skin, and features which are often regular and sometimes beautiful." Yet, they didn't compare with the women back home.

> For those who admire black anywhere except "in the skin," there is nothing more enchanting than the women of Tenerife. Pretty, however, they never are past the age when the *diable* endows them with fleeting charms; they all become either handsome or dead ugly. In England, on the contrary, there are hundreds of pretty women to one beauty—the latter is far rarer than amongst their southern sisters.
>
> "J'aime le vin blanc," said Montaigne; Montaigne's friends
> Consigned him and his wine to all the fiends.
>
> Despite which danger, I will confess, that one soon wearies of Black eyes and black hair, and after a course of such charms, one falls back with pleasure upon brown, yellow, or, what is better than all, red-auburn locks and eyes of soft limpid blue.[12]

Was Isabel on his mind? She might have been, although the color sequence reflects Burton's views on race.

The various establishments seemed more civilized to him than those on Madeira, and the people, he said, spoke "a pretty Spanish dialect instead of a debased *patois* of the debased Portuguese *patois*."[13] Never say that to anyone in Portugal or Brazil. The neighboring islands could easily be visited, and so Burton didn't experience the same sense of confinement and felt the climate almost ideal for those seeking relief from tuberculosis. Tenerife, however, lacked the facilities to serve them, and he didn't think the Spanish wanted strangers in their midst. Indeed, they wouldn't court them for quite some time to come. Now tourists are actively sought after.

Upon their departure from Tenerife the weather turned bad. The ocean in these parts is a breeding ground for tropical storms that can become hurricanes upon crossing the Atlantic. Coasting, they passed Cap Blanc and at Cap Vert caught a glimpse of the infamous slave depot on Goreé Island, then part of the French colony of Senegal. Ninety miles farther on, the *Blackland* called at Bathurst on St. Mary's Island at the mouth of the Gambia River. Britain purchased the site in 1816 for dropping off slaves liberated by its squadrons that patrolled coastal waters, and by the time Burton arrived the colony totaled about five thousand residents.

Here began a region called Guinea that stretched in some minds southward to the Gabon River and in others to as far as Angola. Although it is likely of African origin, no one knows from where the word came, and by the nineteenth century only Europeans used it. Gold from the region gave the currency guinea its name, and two current countries, Guinea and Guinea-Bissau, plus a body of water, the Gulf of Guinea, have kept it alive. Gambia supposedly meant "clear water," but to Burton the river looked "muddy as the Mersey." Bathurst reeked of "decayed" air, and he thought the site must have been "selected for its unhealthiness" because "mud, mangrove, miasma, and malaria" were everywhere.[14]

Burton encountered two African peoples from the region. One he called Mandengas, later more commonly rendered as Mandingos. They are now known as Malinke, part of the larger Mande group, which includes the Soninke, founders of the medieval kingdom of Ghana, centered to the northwest of the Niger River in what is now Mali. The Ghana of today took its name for historical rather than geographical reasons. Burton considered the Malinke a "race of gentlemen and horsemen," bearing "points of likeness to the Somal" with their "long limbs, especially the fore-arm, tall lithe figures, high shoulders, small heads, and semi-Caucasian features."[15] Most of those seen at the coast were traders of one kind or another. He later would put the Malinke and Somali together as among the "noble tribes of Africa" who were spreading Islam southward and thus paving "the way for a higher civilization."[16] The other group, the Wolof, struck him as

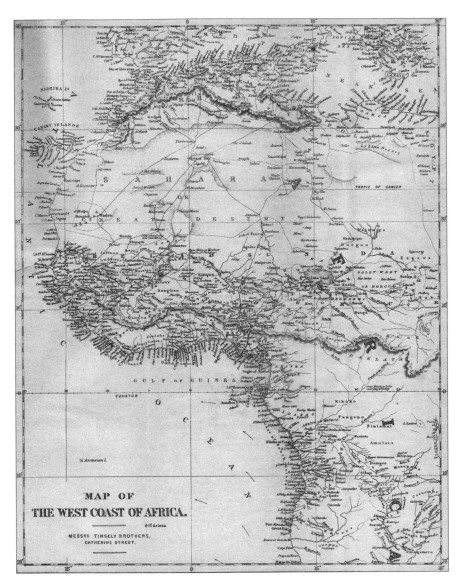

Map of West Africa from Wanderings in West Africa. *(Reproduced with permission of the Special Collections Research Center, Syracuse University Library.)*

more like the Abyssinians and "remarkable for good looks, ringlets, and tasteful toilets and ornaments." They appeared to be "interesting and civilizable."[17] Once again, we see Burton's prejudice at work: The less people fit the Negro stereotype then prevalent, the higher they ranked on the human developmental scale.

Burton didn't tarry long in Bathurst, deciding instead to use the remaining hours to visit a convalescent facility on the mainland. Upon crossing the river he remarked, "The scene at once improved: it illustrated on a small scale how much better is the heart of Africa than its epidermis."[18] This caused him to wonder when the Europeans would decide to abandon St. Mary's Island and move inland, where one could get away from the "white man's grave" of the coast. And with better health, they could more effectively extract Africa's wealth. "I begin to think that the antiquated horror of Western Africa, which methinks is really but little worse than Western India, will soon pass away from the memory of the British public, which is wax to receive and marble to retain such prejudices. Then, as a consequence, hygienic science will readily discover fitting residences for the white man; and then, but not till then, the mines of African wealth, from which we now content ourselves with picking up the fragments, will be effectually and thoroughly exploited."[19]

At this point in *Wanderings*, Burton took a swipe at some European travelers who'd professed having great difficulties in West Africa. The Scot Mungo Park came in for particular abuse. Burton made fun of his dress, with its "black beaver tile, and blue coat with brass buttons, with shoeless feet." He further criticized him for not knowing any of the languages; misunderstanding the Moors, who'd actually treated him quite well instead of badly, as Park claimed; and causing his own death by firing on the inhabitants of Busa without just provocation. Burton thought traveling the countryside would be a piece of cake for him, and he was confident that he could pick up serviceable Mande in a month and with "sword and dagger, a koran, and an inkhorn, reeds, and a few sheets of paper" in hand pass as "an honoured guest."[20] He never got the opportunity to test the hypothesis.

Burton next turned to the general state of humankind. Whether he did so at the time or later can't be discerned. In either event, the remarks provide full testimony to how deeply race infected his thoughts:

With Mr. Luke Burke, I hold, as a tenet of faith, the doctrine of great ethnic centres, and their comparative gradation. I believe the European to be the brains, the Asiatic the heart, the American and African the arms, and the Australian the feet, of the man-figure. I also, or let me say

we, opine that, in the various degrees of intellectuality, the negro ranks
between the Australian and the Indian—popularly called Red—who
is above him. From humbly aspiring to be owned as a man, our black
friend now boldly advances his claim to *egalité* and *fraternité*, as if there
could be brotherhood between the crown and the clown! The being
who "invents nothing, originates nothing, improves nothing, who can
only cook, nurse, and fiddle;" who has neither energy nor industry,
save in rare cases that prove the rule!—the self-constituted thrall that
delights in subjection to and in imitation of the superior races. The
aboriginal American has not been known to slave; the African, since he
landed in Virginia A.D. 1620, has chosen nothing else, has never until
egged on, dreamed of being free. He has fatal respect for the Asiatic, and
the European has ever treated him like a child. And yet we—in these
days—read such nonsense as "Africa for the Africans." *Datur digniori* is
the fiat of Fate where such mighty interests are concerned. When the
black rat expels the grey rat, then the negro shall hold his own against
the white man.[21]

As for hopes of improving the African condition, Burton pinned them on
Islam, claiming that where adopted, it had "wrought immense good" by making
"that first step in moral progress," even though associated with such things as
"polygamy, domestic slavery and the degradation of women," something he
firmly denied. These hardly compared, though, with "the horrors of cannibalism
and fetishism, the witch tortures, the poison ordeals, the legal incest . . . and the
murder of albinos, of twins, of children who cut their upper teeth first," which
Islam suppressed.[22]

West Africa introduced Burton to Christian Africans, and for him they
suffered when compared with Muslims. The five Malinke men who took ship
for passage to Sierra Leone, he called "kind, obliging, and manly in demeanour"
as opposed to "sheepish and servile, or forward and impudent" Christians.[23] He
went on to write,

It was impossible not to be struck by the superiority of their [Malinke]
deportment and appearance. Their loose and ample robes, even when of

poor stuff, gave them breadth as well as height, and the picturesque folds contrasted wonderfully well with the grimy slops of the poorer Christian, and the caricatured imitation of our dress—itself a caricature—affected, at much loss of comfort and aspect, by "Gentlemen," the richer negro classes. There is a manliness and honesty in the Mandenga's look, wholly wanting among the "liberated." The dignity of El Islam everywhere displays itself; it is the majesty of the monotheist who ignores the degrading doctrines of original sin.[24]

At the time events were headed in the direction desired by Burton, as jihad-style movements had spread Islam widely across the interior of West Africa and migrations brought more and more adherents to the coast.

The next call was scheduled for Freetown, Sierra Leone, which Burton took to calling "S'a Leone" after the pronunciation of a "pretty Mulatto lady" passenger from there.[25] Why the Portuguese named the mountain that juts up from the sea after lions is unclear. They didn't get it from any local dialect, and there's no evidence of lions ever being around in unusual numbers, if at all. Might it have been thunderstorms roaring like a lion? In the years following the Portuguese arrival, the secure harbor served as a calling point for ships bearing a wide array of flags. The infamous John Hawkins stopped three times in the 1560s to load slaves. It also became an early site of Christian missionary activity, and a small mulatto population emerged over the course of several centuries.

Although Burton had looked forward to the visit, nothing about the place pleased him. He called the site "vile" because of oppressive high heat, humidity, and its residents' proneness to disease. Serious yellow fever epidemics had occurred in 1839–40, 1847–48, and 1858–59, when half of the 120 white residents either fled or died. The toll taken on Africans wasn't recorded. The settlement, he argued, should have been built higher up the mountain instead of near the water, as happened in 1787, when abolitionists started a colony with four hundred freed slaves, most of whom had fought on England's side during the American Revolutionary War and managed to reach London. They were joined, as W. Winwood Reade put it, by sixty of the city's "women of the town."[26] Disease and conflicts with the local Temne quickly led to the settlement's demise. In 1792 the Sierra Leone Company reoccupied the site by landing about a thousand escaped slaves who'd found refuge in Nova Scotia and gave it the name Freetown.

This time the settlement took, and its numbers were augmented by over five hundred Maroons from Jamaica in 1800, following the putdown of their revolt several years earlier. The two groups didn't get along. The Nova Scotians were highly westernized, whereas the Maroons maintained Africa-based customs, such as polygyny. The company never saw a profit, and in 1808 the British government designated Sierra Leone a Crown Colony, following Parliament's passage of the Act for the Abolition of the Slave Trade the previous year. The act led to the arrival of yet another population, so-called Liberated Africans, mostly of Yoruba and Igbo descent. Although looked down on by the Maroons and colonists from Nova Scotia, they soon achieved numerical and economic dominance. When it became clear that agriculture offered few prospects for betterment, many opted to pursue careers as traders, working within and beyond Sierra Leone's borders. Because they lived in a Crown Colony, they were British subjects, a status most of them prized. Spoken English, Christianity, and European names and dress served as hallmarks of identity. The Liberated Africans, like the other settlers, adopted a Creole identity to set them apart from the indigenous inhabitants and mulattos, both considered inferior.

In the 1830s the colony began attracting westernized professionals from the Caribbean who saw opportunities to further their careers and at the same time help Africans advance economically and socially.[27] Openings existed because few Europeans came to Sierra Leone, and indeed, British policy favored the creation of a colony meant for "free blacks."

With its "decrepit" and "tumble down" houses, Freetown showed years of neglect by residents and government alike. Burton thought this characteristic of the tropics, where, he claimed, "It is far easier . . . to build than to unbuild, which involves re-building." Apathy reigns: "No one intends to stay longer than two years, and even these two are one long misery. Consequently men will not take the trouble to make roads, nor think of buying a farm, or of building a house upon a hill."[28] All things considered, Bathurst looked good by comparison.

Burton, of course, couldn't resist demeaning people. He called an Igbo man on board "our Gorilla, or Missing Link," and found nothing admirable in the nonwhite inhabitants of Sierra Leone.

> The S'a Leone man is an inveterate thief; he drinks, he gambles, he intrigues, he over-dresses himself, and when he has exhausted his means,

he makes master pay for all. With a terrible partiality for summonsing and enjoying himself thoroughly in a court of law, he enters into the spirit of the thing like an attorney's clerk; he soon wearies of the less exciting life in the wilder settlements, where debauchery has not yet developed itself,—home sickness then seizes him, and he deserts, after probably robbing the house. He is the horror of Europeans; the merchants of the Gaboon River prefer forfeiting the benefits of the A. A. S. to seeing themselves invaded by this locust tribe, whose beautiful view is apparently that which leads out of S'a Leone. At Lagos and Abeokuta S'a Leone has returned to his natural paganism, and has become an inveterate slave-dealer, impudently placing himself under native protection and renegading the flag that saved him from life-long servitude.[29]

Fraternization should be avoided at all costs. It was, to Burton, "a political as well as a social mistake to permit these men to dine in the main cabin, which they will end up monopolizing: a ruling race cannot be too particular about these small matters. The white man's position is rendered far more precarious on the coast than it might be, if the black man were always kept in his proper place."[30] And those freed from slaving vessels didn't, in his mind, deserve British citizenship.

Our forefathers never dreamed that the liberty and institutions for which during long centuries they fought and bled, would be thus prostituted—be lavished upon every black receptive, be he assassin, thief, or wizard, after a residence of fourteen days in a dark corner of the English empire. . . . Free the slaves if you like, strike the slaver to the ground with his victims' fetters; but ever remember that by far the greatest number of the liberated were the vilest of criminals in their own lands, and that in their case exportation becomes, in fact, the African form of transportation.[31]

Even the way Africans served food got under Burton's skin. "It seems impossible," he said, "to persuade the negro mind that fish and beef are not eaten together, and that the same plate is not intended to hold, at one time, pork and mutton."[32] Critical of snobs, he was often one himself when it came to the behavior of presumed lesser mortals, and thus showed himself to be, if not by birth, then by attitude, a proper English gentleman. He always preferred native peoples uncontaminated by modern influences. That way, he wouldn't have to deal with them as equals.

Overall, Burton felt Sierra Leone a wasted opportunity, and he held out little hope for its future. "With good management the colony might have become a flourishing portion of the empire, extending deep into Africa, and opening up to commerce lands teeming with varied wealth. Now it is a mere ruin of an emporium, and the people, born and bred to do nothing, of course cannot prevail upon themselves to work."[33] While he may have been wrong about causes, the colony didn't flourish, and the modern state ranks near the bottom on virtually every measure of human well-being.

On September 13 the *Blackland* sailed from Freetown headed for a brief six-hour stop at Cape Palmas. With no time to see much of anything, Burton focused his attention on the area's inhabitants, the Kru, a name encompassing nine linguistically related groups resident on both sides of the cape. They'd developed a reputation for being skilled seafarers, first while working for Spanish and Portuguese slave traders and then aboard merchant ships when the trade in slaves declined. "Kru Boys" became their common appellation among Europeans. Burton called them "grotesque" in appearance because of what he saw as a contrast between physique and face. "A more magnificent development of muscle, such perfect symmetry in the balance of grace and strength, my eyes had never yet looked upon. But the faces! Except when lighted up by smiles and good humour—expression to an African face is all in all—nothing could be more unprepossessing. The flat nose, the high cheek-bones, the yellow eyes, the chalky white teeth pointed like the shark's, the muzzle projecting as that of a dog-monkey, combine to form an unusual amount of ugliness."[34]

He then railed at their supposed cowardice and propensity to steal. Still, the Kru had demonstrated "comparative energy," a "willingness to do work," and an "independent bearing," and, thus, Burton considered them the best of the lot in this part of the world, or, in his words, "bad as they are, all the rest are worse."[35] Indeed, he tried to hire some to work for him in Fernando Po, but had no luck, as they found, in their words, "Nanny Po" an ill-gotten place.

Cape Palmas marked the southernmost point of the Republic of Liberia. It began when in 1822 the American Colonization Society relocated a small number of freed slaves at Cape Mesurado. They brought with them an Americanized culture and built Monrovia as their capital. Continuing immigration supported the establishment of other settlements along the coast, and in 1847 the republic achieved international recognition. But the country was imposed and divided, with the Americo-Liberians, as they became known, either ignoring or lording it over the indigenes encompassed within its artificial boundaries. The tensions simmered before erupting into two decades of violence in the 1980s and 1990s.

Burton didn't meet any Americo-Liberians, but he'd come to view white Americans as well suited for Africa. "For African exploration the Anglo-American is probably the best of men, physically and morally; his energy and sobriety are far superior to that of the older family, and he has had from his youth sufficient experience of Africans to—despite overwrought English sensibilities regarding black men—appreciate their merits and demerits, and to treat them as they should be treated. He is a favourite wherever he goes, by reason of a certain freedom of manner which is liked everywhere save in England."[36]

On September 16 the *Blackland* upped anchor for the Gold Coast. Starting with the Portuguese construction of El Mina in 1481, some twenty-five forts and factories lined a 225-mile-long seafront. Built initially to collect gold, they also served as way stations for slaves destined for the New World. Previously, both had been shipped northward to the savanna kingdoms to become part of the many centuries old trans-Saharan trade. Of the eleven forts still operating, El Mina and three others were in Dutch hands, with the remaining seven, including the scheduled port of call, Cape Coast Castle, British run. While gold still trickled in, the slave trade had ended, with no other valuable commodity yet replacing it. Furthermore, since early in the century, Britain and the Asante Kingdom had been contesting for regional dominance, which led to several episodes of war. Little had been invested in the upkeep of the forts, leading Burton to remark, "Really, for appearances' sake, Britannia ought to look after this out-of-the-way corner of her estate, or give it up altogether."[37]

All in all, Burton didn't have much to say about conditions at Cape Coast Castle, beyond noting that relations between black and white seemed to be worse there than anywhere he had yet visited. This he attributed largely to many of the resident whites being inferior to Africans and mulattos, a condition that stunned him into confessing, "The possibility of such a thing had never yet reached my brain."[38] Burton didn't bother pursuing the "possibility" very far; his thoughts instead drifted to gold, as revealed by a long chapter on its history in *Wanderings*. Near the chapter's end he challenged a certain Mr. Wilson's statement that "the world is not suffering for the want of gold," by saying, "There are those, myself for instance, and many a better man, who would be happy at times to see and feel a little more of that 'vile yellow clay.'"[39] In future years Burton would try to do just that on more than one occasion, including during another journey to the Gold Coast.

From Cape Coast Castle, the *Blackland* sailed for Accra, where both the British and Dutch operated forts. Burton felt the latter a problem. The main issue revolved around their free port policies, which, he said, drew trade away from British posts. If the Dutch could somehow be removed, then profits, he felt, from duties on items such as rum and weapons would soar. Soon he would change his tune about these products. Burton then advised that, for purposes of native cooperation, taxes should be imposed for local use only, perceptively noting that people needed to see results for their payments. As a cost-saving measure, he recommended a civil police made up of West Indians be formed instead of having the regular army on hand. The army would stay and include West Indian units to fight in another war with the Asante from 1868 to 1874.

Burton found the people in the vicinity of Accra noteworthy, claiming he'd "never seen such tall, muscular, and powerful negroes." Although "remarkably hairy," the women appeared "equally well-grown," with complexions "rather a dark red than black."[40] Still, he didn't think Africans along the West Coast measured up to their eastern counterparts. Indeed, with only a few exceptions, such as the Asante, Burton labeled them the most "timid" of races. To him the differences could be explained by the "intermixture of Arab blood" among easterners,[41] another mistaken value judgment based on limited information tinged with prejudice. It also shows Burton's thinking about racial mixing: African plus European yielded an inferior type to both, whereas African plus Semite improved the former.

Leaving Accra, the *Blackland* entered one of West Africa's most infamous waters, as commemorated by the ditty, "The Bight of Benin! The Bight of Benin!

One comes out where three goes in." This time all was well, and during the evening of September 21, the ship dropped anchor in the roadstead of Lagos Island. An important Yoruba trade center since the fifteenth century, it had been annexed by Britain less than two months earlier in order to suppress the last vestiges of the slave trade and initiate "legitimate commerce" centered on oil palm. "Legitimate" in this context had a moral, not economic, meaning, and it was assumed that such trade would prevail over the "illegitimate" version in any direct competition. As Cairns has pointed out, such thinking went along with "the same optimism which evoked easy beliefs that higher religions would replace lower ones, and higher cultures, lower ones," all being "assumptions about the way the universe was moving."[42] Burton basically agreed. Although the task ahead might be a difficult one, "the civilization of the coast, or rather its redemption from a worse state than the merest savagery, can be effected only by its passing into the hands of Europe. Japhet must not only live in the huts of Ham, he must gird his loins for a harder task than he has ever dreamed of in the idle tents of his brother Shem."[43]

Despite looking "squalid" and "unclean" Lagos seemed to be "thriving," and Burton thought it had a bright future. "Its position points it out as the natural key to this part of Africa, and the future emporium of all Yoruba, between the Niger and the sea. It cannot help commanding commerce: even under the wretched management of the native princes, it attracted the whole trade of the Benin country. In proper hands it will be the sole outlet of the trade from Central Guinea and the Sudan, lands teeming with various wealth—palm-oil, cotton, shea-butter, metals, native cloths, sugar, indigo, tobacco of good quality, and ivory."[44] He hoped it would turn out to be a "model colony," meaning profitable. While Lagos did eventually become the capital and primary economic center of Nigeria, the profits from the wealth Burton envisioned either left the country or went to a privileged few.

Kola nuts caught Burton's attention. People considered them an aphrodisiac, a mild stimulant, and useful for treating a variety of ailments. Always willing to experiment with such things, he noted, "The taste is a pleasant bitter, and somewhat astringent. Water 'drunk upon it,' as the phrase is, becomes, even if before offensive, exceptionally sweet. It must be a fine tonic in these relaxing climates. I am not aware of an extract having been made from it: if not, it would be well to try."[45] If he'd been the one, then fortune from Africa would have smiled on him. Instead, later in the century the fortune went to a company in Atlanta, Georgia, with its drink Coca-Cola.

With less than a day to look around, Burton had limited contacts with the city's people. Still, that didn't keep him from voicing the opinion that they appeared to be a "lower type" than those along Gold Coast, though nonetheless a "merry race of pagans."[46] The "merry" observation seems to have been based on seeing a man already high on hashish early in the morning.

Late on September 24 the *Blackland* made a brief stop on the western side of the Niger River Delta to pick up two passengers. Burton badly wanted to visit Benin City, known for its exquisite bronze figurines, but time didn't permit it. Besides, pirates were currently preying on those who took the route. Early the next day the ship set off for Grand Bonny, the last call before Fernando Po. With two days on his hands, Burton decided to have a look around. He discovered a rapidly growing town, fueled by the export of palm oil, instead of slaves, as had previously been the case. They now served African masters, and seeing them caused Burton to wonder about the wisdom of totally suppressing the trade: "The chiefs openly beg that that the rules may be relaxed, in order that they may get rid of their criminals. This is at present impossible, and the effects are a reduplication of misery—we pamper our convicts, Africans torture them to death."[47]

He elaborated on the torture and, in the process, took another shot at the antislave philanthropists at home:

> The master thinks nothing of nailing their hands to a water-cask, of mutilating them in various ways—many lose their eyes by being peppered, after the East Indian fashion, with coarsely ground cayenne—their ears are cut off, or they are flogged. . . . When a great man dies, all kinds of barbarities are committed, slaves are buried, or floated down the river bound to bamboo sticks and mates, till eaten piecemeal by sharks.
>
> The slave, as might be expected is not less brutal than his lord. It amazes me to hear Englishmen plead that there is moral degradation to a negro brought by a white man, and one when serving under a

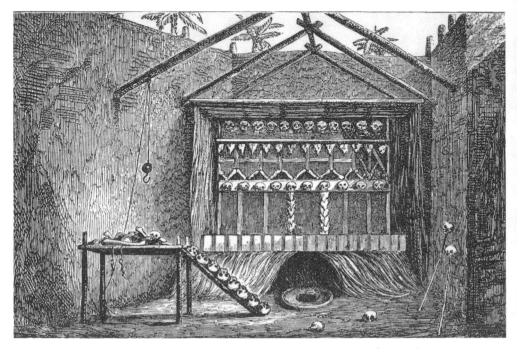

A juju or sacrifice house along the Grand Bonny River as portrayed in Abeokuta and the Camaroons Mountains. *(Reproduced with permission of the Special Collections Research Center, Syracuse University Library.)*

black man. The philanthropists, doubtless, think how our poorer classes at home, in the nineteenth century, would feel if hurried from liberty to eternal servitude by some nefarious African. But can any civilized sentiments belong to the miserable half-starved being, whose one scanty meal per day is eked out with monkey and snake, cat and dog, maggot and grub; whose life is ceaseless toil, varied only by torture, and who may be destroyed at any moment by a nod from his owner? When the slave has once surmounted his dread of being shipped by the white man, nothing under the sun would, I believe, induce him willingly to return to what he should call his home.[48]

At 4:00 p.m. on September 26, the *Blackland* sailed away, and early the next morning the passengers awoke to the sight of Santa Isabel. Burton's final words in *Wanderings* have given biographers much to speculate about: "Arriving in these outer places," he wrote, "is the very abomination of desolation. I drop for a time my pen, in the distinct memory of our having felt uncommonly suicidal through that first night on Fernando Po. And so, probably, did the Consul."[49] We'll never know if he did indeed feel suicidal or simply wrote this for dramatic effect, which I think is more likely the case.

7

THE ROVING CONSUL

GIVEN THE FACT THAT his appointment papers from London had yet to reach authorities in Santa Isabel, Burton decided to have a quick look around the Niger Delta, then called the Oil Rivers because its many waterways crisscrossed an area rich in palm oil. In the midst of a painful change from economies based on the export of slaves to so-called legitimate commerce, he discovered a lawless frontier of competition between local merchants and European supercargoes. To better police the area Burton wanted a gunboat permanently stationed at Fernando Po. The lack of such, he told the Foreign Office, "crippled" his duties because current arrangements required that he wait for a ship to appear and then go where it went. In the short run, a gig would do. The Foreign Office more or less turned a deaf ear to the gunboat request, saying it wished to delay bringing the matter before the Admiralty. Regarding the gig, it asked him to check the boat provided to the previous consul. Repairs could be made, if necessary, provided costs were "reasonable."[1] Burton never mentioned such a boat being on hand, and it would be a while longer before he got his gig.

On October 2 Burton returned to Santa Isabel to begin official duties but stayed only a week before taking off again. He hated the place, a view undoubtedly fueled by what it symbolized career-wise. Making matters worse, the consular building had a leaky roof and badly rotted floorboards. Burton thus requested funds to make the needed repairs.[2] In the meantime, he planned to spend as little time in the city as possible, a luxury afforded by having an experienced assistant in Frank Wilson and an unofficial one in Edward Laughlan, a trader by vocation, to handle most of the day-to-day duties, such as examining ships' manifests, looking for contraband, and dealing with mundane financial matters. An opportunity to leave came when HMS *Arrogant* called on its way to Lagos. Once there Burton transferred to HMS *Prometheus* to join Captain Norman Bedingfield (who later became an admiral) on a mission to meet with Okukeno, the *alake*, or titular leader, of Abeokuta, capital of the Egba peoples, part of the wider Yoruba nation. Abeokuta had recently gained prominence for having defeated neighboring Dahomey, considered at the time the most powerful state in the region. As a result, it now controlled the Ogun River, an important artery of commerce.

Burton pretty much dismissed the four books written about the area. Two he described as from the pens of "the weaker sex," who'd "produced neat little drawing-room sketches, all *couleur de rose*," since neither woman had been there to see the region firsthand. As for the other two books, he characterized them as "in the missionary African-line" and consequently "in a well-known groove." As a result, Burton felt that some "novel facts" could still be conveyed about the Yoruba by a person willing to state "the truth as far as truth lies in him."[3] He would, of course, add his own "*couleur*" and fashion a "groove."

On October 16 Burton suffered his first malaria attack in West Africa. He actually found the onset stimulating, as it produced a narcotic-like effect. "There is nothing unpleasant in these attacks; rather the contrary. The excitement of the nerves is like the intoxication produced by a plentiful supply of strong green tea; the brain becomes uncommonly active, peopled with a host of visions, and the imagination is raised almost to Paranassus."[4] But then followed days of agony and exhaustion, shortened this time when the medical officer of the *Prometheus* administered his specially concocted treatment. With numerous attacks under his belt, Burton challenged the "old nursery rule, 'starve a fever and feed a cold'": "My experience long ago in East Africa untaught me that tenet, and I have ever since preferred to support exhausted nature with essence of meat, beef-tea, and when such things are procurable, with champagne, brandy-cum-soda, and 'ye oldest hoc in ye cellar,' *non sine* tobacco if it can be enjoyed."[5] Although this particular remedy would hardly be prescribed today, he did hit the nail on the head about the "old nursery rule," which strangely still persists in some quarters.

Burton stayed in Lagos from October 23 to 28, and the city provided him a chance to interact with Muslims once again, although their numbers were small and impacts so far minimal. They even lacked a proper mosque for Friday worship. Also while in Lagos, Burton hired Selim Agha to be his personal servant or factotum. Born, according to his own account, in a remote valley between Kordofan and Darfur, Selim would henceforth accompany Burton virtually everywhere in West Africa, having learned during school years in Scotland and past jobs, which included two trips up the Niger River, "to cook, doctor, spin, carpenter, shoot, collect specimens, and stuff birds," in brief to do just about everything.[6]

Given that no suitable roads connected the coast with Abeokuta, the small party set off in two gigs manned by Kru to connect with Agboi Creek. The swiftly flowing current made for slow going, and they spent the second night in the midst of a "fine specimen of maritime Africa—all mud, miasma, and mosquitos."[7] The people, though, didn't seem to suffer. Indeed, Burton noted, "they look fat and well, they have children at their desire, and they breed dogs, sheep and goats, pig and poultry." In good Victorian fashion, what really caught his eye was their industriousness. Pottery abounded, fish traps littered the creek, and unlike elsewhere among the Egba, the women, he observed, "ply the paddle." The surprise caused him to remark, "Truly it is said that one half the world knows not how the other half lives."[8]

The next day a sudden storm forced a landing, and a little farther on the creek became so shallow the gigs had to be shoved along rather than paddled. Relief came upon entering the Ogun River, and in celebration they saluted Bacchus. That night Burton took shelter at the home of one of his least favorite types, a Christian African from Sierra Leone named Johnson. He did, however, appreciate the feast Johnson provided.

Something that bothered Burton during the journey was the sight of bared breasts in public. Hardly known for prudishness, he had a growing sense of Islam being Africa's salvation. As he noted at one such instance, "This 'bestial exposure of the sacred part of the woman's form', as some term it, first disappears permanently amongst the Moslem converts from heathenry."[9] In general, though, the Egba women in these parts seemed fit, despite a poor diet and no evidence of engaging in any kind of physical exercise. The reason, he felt, rested with what later would be termed postpartum abstinence, the practice of refraining from sexual intercourse during breast-feeding, which Mormons also observed.

As noted, postpartum abstinence serves as a form of birth control and results in a degree of child spacing that allows supplemental child feeding and a period of recuper-ation for the woman. Since Europeans prided themselves on being "the largest and strongest of races," Burton felt by adopting "this African custom they might become both larger and stronger."[10] But since this would also mean being open to polygyny, he knew it would never fly in Europe. Still, Burton couldn't pass up an opportunity to chide readers of *Abeokuta and the Camaroons Mountains* with a long discussion of why polygyny was the normal marital relationship and monogamy the abnormal. He closed the discussion by telling missionaries that accepting the fact would lead to more conversions. "Those who hold it their duty to save souls," he claimed, "should seriously consider whether they are justified in placing such stumbling blocks upon the path to improvement."[11] There wasn't much chance of missionaries buying such advice.

The journey upriver ended at Agbameya, the southernmost port of Abeokuta. Two CMS missionaries awaited Burton's arrival with skinny horses to take his party the remaining eight miles or so. Burton called the animals "wretched 'tattoos', rats . . . all skin and bone, very much like asses, ten hands high, with goose rump and hanging head, skeletons which a strong man could easily pull over."[12] Although the ride was uncomfortable, the people greeted the party with civility, just as those along the river had. They were now in a highly populous land of agricultural villages, with the fields located at some distance away. Between lay what looked like unused clearings. Burton thought that these might be used for growing cotton, but then wisely cautioned, "Before sinking good money, however, it would be advisable to perpend whether we could render valuable . . . what the Yorubas cannot."[13] The clearings actually served as buffer zones between communities and also provided habitats for hunting small game. The villages allowed people to congregate for purposes of defense and socialization.

Abeokuta (which means "under the rock," in this case the sacred rock of Olumo) turned out to be a collection of villages, which Burton figured housed as many as 150,000 people, far more than any settlement he had encountered in East Africa. Around it stood a hardened mud wall five to six feet high, through which various gates allowed entrance. Burton calculated the two most distant gates to be six miles apart and the wall's circumference around twenty-seven miles. Once inside he said its "uncleanliness . . . beats anything I ever saw."[14]

The first stop was at the Church Missionary Society compound in Ake, where Burton found quarters for the stay. The others in the party took residence nearby. Early the next morning the party went to examine Aro, where navigation on the Ogun ended, before heading off to see Okukeno. The alake had been forewarned of their coming and sent word that the meeting would take place at 10:00 a.m. They reentered Abeokuta through the southwest or Aro gate, which was unattended and falling down. Burton blamed its condition on Egba overconfidence following their defeat of Dahomey. The road took them to a marketplace full of agricultural produce, hardware, dry goods, leather products, and numerous other items. As elsewhere in much of Africa, women were both buyers and sellers. Although they were often forbidden to work in the fields, much of West Africa's internal trade passed through their hands. It still does.

It was after 1:00 p.m. before Okukeno made himself available. The delay didn't surprise Burton, who commented he probably wouldn't have shown up until 5:00 p.m. had it been his decision, not Bedingfield's. Said to be between sixty and seventy years of age, Okukeno looked like "an old, very damaged and very rickety lion," in Burton's eyes.[15] As with many rulers in West Africa, he made few public appearances and then only briefly, so after a short while he withdrew behind a curtain. The Prince of Ikemta, known as the "king's mouth," conducted the initial palaver, which involved an exchange of salutations, followed by a heavy round of drinking, a common African custom when dealing with important matters. The business palaver was scheduled to take place two days later.

Once again, Okukeno kept them waiting. When he finally appeared, the discussions went directly to the primary business at hand: keeping the trade route along the Ogun River open to traffic. Currently, it was closed because of a four-year-long war between Abeokuta and Ibadan. Britain also feared the conflict could widen as other polities chose sides. A trade that had to stop, however, was the export of slaves. Overall, the meeting went well, and a settlement seemed possible. Most unusually, Okukeno proposed visiting Bedingfield the next day. He did indeed show up, accompanied by an entourage of some eighty people,

An audience with Okukeno as portrayed in Abeokuta and the
Camaroons Mountains. *(Reproduced with permission of the
Special Collections Research Center, Syracuse University Library.)*

who all packed into a small meeting room. This time Bedingfield emphasized the
need to end the practice of human sacrifice, to which promises of reform were
duly given. The treaty-signing ceremony took place on Thursday, November 7.
Okukeno agreed to put an end to the traffic in slaves, to punish subjects who
broke the law, to no longer allow human sacrifice, and to keep the road to Lagos
open. Burton had his doubts. He knew that despite their pretensions alakes had
little real power over subjects beyond their own villages. Of greater importance
were the Ogboni lodges, conservators of tradition through which all-important
decisions must pass. Burton considered them so powerful that, without use of
force, which was out of the question, "they will succeed in defeating all our best
intentions."[16] The treaty did indeed turn out to be a paper one.

When not attending palavers, Burton kept busy inquiring into Egba/
Yoruba culture and economy. Their religious beliefs particularly fascinated him,
at least as judged by the number of pages in *Abeokuta* devoted to the subject.
In addition to his own spiritual quest, Burton found that religion allowed for

probing the human condition more generally. When he came to witchcraft, for example, the subjects of superstition and belief came to mind.

> A folio volume might be filled with these fooleries of faith, which serve two objects—the attainment of good and the avoidance of harm in this life. I look upon them as vestiges of that fetishism which is the first dawn of religion in the breast of the savage and the barbarian, and which cannot fail to crop out even from the enlightened surface of monotheism. Besides which, belief or superstition is, like happiness, most equally divided amongst men. Those who balk at the possible will swallow the impossible, and those who deride the credos of others must make up for themselves faiths of their own, which appear quite as ridiculous to their neighbours. In the present state of human nature, faith appears a necessary evil, an inseparable weakness. Nor can we see any corrective of, or substitute for it until, after the convulsion which follows the present period of quiescence, a higher race—as the elephant is to the mastodon—succeeds the present.[17]

It's the kind of rumination that helped win him enemies. So did, of course, his repeated praising of Islam, which he reiterated as Africa's salvation, playfully writing, "And the day will come when the Law of the Prophet shall rule throughout the lands, when Ethiopia shall stretch forth her hands unto Allah, and shall thus rise to her highest point of civilization."[18] To many in Britain this smacked of heresy, and it certainly ran at odds with the views of those, such as David Livingstone, who saw Africa's future tied to the spread of Christianity. In their eyes, Islam was not only false but also stood in the way of generating real progress in the lives of people.

Burton took another opportunity to tweak his audience when discussing the class structure of Yoruba society. It led him to propound on caste as found in India.

> Caste is one of the most enlightened inventions of the civilized East. It supplies an admirable system of police, acts as practical conservatism, and leads to high excellence in the crafts, arts, and sciences, by breeding

generation after generation, till an instinctive superiority is acquired. The Englishman exclaims, 'What a shame it is, because my father is a tinker, that I am forbidden by the laws of the land to be prime minister;' and he objects to caste because it 'keeps people down.' He forgets, however, that he is talking not of petty European kingdoms of twenty or thirty millions, but of some two hundred millions of human beings, and that each caste is quite numerous enough to form by itself a first-class nation.[19]

Rather conveniently, he failed to mention the plight of "untouchables."

As for the Yoruba, Burton estimated that the three free classes of rich, poor, and "fetish men" made up a relatively high 80 percent of the population. Slaves were mostly of the pawned variety, with many manumitted upon their master's death. Regarding the slave trade, while having "every confidence in the eventual triumph of free versus slave labour," he didn't see its end coming anytime soon, what with able bodies in short supply and commerce growing.[20] Indeed, Yoruba country appeared an "unexploited field," able to produce a wide array of export products. Cotton, in particular, held great promise, but its development would depend on ending the wars and signing treaties with an array of chiefs. Since most free people were otherwise engaged, the only substantial pool of labor for such development resided in domestic slaves. In the short run, therefore, slavery by needs would likely increase, rather than decrease, as the abolitionists assumed. To maintain some degree of peace during the transition, Burton felt troops would have to be stationed at Lagos. Except for officers, these could be recruited from the Muslim Hausa and Bornu peoples farther north. A regiment of four hundred infantry ought to suffice, he thought.[21] There must, however, be a change in the imports coming to West Africa, and Burton proclaimed he would "never cease to protest against the sale of rum, guns, and gunpowder when innocent trade . . . would be equally profitable."[22] He kept his word, although a quarter of a century later others like Joseph Thomson would be uttering the same refrain. As for domestic slavery, it did become ever more common with the expansion of "legitimate trade" in the decades immediately prior to European colonization. Even to this day, reports of such slavery come out of West Africa from time to time.

Burton suffered a major disappointment while in Abeokuta. He badly wanted to visit an Ogboni lodge to witness and hopefully partake in a ceremony, maybe even become an initiate. Each of his attempts was rebuffed.

With business completed, the party left for Lagos on Friday, November 8. Burton described the stop at Baragu later in the day as having produced a most "merry evening." "There was singing, feasting, and dancing; in fact quite an African 'swarry,' only lacking the mutton and caper sauce. Our hosts were perfectly civil and obliging; and so were our hostesses—rather too much so I could prove, if privileged to whisper in the reader's ear. But what would Mrs. Grundy say?"[23] Is this just another instance of Burton trying to shock readers by pulling their legs, or did he avail himself of the obliging hostesses? One can only speculate, but the former seems more likely, as he made the comment in a book for all, including Isabel, to see.

While journeying along the Ogun, Burton helped Bedingfield produce the first sketch map of the river's course. It was a simple one designed to show matters related to navigability and the nature of the shoreline, as illustrated by notations such as "dangerous large rocks" and "dense bush—rising ground beyond."[24] Mapmaking at a variety of scales was an essential ingredient in the larger imperial process of "opening up" Africa to European designs. Indeed, it couldn't have been opened up without maps, which served both utilitarian and symbolic purposes.

Because of a severe outbreak of various fevers among the crew of the *Prometheus*, the captain had moved the ship to Ascension Island farther out to sea. HMS *Bloodhound* under Captain Mackworth Dolben had taken its place, and on November 21 Burton went aboard. Save for a few days here and there, the ship served as home during the weeks immediately ahead. The first objective of the cruise was to inquire into the status of trade along the Oil Rivers. Burton felt two gunboats were needed to secure peace along the seaward margins of the delta, while the Brass River required a man-of-war to control the "insolent" behavior of the locals. He also passed on information about the Europeans in the delta wanting the whole Bight of Biafra to become a British protectorate.[25] Given prevailing government policy, that suggestion was a total nonstarter.

The itinerary called for a stop at the Victoria mission station situated on Ambas Bay, from where Mt. Cameroon, rising to 13,225 feet, could easily be seen. Its local name is Mongo ma Ndemi, the "Mountain of Greatness." Burton

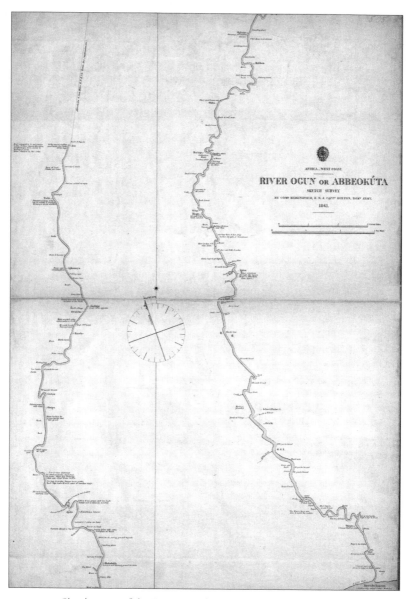

*Sketch survey of the Ogun River by Captain Dolben and Richard
Burton. (Reproduced with permission of The National Archives.)*

wanted to have a go at its peak, which reputedly had yet to be scaled by a
European. Joseph Merrick, a Jamaican Baptist missionary stationed at Santa
Isabel in the 1840s, may have climbed to the top, but the evidence is spotty.

And while there's nothing to indicate that Africans made the ascent, it's hard to believe that none ever at least spied the peak from close-up. Burton also wanted to see if elevations lower down the mountain could serve as sanatorium for those stationed at Lagos and other disease-ridden places along the coast.

As the mist lifted just before sunrise on December 10, the mountain made its appearance: "For a distance of ten miles a huge blue silhouette stood before us, the upper heights gilt by the yet unrisen sun, and the lower expanse still blue-black with lingering night."[26] As soon as possible, Burton and Dolben went ashore to visit the Baptist missionaries. There they met Gustav Mann, a Hanovarian affiliated with Kew Gardens and then working as a botanist in West Africa under British government auspices. He'd failed to reach the peak on a climb the previous year and was preparing to try again. Mann said he'd wait for Burton on the mountain before making the final ascent. Burton planned to be back as soon as possible, both to climb the mountain and to settle several blood disputes then in progress. These continued to make a mess of trade, so once again he stressed to authorities the need for a gunboat.[27]

Illness among thirteen of the thirty-five Europeans, including Dolben and the chief engineer, terminated further explorations, and on December 13 the *Bloodhound* sailed away for Santa Isabel. Once there, Burton began making preparations for what he thought would be a monthlong expedition on Mt. Cameroon. Anglo-Indian Atilano Calvo Iturburu, a judge and also government secretary, volunteered to go along. When back at Victoria on the eighteenth, Reverend Alfred Saker, founder of the Victoria mission, and another Mr. Johnson (the name was common among Anglicized Africans, thus its use by Joyce Cary for the novel *Mister Johnson*), to serve as interpreter, joined them. Johnson knew only the languages in the immediate vicinity of Victoria and would leave the party after two days. That didn't concern Burton. In the United States he'd learned some Native American sign language and felt two hundred signs, a hundred or so words, and an ability to sketch would permit "a traveller to make his way through any country, even China, a few days after arrival."[28] No one, including Burton, ever seems to have tried using the formula.

The ascent of the mountain began immediately the next morning amid "ravages of mosquitoes and sand-flies." Burton described the party as comprising "4 heads" and "18 tails." The trail initially went through a dense forest, which looked suitable for planting cacao. Coffee might yield more revenue, but being highly labor intensive its development would require the use of slaves. The possibility of overcutting and burning worried Burton; it must be avoided, he cautioned, so as not to create a wasteland. It didn't happen here, but such would be the fate of many other tropical areas. Later in the afternoon Mann showed up, headed in the opposite direction. Despite his earlier assurance that he would wait, he claimed to have reached the summit. This announcement, Burton observed, caused faces to fall all around. Smiles soon returned when Burton calculated that not enough time had passed for Mann to have made the climb and reached this point on the way down. Mann continued to insist he had succeeded but didn't push the issue until later, when he wrote a letter to famed botanist Joseph Hooker at Kew Gardens pressing his claim. Hooker then complained to the RGS. Matters went no further than this, leaving who first scaled the mountain an unanswered and unanswerable question. More certain is that Burton made additional enemies.

The expedition seemed on the verge of ending before it really began when two Bakwiri chiefs warned the climbers to go back from whence they came or else face the consequences. At one point it looked as though an armed fight might even break out. Burton attributed the problem to drunkenness and some bad decisions. The judge, he said, "had been a little over-intimate with the people, dancing with them, and making them laugh, under the erroneous impression that it would win their good graces." Instead, a near riot erupted. He also chastised himself for making camp in the center of the village, rather than on the periphery, which had been the rule in East Africa.[29] After tempers cooled, Burton sought to hire additional porters, but chose not to because of a much too high asking price. This meant shuttling up and down slope to establish caches on the way to finding a base camp. Whenever opportunities presented themselves, Mann collected flowering plants and ferns, while Burton focused on mammals, birds, snakes, and land shells. Their findings were included as appendices to *Abeokuta and the Camaroons Mountains*.

The inhabited zone ended above four thousand feet, where the climb also became tougher, especially when crossing surfaces lined with sharp volcanic rocks. Water was scarce as well. The Bakwiri refused to provide them any, and Burton said he squeezed some from moss for several Kru who had fallen behind owing to thirst. Temperatures dropped, producing "a hard, dry piercing cold, that seemed to mock at clothing."[30] Things took a turn for the better on December 23 when they reached a spring around which a base camp could be built. They called it Mann Spring, the first in a series of European-derived names: the two highest peaks of the mountain became Victoria (earlier Mann had dubbed it Elephant Mountain) and Albert and a lesser one Mount Isabel. Burton explained away a practice he previously condemned by saying, "As the natives have no distinguishing terms for the several heights, we thought it not ungeographical to seize the opportunity."[31]

Saker left on Christmas Day for the Cameroon River, and with Mann under the weather from dysentery, Burton and the judge set off with three Kru to reconnoiter the peaks. After several pauses, they started their assault on Victoria Peak. As they gazed at it close-up, Burton recorded, "We were the first Europeans certainly, and perhaps, the first men, who ever stood within gunshot of that tall solitary pile. We made eternal silence vocal with a cheer,—there was no one to deride our demonstrativeness."[32] For sure, the claim didn't please Mann.

At 1:00 p.m. the judge suggested the final ascent be put off for another day. Burton claimed he shouted back, "No! to be the first is everything; to be second is nothing."[33] At the summit, which proved to be a crater, as did Albert Peak, Burton erected a small stone cairn in which he "placed a fragment from the facetious pages of Mr. Punch, perhaps the greatest traveller on record, and certainly one of the traveller's best friends."[34] During a climb in June 1886, Harry H. Johnston found the cairn.[35] Suddenly realizing it had taken seven hours to reach this point and that only four hours of daylight remained, Burton and his party hurried down the mountainside, but not before darkness settled in.

Along the way, Burton's boots became tattered and soaked, and he forgot to remove them before falling fast asleep. An infection developed, causing his feet to swell badly. He also experienced episodes of ague and fever, which together laid him low for a month. Mann made a climb up Albert with the judge on January 3, but when his illness recurred he left for treatment in Victoria. Saker reappeared and climbed Victoria Peak on January 13, but highly fatigued by the ordeal, he departed for good a day after getting back to camp. In the game of musical climbers, Mann showed up again on January 25. Burton could now walk without pain, and so they set out two days later, taking along Selim and six Kru. Near the top, Burton and Mann decided to take separate routes in order to

On Mount Cameroon as portrayed in Abeokuta and the Camaroons Mountains. *(Reproduced with permission of the Special Collections Research Center, Syracuse University Library.)*

do a more complete survey of the area between the two summits. Upon meeting up again Burton wrote, "At 2 P.M. we took formal possession of the place; flew the union jack; drank the health of the Sovereign Lady with our last bottle of champagne; and left our names upon a leaden plate, with two sixpences—rather a bright idea, but not emanating from my cranium."[36] Afterward Mann returned to camp, while Burton and Selim had a further look around. They left the mountainside for good the last day of the month and reached Victoria on February 2. Two days later Burton said his good-byes: "Farewell, Camaroons! Farewell beautiful heights! where so many calm and quiet days have sped without sandflies, or mosquitoes, or prickly heat. Adieu! happy rustic wilds! where I have spent so many pleasant weeks, even in West Africa. Adieu and may adieu in this case bear all the significance of au revoir!"[37]

Back in Santa Isabel, Burton sent a report to the Foreign Office, asking that it be forwarded to the RGS for publication. He prefaced his remarks with,

THE Royal Geographical Society may, at first sight, not be disposed to think much of an exploration which appears only to have reached a mountain district fourteen miles of direct, and twenty-one of indirect, distance from the sea. But a little knowledge of the subject gives another view of it. Water is often wanting; provisions are never to be found on these tropical heights. The wild people are a notoriously bad, though cowardly race, and everywhere, as the late expedition to Kilima-njaro proves, if such proof be required, savages are unwilling to see their mountains ascended for the first time. Add to this, that the only escort in these lands must be krooboys; sturdy fellows, but the most arrant poltroons.[38]

By this time Burton's handwriting had become so bad that is was mostly unreadable, and the Foreign Office told him in no uncertain terms that in the future he must "write in a larger hand and more distinctly."[39] The report was cleaned up and published in the society's *Proceedings*.[40]

Besides detailing the ascent, replete with measurements and observations, Burton told the authorities that at roughly 7,300 feet in elevation and with ample building materials nearby, the area around Mann Spring could serve as "an admirable spot for a Sanitarium or a Colony." He thought about three hundred colonists drawn from "free blacks" in Canada would do for starters and be enough to justify building a road suitable for mules. In *Abeokuta and the Camaroons Mountains*, Burton spelled out some requirements for the colonists. The men should have manual skills and the families given grants of land. He recommended three settlements—the first on Mondori Island in Ambas Bay, the second at about one thousand feet in elevation and two miles walking distance from the mission, and the third between five and seven thousand feet. It would be an experiment, but one worth trying in his mind. If successful, then the sanatorium could be built and the consul "removed from the starving Cove of malarious Clarence to a place of health and plenty."[41] What Burton failed to realize is that with over four hundred inches of annual precipitation the western slope of Mt. Cameroon is Africa's wettest place. In any event, once again his recommendations went wanting.

Earlier, while still on Mt. Cameroon and recovering from his foot infection, Burton had written a long letter to the Foreign Office urging greater British involvement in the region. The establishment of a Bight of Biafra protectorate would, he said, "do much toward improving the coast & consolidating our interests." The real prize, though, was the Niger River.

> I venture to express a hope that this great approach to the heart of Africa, will not, at so late a period be neglected by Govt. It will tend to encourage legitimate trade, cotton, palm oil and shea butter, in exchange for cloth & kola nuts—far more profitable investments than the poisonous rum, and the arms and ammunition which now form the staple of import, and which the West African Merchants, with curious perversity, will not, though aware of the fact, be persuaded to discontinue. And besides being an asset to trade, the Niger is determined to become the neighborhood of Central African Exploration and the means, if there be any, of diffusing light throughout the interior of the "dark continent."[42]

Britain would eventually take the bait, but not until lured by the "scramble for Africa" later in the century. As for Cameroon, it went to Germany.

Two things about Fernando Po pleased Burton: palm wine made by Jesuits and the Bubi, the island's aboriginal inhabitants. When the Portuguese arrived they found the Bubi (also Adija) living a basically Stone Age existence, a result of having been isolated from developments on the mainland for several thousand years. In the four centuries since then nothing much had changed, which Burton attributed more to "sound instinct" on the part of the Bubi rather than "prejudice" against them. Because of disease and fears of enslavement they'd chosen to live in the island's interior, but not above three thousand feet, so as to be within the zone where plantains and palm trees thrived. The Bubi kept no slaves and worked hard, especially at hunting. Most of all, he admired their honesty: "You may safely deposit rum and tobacco—that is to say, gold and silver—in his street, and he will pay his debt as surely as the Bank of England."[43] Unlike most of the African ethnic groups of whom Burton was less critical, the Bubi showed no signs of Semitic or other outside influences. Perhaps it was their independence and simple lifestyle that helped win his sympathies.

Once again Burton didn't stay long at his post: this time he boarded HMS *Griffon* for Gabon in search of gorillas. To excuse the ramblings, he pointed to travel as necessary for health maintenance in Africa, calling a change of climate the "chief doctor," even if it meant going to someplace worse.[44] In this instance, it allowed him to escape from an outbreak of yellow fever that eventually killed seventy-eight Europeans. As usual, Selim went along, as did a copy of Paul Belloni Du Chaillu's recently published book, *Explorations and Adventures in Equatorial Africa*, which had whetted appetites for information about a legendary ape only recently proven to exist. Burton couldn't resist the opportunity to see if he could track one down, even though Gabon lay beyond his jurisdiction. Stuffed gorilla specimens were wanted for study and capturing one alive, especially a juvenile, would be a major coup. For purposes of comparison, he also wanted to have a look at a French colony.

Established via treaty signings with the area's Mpongwe inhabitants beginning in 1839, Gabon had become the principle trade center on Africa's western equatorial coast. Nonetheless, the English, not the French, did most of the trading. As Burton put it, "Gaboon is French with a purely English trade. Gambia is English with a purely French trade."[45] As such, he thought a switch of colonies made sense, which in the end might benefit Britain because of Gabon's healthier climate and potential riches.[46] Hindsight shows him to have been right about the comparisons, but the later wheeling and dealing for colonies kept both with their original possessors.

The short sea voyage was uneventful, and early in the afternoon of March 17, 1862, the *Griffon* tied up opposite the capital, Libreville, at the mouth of the Gabon River. Burton had to move fast so as not to miss the ship's return to Fernando Po. To his great frustration he had to wait until the nineteenth before the journey across the wide mouth of the river in a small gig borrowed from the Gabon mission could begin. A sudden, violent storm threatened to capsize the boat, which would have meant certain death by drowning for Burton, Selim, and the four rowers aboard. Fortunately, the winds eased off, allowing them to reach safety on the south bank of the river. Continuing on, they made several stops, one to visit Rapwensembo, known as King William to the English and Roi Denis to the French. Described six years earlier as regal-looking at age sixty, Rapwensembo was, to Burton, "a petit vieux vieux, nearer sixty than seventy, with a dark, wrinkled face, and an uncommonly crafty eye, one of those African organs which is always occupied in 'taking your measure' not for your good."[47]

With time an issue, they kept going until 9:30 p.m., only to spend the night under assault by swarms of mosquitoes.

The first hours the next morning produced a struggle through "a labyrinthine ditch, an interminable complication of over-arching roots, and of fallen trees forming gateways; the threshold was a maze of slimy stumps, stems, and forks in every stage of growth and decay, dense enough to exclude the air of heaven."[48] A little farther on, the channel opened to reveal the welcomed sight of human settlements along the banks. Shortly thereafter, a fallen tree grounded the gig. Some canoes were located to continue the river journey to the point where a trail led overland to Mbata, their destination. There Burton met Forteune, their appointed gorilla guide. Forteune claimed he and his men had killed many of the apes, and upon examining the ancient muskets in use, Burton concluded that the gorilla's "vital power cannot be great."[49] He was, of course, dead wrong. More than likely, Fortuene exaggerated his hunting prowess in order to impress the white man, who wouldn't know one way or the other.

Almost immediately, monkey skins appeared for sale. Most were spoiled, and besides, Burton wanted people to know he was a traveler and consequently didn't need to engage in the "whimsy-whamsies" of providing liquor and other things gratis required of traders.[50] He thus refused to buy any. Still, "dash" payments had to be handed over to anyone claiming to be of importance, no matter how little actual status he might have.

Socializing, which, as usual, meant a lot of drinking, occupied the first night. It also brought, according to Burton, an offer of two women for his enjoyment. One was Forteune's second wife and the other his daughter. Burton said he politely declined their affections, although he admitted he partook of the "unvarying kindness" they provided in attending to his comforts while in Mbata.[51] In a later letter to Milnes, Burton upped the ante to four women, "a wife, a sister, a daughter-in-law and a daughter!"[52] An exaggeration? Given their joking relationship, that's likely, although it was common custom in this part of Africa for important strangers to be offered the companionship of women family members, including wives and daughters.

A series of storms delayed the start of the hunt for two days. When it finally did get under way, the signs looked promising, but following them produced no gorillas in the flesh. When the next day proved equally frustrating, Burton

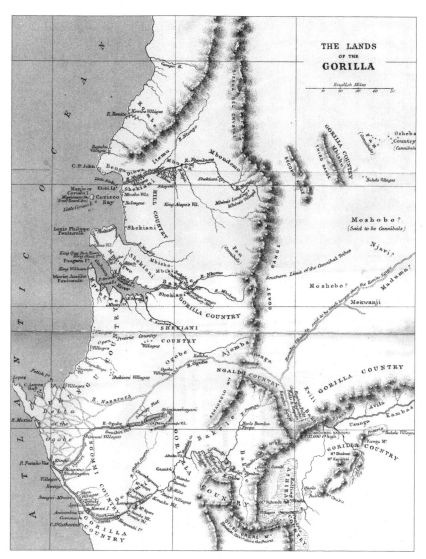

The "Lands of the Gorilla" from Two Trips to Gorilla Land and
the Cataracts of the Congo. *(Reproduced with permission of the
Special Collections Research Center, Syracuse University Library.)*

decided to leave Mbata for the town of Sanga-Tanga, two days march directly
south. The trip wasn't so much about finding gorillas as about having a look at the
town because of its reported beautiful location and ties to the slave trade. Along
the way, they did come across the remains of a gorilla whose most desired parts

had already been removed and sent on their way to England. Locals, though, said many live ones, including a male supposedly sitting in a tree nearby, were in the vicinity. The search for the male yielded only some crashing sounds and grunts in the distance. Another storm made for a miserable night, and upon reaching the location where Sanga-Tanga should have been on March 28, they found nothing standing, only silence. The town had been burned to the ground after the slavers moved farther south in search of prey. Burton wanted to continue on to Cape Lopez, but with days ticking down, he thought it best to try at a future date. The opportunity never came. Conditions this time favored travel, and at sunset the next day they were back in Mbata.

The return downstream required only about ten hours, and that evening Burton received a specimen sent by Forteune called *Nchigo Mpolo*. An old male, it measured just short of four feet eleven inches in height with a six feet one inch arm span. Poorly preserved, only some parts managed to reach England, where it was identified as a chimpanzee. On visiting the British Museum later, Burton could hardly recognize the reconstruction. It may or may not have been fashioned from what he sent.

As he had seen no live gorillas, much less captured one, Africa had once again thwarted Burton. Still, he seems to have enjoyed the hunt. The scenery often struck him as sublime. For example, while on the way to Sanga-Tanga he remarked, "I could not sufficiently admire, and I shall never forget the exquisite loveliness of land and sea; the graceful curve of the beach, a hundred feet broad, fining imperceptibly away till lost in the convexity of waters. The morning sun, half way to the zenith, burned bright in a cloudless sky, while in the east and west distant banks of purple mist coloured the liquid plain with a cool green-blue, a celadon tint that reposed the eye and the brain."[53] And overall, he liked the Mpongwe, noting that their involvement in trade had given them "an ease and urbanity, a polish and urbanity of manner," lacking among so many others like the Kru. Indeed, he considered them one of the "most civilized of African tribes."[54]

Women, naturally, caught his fancy.

The Mpongwe women have the reputation of being the prettiest and the most facile upon the West African coast. It is easy to distinguish two types. One is large-boned and heavy-limbed, hoarse-voiced, and masculine, like the "Ibos" of Bonny and New Calabar, who equal the men in weight and stature, strength and endurance, suggesting a mixture of male and female temperaments. Some of the Gaboon giantesses have, unlike their northern sisters, regular and handsome features. The other type is quasi-Hindu in its delicacy of form, with small heads, oval faces, noses a la Roxolane, lips sub-tumid but without prognathism, and fine almond-shaped eyes, with remarkably thick and silky lashes. The throat is thin, the bosom is high and well carried, or as the Arab says, "nejda;" the limbs are statuesque, and the hands and feet are Norman rather than Saxon.[55]

The differences reported likely distinguished average women from the royalty, who, as elsewhere, made selections based on physical traits deemed desirable.

Burton next wanted to visit the Fan (now usually rendered as Fang), purported to be cannibals and also described by Du Chaillu. They had recently entered Gabon from the north, displacing Mpongwe and Bakele communities along the way. Lousy weather kept him in place until April 10, when the journey upriver began on the *Eliza*, a twenty-ton steamer borrowed from the British trading firm of Hatton and Cookson. Late on the twelfth they reached Mayyan, where Burton proclaimed, "At length I am amongst the man-eaters."[56] He would have only one week to get acquainted with them.

From the illustrations in Du Chaillu's book, Burton expected to see a "large-limbed, black-skinned, and ferocious-looking race, with huge mustachios and plaited beards." Instead, they appeared "a finely made, light-coloured people, of regular features and decidedly mild aspect." He went on to write that "many, if bleached, might pass for Europeans."[57] As for Fang cannibalism, Burton saw nary a skull in the village and correctly concluded it was not common, rather "a quasi-religious rite practiced upon foes slain in battle, evidently an equivalent of human sacrifice." And the eating, according to informants, involved only men, who sat outside the settlements and destroyed all cooking pots when finished.[58] Given the abundance of fish and wildlife, the Fang certainly didn't need human flesh for nutritional reasons. Indeed, the high quality of their diet prompted Burton to launch into one of his social commentaries:

When will the poor man realize the fact that his comfort and happiness will result not from workhouses and almshouses, hospitals and private charities, but from that organized and efficient emigration, so long advocated by the seer Carlyle? Only the crassest ignorance and the listlessness born of misery and want prevent the able-bodied pauper, the frozen-out mechanic, or the weary and ill-clad, the over-worked and under-fed agricultural labourer, from quitting the scenes of his purgatory, and from finding, scattered over the earth's surface, spots where he may enjoy a comparative paradise, heightened by the memory of privations endured in the wretched hole which he pleases to call his home. But nostalgia is a more common disease than men suppose, and it affects none more severely than those that are remarkable for their physical powers. A national system of emigration, to be perfect, must not be confined to solitary and individual hands, who, however numerous, are ever pining for the past. The future will organize the exodus of whole villages, which like those of the Hebrides in the last century, will bear with them to new worlds their Lares and Penates, their wives, families, and friends, who will lay out the church and the churchyard after the old fashion familiar to their youth, and who will not forget the palaver-house, vulgarly called pothouse or pub.[59]

While not quite so organized, European immigration to the Americas and Oceania in the later nineteenth and early twentieth centuries pretty much resembled this depiction.

Desirous of having one more go at gorillas, Burton and Selim headed down the Mbokwe River on April 14, accompanied by a canoe loaded to the gills with Fang. After a short journey up the Londo tributary, the party, with eight new porters, went overland, and two days later Burton gave up the chase. It seemed futile, plus the *Griffon* would be sailing soon. A rapid trip down to the coast brought him on board on April 22. Following a look around the offshore island of Corisco, Burton returned to his post on April 25 and dashed off a letter to Lord Russell about the Gabon venture, advising him of the need to inquire into the grievances of the British merchants and about the small slave trade that still existed. To deal with both he recommended a vice consul be installed to look after the area between the Cameroon River and Cape Lopez and urged acquisition of Grand Bassam and Asagny as a way to counter French ambitions at the Ivory Coast.[60] Burton's imperial vision clearly exceeded that of the government, since once again his advice fell on deaf ears.

The consular house in Santa Isabel was still in shambles, and the Foreign Office refused to contribute any funds whatsoever for repairs, telling Burton he could sell the place.[61] Instead he dug into his own pockets to get the job going, although with no intention of spending much time there. Besides its condition, the house, Burton noted, was "situated unpleasantly near a military hospital: breakfast and dinner were frequently enlivened by the spectacle of a something covered with a blanket being carried in, and after due time a something within a deal box being borne out on four ghastly men's shoulders."[62] Following the Bubi example, Burton renovated a small cottage in the nearby hills to get away from the town's heat, humidity, disease, and the dull routine of business, which he left mostly in Wilson's hands.

Another matter involved a leave of absence. Burton requested three months per year of service, claiming the consul in Lagos received this much time. According to the Foreign Office, no such arrangement existed, and the request was denied. Eventually, they agreed to two months' leave for the current year once he finished it.[63] Isabel, always imploring on Richard's behalf, said she wept one day at the Foreign Office over their long separation.[64] She probably did shed crocodile tears, and as matters turned out Burton wound up with four months of leave.

In the coming weeks, Burton shuttled between Fernando Po and the mainland. He had permission to use mail packets when duties called if no man-of-war was available.[65] A major issue involved conflicts between traders and local rulers, each blaming the other for injustices. The Old Calabar River was a particular trouble spot. Burton called it "an African Sodom and Gomorrah" for all the "murders, tortures, and other crimes" committed.[66] After some difficulty, he managed to get signatures on a document labeled an "Agreement Between the British and Other Supercargoes, and the Native Traders of Old Calabar."[67] He then wrote the Foreign Office about the need to establish courts of equity along the rivers to deal with disputes. For a change they accepted his recommendation, although hardly anyone paid attention to the courts' rulings during Burton's tenure.

In June he again journeyed outside his jurisdiction, this time to Accra in the Gold Coast. Unusually, Selim was left behind. Why, Burton didn't say. Reports and his previous visit led him to consider the area a "mine of wealth," and he very much wanted the governorship. If appointed Burton promised "to send home one million sterling during the first year, and double that sum during the future."[68] Isabel would also be able to join him, as the post was judged healthy enough for families, as opposed to Fernando Po, "the damnedest hole ever created or dreamed of by the creator."[69] He would keep trying to no avail.

Burton spent his first days investigating the area around Accra. One place he visited was Beulah Gardens, run by Reverend Thomas Freeman, who'd created a literal agricultural paradise planted with cassava, maize, plantains, cabbages, peppers, sugarcane, cotton, and a whole array of other crops. Burton didn't expect to see such luxuriance, remarking that it showed "what an able and energetic man can do."[70] Always on the lookout for a place to build a sanatorium, Burton visited the area of Ajimenti. Only a short distance from Accra and with elevations reaching to around eleven hundred feet, it looked highly promising. Once again, the idea never caught on.

Burton then decided to head for Ada at the mouth of the Volta River to inquire further into the area's gold potential. Along the way he had a look at the forts Britain acquired from the Dutch in 1850. They were mostly in a decrepit state. The small village of Tassy presented a different picture. Its neatness and seeming prosperity led Burton to note having "seen many a village in Essex with less of comfort and civilization."[71] The exceptions to his model of external influences being necessary to explain "progress" in Africa were beginning to mount.

Burton spent three days scouting out Ada and the surrounding countryside. The land looked productive, and fish abounded in the river and ocean. Ada itself seemed healthier than Accra and, he thought, easily defended. At the time the village housed about three thousand inhabitants, and he figured the number might grow to thirty thousand with a company of police on hand to regulate trade and gold-mining activities. To this day it remains basically what it was then, a quiet fishing town.

When back in Accra waiting to leave, Burton encountered a strong earthquake that rattled the town, followed by numerous aftershocks. Considerable damage was done all along the coast, and Burton sighed with relief when the *Bloodhound* showed up on July 13. Two days later it sailed away with him aboard and the ground behind still shaking.

On July 23 a message from the Foreign Office reached Santa Isabel instructing Burton to speak to King Pepple of Bonny about ending human sacrifice. "You will inform the King," it said, "that if he thinks fit to call a meeting of his chiefs and the Head Men of the River, you are authorized to make known to them the horror and destruction with which this horrible custom is viewed by the British Govt and by all civilized people, and that Her Maj Govt will give him support in his determination to suppress similar barbarous proceedings in the future."[72] Burton requisitioned the newly arrived *Bloodhound* and set off on August 1 for the Benin River, this time with Selim in tow. Another passenger was Dr. Henry, a merchant from Benin City, whose factory had recently been plundered. He wasn't there at the time, and out of fear for her life, his wife had fled, only to fall ill and die shortly afterward. Dr. Henry, naturally enough, wanted the suspected culprits caught and punished, and Burton agreed to assist him in whatever way possible. He hardly needed much convincing, as it would provide another opportunity to do some sleuthing. Pepple could wait.

Trade completely dominated the Benin River, to the extent that people expended little effort on anything else. However, at the moment, with no one seemingly in charge, a state of anarchy prevailed, and commerce had come to a standstill. When a palaver failed to accomplish anything regarding the suspects, Burton joined Lieutenant Commander John Edward Stokes and Dr. Henry on a journey to Warri, some eighty miles distant via a circuitous route. They left Friday, August 8, in three gigs, following a series of small, barely navigable, streams bounded by dense mangrove swamp. The rainy season made the trip doubly uncomfortable, and six hours of rowing left them exhausted. Conditions only worsened the next day, and at times the gigs had to be pushed rather than paddled. Sunday brought them to a factory on the outskirts of Warri. Once the center of a powerful kingdom, it had attracted a number of European visitors, including missionaries. Now much lay in ruins. With nothing really to do or see, they headed back on the twelfth.

During a stop caused by heavy rain, several men showed up bearing gifts from a local headman. Burton reacted to them in a by now typical manner:

These *dashes* were brought by sundry swells in glazed black nautical hats, heavy cloth and big bone-buttoned coats smiting their ankles, and pink or rainbow-coloured umbrellas—that being the whole toilette. It is a constant mortification in these lands, the hideousness of one's so-called fellow-creatures. They must also deform deformity by their barbarous hankering after cast-off finery of Europe: Royal Marines' swallowtails, beadles' great-coats, and the sky-blue tiles of masquerade. What a contrast to the picturesque and beautiful costumes of Asia— the turban, the haik, and the burnus![73]

Faced with a tide working against them, the gigs didn't make it back to the *Bloodhound* until 11:30 p.m. on Thursday.

Saturday saw the same party set off for Great Benin, the name given by Europeans to both city and state. Though it had once been powerful, a redirection of trade toward Lagos, the elimination of slave exports, and civil war had caused significant decline. After nineteen straight hours of travel Burton's party collapsed at the village of Gwato. Similar to Warri, the town looked to have been prosperous not too long ago but now counted only some twenty to thirty houses. Still, Burton thought the countryside excellent for growing cotton, although he cautioned that any project of the kind would require bringing in foreigners because "with native workers it must fail."[74]

The land journey from Gwato to Benin City was supposed to take a day; however dense bush, fallen trees, and heavy rains slowed travel, and they didn't arrive on the outskirts of town until the next morning. A meeting with the "Captain of War," a figure second only to the king, followed. It was mostly about ceremony, and upon leaving, Burton noticed a man crucified "after the African fashion, seated on a rough wooden stool."[75] Reportedly, he sketched the scene, although the sketch has never turned up. "Green and mildewed skulls" lined the path to an open space, later named the "Field of Death."

It was indeed, a Golgotha, an Aceldama. Amongst the foul turkey buzzards basking in the sun, and the cattle grazing upon the growth of a soil watered with human blood, many a ghastly white object met the sight, loathsome remains of neglected humanity, the victims of customs and similar atrocities. Our first idea was that we were led into the city by this road that an impression might be produced upon us. Afterwards it became apparent that all the highways conducting to the palace are similarly furnished. In Africa the divinity that doth hedge in a king, is a demon in a chamber of horrors.[76]

Shortly thereafter they entered the city and were taken to their quarters, where word arrived that the king would give them an audience in the afternoon. Following an exchange of gifts, Burton and Stokes proceeded to the palace in full uniform, a symbol of their high office and the force behind them. As further proof, they took along two Kru armed with cutlasses.

The king's court was situated in a quarter separated from the rest of the city by broad streets and squares. A truly "ghastly sight" greeted them just inside the gateway—"the form of a fine young woman, seated and lashed hand and foot to a scaffolding of rough branches, which raised her ten or twelve yards from the ground." Buzzards had been busy working on her remains.[77] Told the king couldn't see them just now because he was busy with customs ceremonies honoring ancestors, they patiently waited, only to see the sun go down. The meeting would have to take place on the morrow, since kings never met with strangers after dark.

The morning brought more signs of horrors committed. Just outside the door to the house lay "the corpse of a man, with broken bones, and a gashed throat." Then while walking to a nearby market they saw "a pool of blood where another victim had been slaughtered."[78]

Dr. Henry finally received an audience at mid-afternoon. The king listened politely and agreed a wrong had been done, but said no rule in Warri existed to prevent such happenings. A second grander audience with Burton and Stokes took place a little later. The palaver was pleasant but yielded nothing of substance. With darkness descending, Burton and company returned to their quarters. Another meeting had been scheduled for the next day. It turned out to be about nothing more than exchanging gifts, with hopes expressed they could return one day for a longer visit. Heavy rain and drunken porters marked the return to Gwato on August 21. A demand there to hand over the culprits only elicited the reply that they could not be found. On August 27 the *Bloodhound* sailed for

Lagos, where Burton and Stokes brought Dr. Henry's case to the attention of the governor. In the end, he never did get any satisfaction.

The next we know of Burton's whereabouts is that he was aboard the *Bloodhound* as it docked at a place identified as Great Batonga on September 11, 1862.[79] He gave the coordinates as 2°52' and 90°52', the latter obviously a typo. Dropping the zero would put him in the south of present-day Cameroon. The purpose for being there was to scale Elephant Mountain, interestingly enough Mann's name for Mt. Cameroon. Burton called it that because "at a distance the resemblance to an elephant *couchant* is striking. When the clouds clear away, a long chine extends high above the lowlands; sundry depressions form the ear and neck; a swelling on the right of the profile, dipping towards the southern base, is the trunk; and the body everywhere bristles with trees."[80] He figured the mountain to be about ten miles away to the southeast. Using a factory of the firm Hutton and Cookson as a base of operations, Burton and Stokes set off on the fourteenth through country yet to be traversed by a European. Groups of staring "bush people," the general term for those living in the interior, lined the route. On the third day they made the ascent to the summit, which Burton calculated to be at 1,707 feet. During the brutal trip down the western slope Stokes became feverish, and he had to be carried back to the *Bloodhound*. While the vessel waited, fevers had also visited its crew, and without delay it set sail on September 18, bound for where Burton didn't say.

But where exactly were they? A Grand Batanga with a small bay does exist at the approximate coordinates, but there's no upland of note ten miles to the southeast. A narrow north-to-south trending ridge can be found to the northeast at about twenty-five miles distant. Just a bit farther north along the coast is the present city of Kribi, from which the ridge can be seen directly to the east. Burton mentioned crossing a stream near the southern base, and there is one in the vicinity. Still, the mystery isn't quite solved. Upon nearing the so-called mountain he said the elephant shape gave way to a normal saddleback appearance. But the highest point of 1,227 feet, nearly five hundred lower than Burton's calculation, is in the middle, which doesn't conform to a saddleback shape. The most likely explanation for the incongruence is that Burton measured and described incorrectly.

On the way back to Fernando Po, Burton visited Bonny to see King Pepple, whom he'd met briefly in December 1861. The city struck him as "the filthiest and the most barbarous place on the coast," quite something when you consider other places he visited. As for Pepple, Burton found him to be nothing more than "a petty trading chief" and, as a result, "completely powerless." He was, as he had been exiled between 1854 and 1861 because of royal debts. There seemed to be little prospect at the moment for preventing human sacrifice, and Burton told Lord Russell this "sounds to an African as absurd as the 'abolition of Christianity' to a European."[81] All in all, the trip proved a useless one.

Leave time now approached. Richard had instructed Isabel to wait until he sent word from Madeira before joining him there. Plans changed, however, when his ship was quarantined as a result of a yellow fever epidemic on Tenerife. None on board had gone ashore, but just having called at the port was sufficient enough reason for a quarantine to be imposed. The ship thus continued on to Liverpool, where Richard and Isabel were reunited on December 12. For him, England also meant getting together with Milnes and other friends for partying and conversation.

In January Burton helped form the Anthropological Society of London as an alternative voice to the long-standing Ethnological Society, itself a derivative of the Aborigines' Protection Society. It was the brainchild of Dr. James Hunt, who'd become an ardent supporter of Scottish anatomist Robert Knox's argument for human polygenesis, and the inherent and immutable racial inequalities that supposedly went with it, a view not accepted by most Ethnological Society members.[82] This wasn't the main attraction for Burton. Instead, he relished the prospect of virtually every topic, especially those outside the mainstream like sexual practices and cannibalism, being open to discussion. As he told members,

In availing myself of the opportunity now afforded me of addressing you, I cannot but congratulate ourselves upon the fact that we find in the room a liberty of thought and a freedom of speech unknown, I may assert, to nay other society in Great Britain. It is well so. Our object of study being Man in all his relations, physical, moral, psychical and social, it is impossible to treat the subject adequately without offending in general the *mauvaise honte*, the false delicacy, and the ingrained prejudices of the age. Without some such refuge for Destitute Truth as the rooms of the Anthropological Society, we find it equally difficult to relate and to publish facts. Indeed, some years ago, I was induced to propose that if the terminology of certain natural objects be held too gross for ears modest and polite to hear, the physiologist might adopt some system of conventional symbols which, like the finger-language of the Chinese ideologist, would obviate the displeasures of articulation. Some such symbolism is everywhere instinctively known to the natural man. This highly decorous proposal was, however, I regret to say, utterly ignored.[83]

For purposes of publication, the society created the *Anthropological Review.* To discuss topics too risqué for even the *Review,* the founders formed an informal dinner group called the Cannibal Club.

Starting with just a handful of members, the society counted some five hundred by 1865. People then started to drift away when political topics like the government withdrawing support for missionaries took center stage. Some were lost to a more convincing monogenetic view of humankind, one held by Charles Darwin. Two years after Hunt died in 1869 the society merged with the Ethnological Society to form the Anthropological Institute of Great Britain and Ireland. Burton went along, but then in 1873 left for the London Anthropological Society, which lasted only until 1875. At that time he returned to the Anthropological Institute to remain a corresponding member for the rest of his life.

While still in London, Burton also sought reinstatement of his military pension and requested promotion to the rank of lieutenant colonel, an honor accorded Rigby. As further justification he stressed his many services to Great Britain going back to 1842.[84] Once again, his requests were denied.

With the holidays over the Burtons looked forward to their deferred vacation. For him it meant needed space and time to write, and for her, of course, many weeks with Richard. The trip began ominously when a storm blew up as the SS *Athenian* prepared to leave Liverpool on January 24, 1863. Once into the Irish Sea the winds roared at gale force. Passengers implored the captain to turn around, but he dared not risk the maneuver for fear of capsizing, which seemed likely to happen anyway. According to Isabel, "The ship appeared quite unmanageable; she bucked and plunged without stopping. There were seven feet of water in the hold, and all hands and available passengers [Richard included] were called on to man the pumps. The under berths were full of water, the bird-cages and kittens and parcels were all floating about, most of the women were screaming, many of the men passengers were drunk, the lights went out, and the furniture came unshipped and rolled about at its own sweet will."[85] Two men washed overboard, and it looked as though all the passengers and crew would soon join them in a watery grave. But the *Athenian* held fast, and when the seas calmed after three days of being buffeted about, so too did fears. Still, sighs of relief accompanied the sighting of Funchal on February 6.

The Burtons spent six weeks enjoying the island's summer-like warmth before going to Santa Cruz de Tenerife. Yellow fever once again plagued the city, and so they moved to Orotava, only sixty miles distant, but much cooler and free of fever. There were no hotels, and thus a small, shabby rented room spruced up by Isabel sufficed for home. While there, they climbed Mt. Teide, at 12,162 feet the highest point in Spain or any of its possessions. Burton had instructions to return to Fernando Po before the end of April, and so the couple would have to endure another long separation. She wasn't happy, having told him earlier, "I could not possibly go on living as I was living; it was too miserable, one's husband in a place where one was not allowed to go, and living with my mother like a girl—I was neither wife, nor maid, nor widow."[86] The weeks together apparently strengthened the bond between them, and evidence suggests they likely met from time to time at Madeira or Tenerife without the Foreign Office ever knowing about it.[87]

Upon reaching Fernando Po, Burton discovered a large gig had finally been provided. A close inspection revealed it might last a year at best; still, it was better than nothing at all. He also found a welcome change on the island. During the previous year's yellow fever epidemic, the governor had conducted an experiment by establishing a makeshift infirmary at an elevation of twelve hundred feet in the hills above Santa Isabel. When it proved successful in reducing the incidence of the disease, the next governor began to build accommodations for soldiers on leave from duty in the city. Anyone with signs of illness was taken there as well, and consequently mortality began to plummet. Burton's sanatorium idea was at last being realized, although in a Spanish, not British, possession.

Somehow Burton got wind of the Foreign Office's wish that he proceed to Dahomey in order to discuss with King Gelele matters related to slavery and human sacrifice. Originating in the early seventeenth century among Fon-speaking peoples, Dahomey had become a militaristic state engaged in regular conflict with its hated enemies, the Yoruba. It both exported and used slaves for domestic production and military purposes. As the state expanded, the demand for slaves increased. War was the only way for them to be obtained, since, by tradition, freeborn citizens could not be enslaved.

An Amazon as portrayed in A Mission to Gelele, King of Dahome. *(Reproduced with permission of the Special Collections Research Center, Syracuse University Library.)*

By the time official word was sent on July 23, 1863, Burton had already made a visit during a reconnaissance of conditions along the Oil Rivers in May and June. He met with the king on three separate occasions over the span of a week and described him in a report to Lord Russell as "a man about forty years old, of noble presence, and a remarkably light complexion." He dressed simply and was apparently "greatly respected" by his subjects. On the other hand, Dahomey's notorious Amazons hardly matched the classical version of strong and beautiful women. Instead, Burton described them as "elderly, and all ugly, poorly dressed, and badly drilled, great at singing, talking, and dancing, and noisy as feminine troops might be expected to be."[88] He calculated their ranks numbered about seventeen hundred fighters, a figure much reduced by the debacle at Abeokuta. They were split into two divisions, a regular army and reserves to serve as royal guards. All of them lived at the palace. Despite their appearance, he considered them better fighters than the men. As for human sacrifice, Burton saw no evidence of it, not even a "single skull," although inquiries produced estimates of from ten to a thousand per year. However many, they were captive enemies, never subjects. As for the future, he concluded,

> I would further remark, that there is no risk whatever in Englishmen visiting the King of Dahome, and that in time great good will come from not permitting estrangement to arise. But visits to be of use must follow one another once a year. When left to his advisors, white and black, the King will be exposed to all manner of evil influence. It will not be long before he permits missionaries to settle at his capital, and presently human sacrifices will cease to offend by their display. As at Ashante and Abbeokuta, they will be performed secretly. They will not, however, be done in the face of day, as is now the case in Benin and Abomey.

Convinced he'd made a good impression on Gelele, Burton offered to visit him in an official capacity, saying "no effort will be wanting on my part to manage matters in a satisfactory manner."

Burton sent a quite different letter to Milnes. It's worth quoting at length.

I have been here 3 days and am generally disappointed. Not a man killed, or a fellow tortured. The canoe floating in blood is a myth of myths. . . . Not a skull have I been able to attest. The victims are between 100 and 200 a year instead of thousands. At Benin *au moins* they crucified a felloe in honor of my coming—here nothing! And this is the bloodstained land of Dahome!! The "monster" as your papers call the King is a jolly looking party about 45 with a pleasant face, a frank smile and a shake of the fist like a British shopkeeper. He made me Captain of his "Fanti" Corps of Amazons. I was looking forward with prodigious curiosity to see 5000 African adult virgins—never yet having met with a single specimen. I found that most of them were women taken in adultery, and given to the King as food for powder instead of being killed. They were mostly elderly and all of them hideous. The officers are decidedly chosen for the size of their bottoms.

Because of yellow fever raging in the Bight of Biafra, Burton went on to quip, "I daren't take a cruiser there. So most probably I shall go up the Niger and attempt Timbuctoo in a canoe. Really it will be a curious spectacle for the immortal Gods to look down upon, a chap starting in a hollowed log of wood for some thousand miles up a river with an infinitesimal prospect of returning! I ask myself 'why?' And the only echo is 'damned fool!' *Enfin*; needs must when the devil drives."[89] Whatever his intentions might have been, he was in Lagos by June 17 on the way back to Fernando Po.

Burton stayed at his post for just a little more than a month before embarking on another journey, this time to the Portuguese possession of São Paulo de Loanda. In his official reports, he claimed a painful attack of neuralgia required better treatment than was available in Santa Isabel. Loanda was hardly noted for its medical facilities, and a somewhat different and more believable story exists in the pages of *Two Trips to Gorilla Land and the Cataracts of the Congo*. Here, Burton claimed miserable conditions on Fernando Po caused him to become "thoroughly dispirited for the first time" and to begin "meditating how to escape."[90]

HMS *Torch* took Burton to Loango, where he transferred to HMS *Zebra* for the rest of the journey. During the voyages Burton was well enough to record

observations of the coast, and once in Loanda he traveled to the old settlement of Calumbo in the Cuanza River Valley. At no point in the book did he
mention being ill. For a badly run-down place, Loanda surprised Burton with its
orderliness, especially since many of the inhabitants were former convicts. After
two weeks he set off for the Congo River, some 180 miles to the north. He told
Lord Russell about highlands, "which tradition represents to be a sanatorium,"
existing in the upper reaches of the river, and he wanted to go there in order
to hasten recovery.[91] More to the point is the fact that no Europeans had gone
beyond the Congo's lower rapids. The one major attempt to do so, the Tuckey
Expedition of 1816, ended in total disaster. A potential exploration coup, one
almost as grand as the Nile, thus awaited someone willing to take the risk. On
August 30, 1863, Burton stepped ashore at Banana, the port of call at the Congo's
mouth, to do just that.

With the rainy season scheduled to begin soon, time was of the essence and
so after a quick look at the area near Banana, Burton and Selim joined Captain
John Laigné Perry and six other crew members of the *Griffon* on a French boat
destined for Boma, the last depot below the lower rapids. Once past the tangle
of mangroves, they came across numerous factories lining both sides of the river.
Most exported slaves in addition to palm oil and groundnuts. They stayed at Boma
from September 3 to 6, allowing Burton time to make a number of observations.
One based on his experience in East Africa pinpointed a problem; noting two
sickly looking cattle, he thought their condition more likely the result of tsetse
than the prevailing explanation of poisonous grass. Another observation of
interest, especially since it goes at odds with several previous statements, involved
the rather garish European-based costumes worn by men fancying themselves
kings. As Burton noted, "But there is also a sound mundane reason which causes
the African 'king' to pose in these borrowed plumes. Contrast with his three-
quarter nude subjects gives him a name; the name commands respect; respect
increases 'dash'; and dash means dollars."[92] He also sagely advised foreigners they
would be better off health-wise to follow diets based on lighter local fare instead
of eating roasts and heavy puddings.

Beyond Boma travel alternating between canoe and land became necessary, as the river cut through highlands, the same Sierra del Crystal encountered
in Gabon. The people along the way provided no opposition, although many

seem to have fled the river to avoid capture by slavers. This changed in an area called Banza Nokki, where Burton estimated a population of about 2,400 in twelve closely spaced settlements. At an elevation of 1,300 feet or more, he thought the place held considerable potential. "When the Lower Congo shall become the emporium of lawful trade, the white race will find a sanatorium in these portals if the Sierra del Crystal,—the vine will flourish, the soil will produce the cereals as well as the fruits and vegetables of Europe, and this region will become one of the 'Paradises of Africa.'"[93] Things didn't quite turn out that way. Europeans went elsewhere in what would become the Congo, and while some did find "paradises," they would exist only for them and not the Africans.

From this point on, Burton had only Selim and a local youth as companions, the others having turned back to rejoin the ship. Lengthy negotiations that nearly exhausted supplies of cloth and rum made starting upriver again uncertain. Then, suddenly on the morning of September 11 an escort of twenty men appeared to lead Burton toward the rapids at Yellala, a mostly overland journey needing four days to complete. Along the way Burton was forced to hand out considerable dash for little in return, which led him to once again go off about the supposed lack of African hospitality: "The chief, will, it is true, quarrel with you if his house be passed without a visit; but his object in taking you in is to make all he can of you."[94] At the sight of the rapids, he felt they "ought not to cause any serious obstruction to the development of the Congo."[95] As he informed Lord Russell in a report, cotton, wax, copper, ivory, palm oil, and groundnuts all looked promising as exports, especially with the slave trade drying up as a result of the British sea blockade.

> I need hardly say that if your Lordship deems the subject worthy of investigation, I should be highly honored by being chosen to carry it out. The local authorities at Angola, will, I am certain, afford me every possible assistance, and with the aid of a naval officer, who could assist me in observations, I might look forward to returning with important results, not only geographical, but ethnological and commercial. It is indeed regrettable that the Great Zaïre should, in this our nineteenth century, be permitted to flow through regions blank and unknown to us in the delightful region as on their creation day.

Burton never got the chance to fill in the "regions blank," that task being left to Henry Morton Stanley in 1877.

Yellala was as far upriver as Burton could go. With time running out and demands too great for what appeared to be limited opportunities for seeing something new and different, he started back down on September 17. At Boma, an attempt to organize an expedition to visit the old capital of the Kongo Kingdom, San Salvador, fell through; no one there knew the way, and besides, the Dahomey assignment beckoned. Burton's prime directive was to tell King Gelele that Her Majesty's government wanted the slave trade stopped immediately, something he knew would be difficult because of the profits the king's subjects made. Whether other sources of income could become substitutes seemed problematic. In addition, Burton had instructions to inform the king that human sacrifices must cease during his stay, and should any occur he must "decline to sanction these sacrifices" by being present.[96] Burton wanted to delay the trip until December or January because before then the route would be quite swampy. Nonetheless, he had to hurry to Banana in order to catch the *Griffon* for the return to Fernando Po. They arrived just in time for the sailing on September 28.

What Burton did over the course of the next several months isn't clear. He might have met Isabel in Tenerife, but there's no trail to follow. However, December 2, 1863, saw him in Lagos, having arrived aboard HMS *Antelope* to prepare for his mission to Gelele. Appearance-wise, Britain's most recent territorial acquisition looked much better than last time, thanks to the efforts of its former acting governor William McCoskry, who'd been acting consul at Fernando Po prior to Burton's arrival. Disease, though, still ran rampant; of seventy Europeans, nine had recently died. And Burton reported the existence of considerable "animus between white and black and white-black," part of which he attributed to "the extra-philanthropic portion of the fourth estate at home."[97]

The *Antelope* next called at Whydah, the starting place for the overland journey to Agbome, or more commonly Abome. A wildly enthusiastic parade of soldiering, singing, drumming, and dancing accompanied them into the town, which, like so many others in this part of Africa, was divided into quarters representing former villages. The French, British, Portuguese, and Brazilians all had built forts or factories, and Catholic and several Protestant mission stations dotted the landscape as well. The need to wait for the king's permission to come forward allowed Burton the opportunity to stroll about Whydah. Economically, it was clearly in decline, and he told the Foreign Office there would be "no difficulty in taking or holding the place" should there be a wish to.[98] On December 11 the permission to proceed onward arrived, and two days later the party set off. Burton's traveling companions included two interpreters, plus Reverend Peter Bernasko of the Wesleyan Methodist mission and Dr. John Cruikshank of the Royal Navy. Eighty-nine bearers hauled the luggage, which included an array of gifts. They also carried hammocks, a necessity since tradition required important visitors to travel in royal style. Missing from the entourage was Commodore William Eardly Wilmot, now in charge of Her Majesty's fleet in West Africa and the only officer with knowledge of Dahomey. He'd met with Gelele in late 1861 over matters pertaining to slavery, human sacrifice, the position of Christians, and relations with Abeokuta and spent two months getting to know the country and its people. This time, after he had waited two weeks, duties elsewhere demanded his attention.

No obstacles blocked the expedition's path. Water was ample, and although the heavy bush provided ideal concealment for an ambush, Burton judged this unlikely.

> The reason is, that the old blood has been killed off, except in the royal family, and the present race is a mongrel mixture of captives and serviles. The women are the only regular soldiery, the men are a mere militia. I have no doubt that the latter are ferocious enough when they have surrounded an unarmed village, and one hearing their speeches would fancy himself in the midst of black heroism. But they dare not fire their guns from the shoulder; they cry bitterly at a trifling flogging; they groan and moan after an accident or at an operation; and such is their horror of the grave, that they allude to death by such periphrase as "the tree has fallen."[99]

Indeed, they were literally feted at each stop. Yet, overall, much of the countryside looked like desert to Burton, as it carried about a third of the population it could support and these mostly women and children. He attributed the condition to "the annual withdrawal of both sexes from industry to slave-hunting, and the customs of the capital, waste of reproduction in Amazons, and losses by disease and defeat."[100]

At Allada, considered by Dahomans their "cradle," Burton lapsed into one of his off-the-wall determinisms. Calling the Fon spoken here the purest, he attributed the harsher aspirates and gutturals of Abome as likely owing to "a colder climate and a more rugged land," whereas the softer tones heard at Whydah resulted from "the damp heat and consequent languor of the seaboard."[101] The sight of four Amazons then turned Burton's thoughts to matters of gender. As with the Yoruba, he considered Dahoman women physically superior to men. And since "they are the domestic servants, the ploughboys, and the porters, the Gallegos, the field hands, and the market cattle of the nation—why should they not be soldiers?" Still, "in other matters," he quickly noted, "they are by no means companions meet for men: the latter show a dawn of the intellectual, whilst the former is purely animal bestial."[102] Could Burton's bigotry/misogyny be any clearer?

Disappointment with quarters at one stop prompted yet another outburst on how Africans received strangers. "I have heard and read much of African hospitality; but I have never seen a trace of it in the true Hamite. He will take you into his hut, and will even quarrel with you if unvisited: he will supply you with food, and will assure you that you are the monarch of all you survey. But it is all a sham: he expects recompense in double and treble, and if he does not obtain it, his rudeness will be that of the savage *gratte*."[103]

At Kana on December 19, Burton received word that the king would appear on the morrow. While he did arrive as scheduled, no meeting took place, and when Burton and his party moved on to Abome, Gelele stayed behind to oversee a trial of several Amazons who'd become pregnant, which meant that they'd broken a sacred oath to avoid sexual intercourse while on active duty. The eight men involved were convicted and sentenced to die in public. Burton presumed the women met the same fate. Their executions, though, would be carried out privately with no men present. This, Burton thought, "more civilized than Great Britain, where they still, wondrous to relate, 'hang away' even women, and in public."[104]

Under a blazing sun, Burton awaited the king's return to Abome. As tradition required, a long procession preceded him. The whole affair dragged on thanks to ten royal circuits, instead of the usual three, of the square outside the palace, the extras likely meant to impress the visitors. The next day, December 22, should have been one of rest, but Gelele was anxious to receive his presents, and thus they were placed beneath a large tent for him to inspect. Burton told Lord Russell, "I need hardly inform your Lordship that the sole object of the Dahomian King's civility is to obtain presents; that unless valuable articles are sent it is useless to send any; that if those applied for are not forwarded, it becomes a grievance; and finally that a too rapid recurrence of these gifts robs them of half their value. The King did not express the least gratitude for the presents sent by Her Majesty's Government, nor indeed did he once allude to them."[105]

This was the last meeting of substance between the two for quite a while because on December 28 the annual customs celebration in honor of the ancestors began. The associated events went on for weeks, with only an occasional day off intruding. At one event Burton and his companions were expected to dance. They each did, he performing a "Hindustani *pas seul.*" During another, Burton joined the army's commander in chief in a "*pas de deux*, with left shoulders forward, corresponding arm akimbo, and ditto leg in the air."[106] Gelele always made an appearance for at least part of the day, and on occasions he summoned Burton to the palace, but only for niceties.

At the beginning of the customs Burton observed twenty men in a shed said to be either criminals or captives destined for sacrifice. Escape looked easy, but they sat nonchalantly awaiting their fates. More intended victims occupied a second shed. Burton learned that two "evil nights" (January 1 and 5) took place during the customs and estimated that they totaled around eighty victims. He never witnessed any executions because they occurred at night, and everyone stayed indoors under "pain of death."[107] The grizzly evidence, though, was there to see in the morning on more than one occasion.

When nearly six weeks had passed without his being able to put the government's position before the king, Burton sent a message to Gelele saying he would no longer attend any events until a meeting took place. Furthermore, a ship awaited his return to the coast, and he couldn't stay much longer. On February 11 the customs finally ended, and late in the day of February 13 Burton had his meeting. It started with him presenting a list of complaints—living in a kind of prison, not seeing visitors, not being able to travel, annoyances of one

Victims of Gelele as portrayed in A Mission to Gelele, King of
Dahome. *(Reproduced with permission of the Special Collections
Research Center, Syracuse University Library.)*

kind or another, and that very day having to wait in the hot sun for four hours.
Gelele seemed taken aback, which didn't surprise Burton, as he suspected the
court's ministers concealed much from him. They then got on to the subjects of
the August 20, 1863, directive. As regards the slave trade, Burton reported the
king as saying that it "was a custom of his ancestors, established by white men,
to whom he would sell whatever they would buy. . . . Moreover the customs of
the country compel him to go to war, and unless he sold his captives he must
put them to death, which England would like even less." As for sacrifices, Gelele
claimed killing "only ill-doers and war captives, who, if they could, would kill
him." Burton knew these were the public killings, that the "real sacrifices" took
place secretly. Overall, he thought they might total five hundred in a year. But
if not performed, he added, "it would be sacrilege, and his subjects would look
upon the omission as Europeans would regard a King that forbade prayers over
the dead."[108] Other matters, such as establishing a permanent resident at Whydah

and the fate of Christian captives, received similar cool replies. It was, in a sense, a mission unaccomplished as Burton walked away from the more than two-hour long conversation with nothing to show for it. According to Reverend Bernasko, much of the blame rested with Burton because he'd behaved "with a hot passion and harsh temper."[109]

In the end, Burton thought Dahomey would cease to be an important regional player in the not-too-distant future. "Weakened by traditional policy, by a continual issue of blood, and by the arbitrary measures of her King, and demoralized by an export slave trade, by close connections with Europeans, and by frequent failure, this breed of black Spartans is rapidly falling into decay. The Abeokutans, far from feeling their old terror of the King, now openly boast that they will 'whip' the man who attacked them with women."[110] On March 15, 1864, Dahomey launched an attack against Abeokuta. It turned into a rout, the Dahomans losing several thousand to battlefield casualties, with untold numbers of prisoners taken and subsequently executed. Nonetheless, the kingdom maintained its independence until defeated by the French in 1892.

As Burton prepared to leave Abome he asked for a final meeting, which was denied. Instead the king requested he come back in about ten months, bringing a tent, carriage, and horses. Burton said he couldn't pledge himself to anything, since official orders would determine his future activities. Furthermore, this would again correspond to the time of customs, which Burton said must be avoided by future visitors until animals replaced humans as sacrificial victims.

On February 15, 1864, the return to Whydah began. After three days of boring, uneventful travel, they arrived, only to find that a fire had just swept the town, killing some sixty to eighty people. It, however, spared the British fort, where Burton stayed doing little until the twenty-sixth when he joined HMS *Juseur* bound for the Niger Delta. The only thing we know about what happened there was a meeting with a reluctant Pepple that caused Burton to fine and banish him from Bonny.[111]

Burton's book *A Mission to Gelele, King of Dahome* is mostly about the customs ceremonies. Still, with so much time on his hands, he had an opportunity to explore other aspects of Dahoman culture in ways not possible elsewhere during his travels in Africa. As might be expected, religion and beliefs more generally caught his attention. In a 1930s study, anthropologist Melville

Herskovits credited Burton with having produced by far the most thorough early examination of Dahomey.[112] Indeed, he cited or quoted him ninety-six times. It's worthwhile noting that Herskovits didn't comment upon Burton's less-than-careful characterization of the people. "They are Cretan liars, cretins at learning, cowardly and therefore cruel and bloodthirsty; gamblers, and consequently cheaters; brutal, noisy, boisterous, unvenerative, and disobedient, dispas-bitten things, who deem it a 'duty to the gods to be drunk'; a 'flatulent, self-conceited herd of barbarians,' who endeavor to humiliate all those with whom they deal; in fact a slave race—vermin with a soul apiece."[113]

The most remarkable chapter in the book is titled "Of the Negro's Place in Nature." Burton began it with a letter to James Hunt, complimenting him on a pamphlet he'd written on race. The second paragraph reveals how deeply social Darwinism had penetrated his thinking:

> Like other students of anthropology, I am truly grateful to you for having so graphically shown the great gulf, moral and physical, separating black from the white races of men, and for having placed in so striking a light the physiological cause of the difference—namely, the arrested physical development of the negro. There is hardly a traveler, however unobservant, who has not remarked the peculiar and precocious intelligence of the African's childhood, his 'turning stupid,' as the general phrase is, at about the time of puberty, and the rapid declension of his mental powers in old age—a process reminding us of the simiad. It is pleasant to see anatomically discovered facts harmonizing with, and accounting for, the provisionary theories of those who register merely what they have observed. M. Gratiolet's Eureka, that in the occipital of the lower breeds of mankind, the sutures of the cranium close at an earlier age than amongst the frontal races, admirably explains the phenomenon which has struck the herd of men, however incurious: it assigns a physical cause for the inferiority of the negro whose physical and mental powers become stationary at an age when, in nobler races, the perceptive and reflective principles begin to claim ascendancy.[114]

Burton then presented a list of his own observations. A few will suffice to reveal the tenure of his thoughts:[115]

The negro is, for the most part, a born servile—not a servant.

The so-called civilization of the negro is from without; he cannot find it within.

The cruelty of the negro is, like that of a schoolboy, the blind impulse of rage combined with want of sympathy.

The negro, in mass, will not improve beyond a certain point, and that not respectable; he mentally remains a child, and is never capable of a generalization.

Following a later address to the Anthropological Society, a member asked Burton if "he thought the pure negro would be improved or exterminated." Burton responded that improvement "was effected by an intermixture of northern blood" and that he believed the true negro "would be 'improved off the face of the earth.'" The society also provided Burton an opportunity to address issues he couldn't in the book on Dahomey, notably circumcision and castration. He again predicted the kingdom wouldn't last much longer, noting, "It contains within itself a preponderance of destructive elements, and hitherto its only safeguard has been the imbecility of the neighbouring tribes."[116]

Burton found a more livable Fernando Po when he returned on April 3. The sanatorium idea had worked, and he moved into a pleasant frame house of a resident away on business in Spain. Called Buena Vista, it stood at about eight hundred feet above sea level and provided a "genial and healthful" setting.[117] Some Kru looked after the property, and though they were not technically slaves, Burton pretty much saw them as such; "no white man," he said, "who has lived long in the outer tropics can prevent feeling that he is *pro tempore*, the lord, the master and proprietor of the black humanity placed under him." All in all, he and the island had become "fast friends."[118]

Burton seems to have stayed on Fernando Po in the coming months, working on his Dahomey manuscript and putting the final touches on another consisting of proverbs titled *Wit and Wisdom from West Africa*. It displays an appreciation of African culture that goes against the grain of the derogatory views expressed in other sources. For example, in the preface he wrote,

Now, as the grammar proves that Negro languages are capable of expressing human thoughts—some of them, through their rich formal development, even with astonishing precision—so specimens of their 'Native Literature' show that the Negroes actually have thoughts to express; that they reflect and reason about things just as other men. Considered in such a point of view, such specimens may go a long way towards refuting the old-fashioned doctrine of an essential inequality of the Negroes with the rest of mankind, which now and then shows itself; not only in America, but also in Europe. Such views may, perhaps, be excusable in those who have never heard black men speak, except in a language foreign to them, and which they had to learn from mere hearing; but when I was amongst them in their native land, on the soil which the feet of their fathers have trod, and heard them deliver in their own native tongue stirring extempore speeches, adorned with beautiful imagery, and of half-an-hour's duration; or when I was writing from their dictation, sometimes two or three hours in succession, without having to correct a word or alter a construction in twenty or thirty pages; or, when in Sierra Leone, I attended examinations of the sons of slaves in Algebra, Geometry, Latin, Greek, Hebrew, etc.—then, I confess, any other idea never entered my mind but that I had to do with *real men*.[119]

So, what did he really believe?

Burton also penned a very long private report to Lord Russell summarizing his numerous visits to the coast and hinterlands. In it he stressed the problems of the many rivalries present. Missionaries came in for special criticism.

The presence of missionaries is another source of trouble. These employees who are almost invariably of mechanic origin come out to the country at an early age and settle for life in comfort, if not affluence, going home to marry and bringing out their families. They learn the native dialects and are consulted by the people when legal defense against the violence and arrogance of the European is required. On the other hand the missionary who boasts that he "has the stand-point of Archemedes" must duly oppose the customs of the people, their

sacrifices, their wars, their polygamy, and their system of slavery. He
will strain every point beyond the limits of the most elastic conscience
to protect and shelter and to secure the escape of a fugitive servile.

So, too, did freed Africans, especially those from Sierra Leone. "Another and
even more increasing evil in all these rivers is the immigration of Sierra Leone
and other liberated men. . . . They call themselves merchants and they do
peddlers' work. They profit from promoting dissentions between white and black,
and they preserve the peculiar independence of manner which distinguishes
them in their own colony." Going on, he complained, "These men are supported
by the people because they can read, write, and lie about England, and they
are upheld as converts by those missionaries who assume extreme negrophilia
views. It is not a little remarkable that the two missionary rivers, Cameroons and
Old Calabar are as barbarous as any in the bight of Biafra." Burton ended the
report with a lament: "It is somewhat with regret that I find myself in a place
where so much is to be done for reform and for progress, and yet in a position
where little or nothing can be done."[120] Once again, Africa had bested him.

A second leave beckoned. This time Burton arranged to meet Isabel in
England. She'd continued lobbying on his behalf, especially for a new posting
that would allow her to go along. He left expecting to arrive in July. Instead,
it would be August before they embraced again, as Burton spent some time in
Tenerife before heading home. He would not return to Fernando Po and later
called the years spent as consul there ones of "penal solitude."[121]

8

THE GREAT DEBATE THAT NEVER WAS

NO ADORING CROWDS WELCOMED Burton home, a marked contrast to the highly enthusiastic, at times tumultuous, greetings provided Speke and Grant four-teen months earlier. Overcoming numerous obstacles and enduring some-times brutal hardships, they'd returned triumphant, for in late July 1862, after long stays in Karagwe and Buganda, guides led Speke to where a river tumbled out at the north end of the Victoria Nyanza. Grant didn't share in the moment. The route downriver went through Unyoro, and he'd been sent to get King Kamurasi's approval for right of passage. Speke named the site Ripon Falls, after George Robinson, First Marquess of Ripon. The falls is no longer visible, as it has been incorporated within the Nalubaale (formerly Owen Falls) Dam hydro-electric station. Also buried is a small plaque bearing the inscription, "SPEKE DISCOVERED THIS SOURCE OF THE NILE ON 28 JULY 1862." According to Speke, the issue of the source of the Nile was "settled" once and for all. Upon receiving the news, Murchison called the discovery a "feat far more wonderful than anything which has been accomplished in my life."[1]

Not long thereafter things started to unravel, in large measure because of Speke's own doings. The turn of fortune started with a personal attack on John Petherick, a man with fifteen years' experience in Egypt and the Sudan as a mining engineer, an explorer, a collector of fauna, and at the time Great Britain's vice consul in Khartoum. Murchison had introduced the two men in July 1859, and over the course of the following months they developed a plan in which Petherick would travel up the Nile from Khartoum to lay in supplies and have two boats at the trade center of Gondokoro for Speke and Grant's homeward journey downriver. All was slated to be in readiness by November 1861. If Speke and Grant hadn't arrived by then, the RGS instructed Petherick to proceed with an armed party toward the Victoria Nyanza to find and bring them forward, in hopes both were still alive.[2]

The search for funding pushed back a scheduled March sailing for Egypt until April 17, 1861, and at the end of the day, the expedition had only twelve hundred pounds provided by the RGS at its disposal. The government had balked at a request for an additional one thousand. This proved to be only the first of many setbacks experienced by the Pethericks (his wife, Kate, was part of the expedition). They waited in Cairo until the last day of June for the ammunition to arrive. Then once they were under way an array of problems kept them from reaching Khartoum until October 15, only to find it overrun by slavers who'd been pillaging the area upriver, creating a nightmare for travelers headed in that direction. Although banned by decree in 1854, the slave trade had become ever more virulent, bringing legal trade to a virtual standstill. Bouts of illness and the need to form a much larger expedition for security reasons put off the starting date for the journey to Gondokoro until March 28, 1862. Soon after departure the north winds so necessary to sailing upriver stopped blowing some six weeks earlier than usual. Torrents of rain, the likes of which no one could remember, then started to fall, and diseases ravaged the party as it struggled along the river. After covering only seventy miles in thirty-eight days, Petherick opted to follow an overland route toward known trading stations west of the Nile. The decision resulted not so much from a desire to save time as to travel through familiar country and to conduct some trade in ivory, which the agreement with the RGS allowed. The government also approved, since the salary allocated for the vice consul post amounted to a mere pittance. Petherick retrofitted one of his boats and sent it on to Gondokoro, where two others were already moored with supplies for Speke and Grant. Nothing had been heard from them in ages, and for all anyone knew, they both might have been dead.

The land journey dragged on and on, until finally on February 20, 1863, the Pethericks reached Gondokoro. Speke and Grant had arrived five days earlier, and there to greet them were Samuel Baker, whom Speke had met in Aden, and his beautiful paramour, later wife, Florence. (She was of Hungarian descent, and he'd secreted her away from an auction in Turkey of captured girls meant for harems or to be servants.)[3] The intrepid couple were on their own Nile quest, hoping to run into Speke and Grant at some point, if not discover the source themselves. Given the current circumstances, Baker decided to take Speke's advice and search for the Luta Nzege (literally "dead locusts" because of all the ones that met their ends there), said to be another large lake from which a river that could be the Nile purportedly issued. Kamurasi wouldn't allow Speke and Grant to go there. As an aid, Grant gave them a rough sketch map he'd made of the likely route to the Luta Nzege. They did find it after a dangerous journey that could have killed both of them. In honor of the prince consort, they called the lake "the Albert N'yanza" (soon changed to Lake Albert). As with Lake Victoria, the name is still in vogue because countries sharing it cannot agree on a new, African one.

While Grant was cordial enough at the time, he would later change his tune. Speke, according to John Petherick, acted with "coolness" and refused the supplies and the boats waiting for him, calling the offer a "succour dodge."[4] Instead, he accepted supplies and a boat from Baker. Upon reaching Khartoum, Speke started a campaign against Petherick, saying the consul went on a trading mission instead of being in Gondokoro as promised. Later, he even accused him of dealing in slaves, drawing on a letter written by the Austrian consul in Khartoum. The charge was bogus and may have been the result of a translation problem.[5] Still, Petherick had made a number of enemies in Khartoum during a failed attempt to end the slave trade, and rumors about him were rife. Speke's heavy-handedness didn't sit well with many. Petherick was, after all, a respected member of the RGS. Murchison called a telegram sent to him "most violent," noting that had it been made public Speke "could have been very injured."[6] James MacQueen took it upon himself to come to Petherick's defense with a withering, largely personal, attack on Speke in the *Morning Advertiser*. For example, he accused him of numerous sexual improprieties in Buganda, including partaking in an orgy with the Queen Mother. Speke's own words about his relationships with women there and in Karagwe, where he took detailed measurements of a royal princess while her stark-naked sixteen-year-old daughter looked on, provided plenty of ammunition for those who wished to damn him. Petherick, too, fought back vigorously, but it took until May 1872 for him to be exonerated of having been involved in the slave trade. The compensation he received hardly covered what the affair had cost him in reputation and money.

This was all yet to come out, and on June 22, 1863, Speke and Grant addressed the RGS. People packed the auditorium to the rafters, and some who couldn't get in climbed up walls to have a peek through windows, a few of which broke, at the goings-on inside. The next week the two appeared before a somewhat less rambunctious crowd at the Ethnological Society. In both instances Speke claimed, "Had I been alone in this first expedition I should have settled the Nile in 1859 by traveling from Unyamwezi with an Indian merchant, Musor Maruri, who was prepared to go there; but my proposal having been negatived by the chief of the expedition, who was sick at the time and tired with the journey, I returned to England."[7] Speke never mentioned such a proposal in earlier statements, and his portrayal of Burton was at odds with how he described him upon returning to Kazeh from the Victoria Nyanza. Later, in a letter to the *Athenaeum*, Speke wrote, "I don't wish to say anything about Captain Burton. I taught him, at his own request, the geography of the countries we traversed, and since he has turned my words against me."[8] While the latter was certainly true enough, it's hardly likely Speke could have taught Burton much about geography, except possibly mapmaking.

Speke did something else to dampen the society's enthusiasm for him: he signed a book contract with Blackwood's instead of publishing with the RGS, as stipulated in the agreement. John Murray had offered him the tidy sum of two thousand guineas, but Speke decided to go with Blackwood's for two thousand pounds plus a cut of profits. What he eventually provided them was so badly written that they hired someone to rewrite virtually everything. Some portions were altered in order to express Africa's urgent need of European guidance, especially in the form of Christianity.[9] In a twist of fate, the man chosen for the rewrite was John Hill Burton, a prominent lawyer and writer from Edinburgh, who was not related to Richard. Nothing has survived to indicate what Speke thought about having to deal with another Burton, but one can imagine it didn't please him all that much.

The article Speke eventually sent to the RGS for inclusion in its journal turned out to be thin and also poorly written. The society prefaced it with a remark that readers must look to his published work for details.[10] More crucial, though, were challenges to Speke's claim that the Nile was "settled." Two criticisms proved to be especially devastating. Lake Victoria, as it was now known, hadn't been circumnavigated; indeed, Speke spied the western shore only briefly on the way to Buganda. Furthermore, he followed the river for about fifty miles from Ripon Falls before heading overland to join Grant in Unyoro, and from there they took a land route through Acholi country before connecting with a river again. No assurances could thus be given that it was the same one left earlier. Topping things off, Speke's elevation calculations showed the Nile flowing uphill for ninety miles. In any event, enough doubt had been sown about the source of the Nile having been "settled" that one year after his high praise Murchison told the RGS, "But, in warmly praising and honouring the men who accomplished it, we are not yet satisfied, as geographers, with their simple line of march, and the valuable data which they fixed. We look naturally to other efforts which must be made to dispel skepticism regarding the upper waters of the Nile."[11]

Finally, there was the matter of Speke's "Scheme for Opening Up Africa," which he spelled out to a small group in London on February 18, 1864. It contained eight propositions, the last two of which bear repeating for their revolutionary nature:

> 7. That our Government be petitioned to form a chain of Negro Depots round the East and West sides of Africa, in sufficient numbers to half man our men-of-war, and yet to have a strong reserve at each depot; who shall all be educated and brought up for the holy purpose of liberating their fellow country men from the thralldom of slavery; as it is obvious that the great sums of money now spent, with a view to suppressing slavery, are doing more harm than good,
>
> 8. That as much as possible, Negroes should be educated and employed in all British Services, and taught to abhor the slave-trade, which they hitherto have been taught to consider legitimate from the fact that they are purchased with European articles of merchandise.[12]

He failed to impress his audience, and upon hearing of the scheme, Murchison told Grant, "Our friend Speke is out of favour (between ourselves) in the estimate of geographers by having entered into what we all consider a wild and impractical scheme of regimenting niggers and proselytising Africa as a new plan. He fell into the hands of a worthy missionary and has been going great lengths into bodies wholly alien to ourselves. He since seems to set his face against an exploration up the Nile to reach the Equatorial Kingdoms and finish off and complete much of what you necessarily left in an uncertain state."[13]

With both men in London, time seemed right for a face-to-face showdown between Burton and Speke. The annual British Association meeting, scheduled to begin September 15 in Bath, seemed like an ideal venue. All things considered, the competition favored Burton overwhelmingly, what with his erudition and cutting style, compared to Speke's somewhat nervous, halting delivery and overall lack of learning. Still, Speke was confident about the Lake Victoria/Nile connection and could hardly turn down Murchison's proposal for a debate on the second day of the meetings. Moreover, since reading *The Lake Regions of Central Africa* he spoiled for a fight, whether with words or fists.[14] Burton at first seems to have been reluctant and later indicated he had hopes for some sort of reconciliation:

> His brilliant march led me to express, despite all the differences that had sprung up between us, the most favourable opinion of his leadership, and indirect messages passed between us suggesting the possibility of a better understanding. Again, however, either old fancied injuries still rankled in his heart or he could not forgive the man he had injured . . . or, which is most probable, the malignant tongues of "friends" urged him on to a renewal of hostilities, and the way to reconciliation was forever barred. This was the more unhappy as he had greatly improved under the influence of a noble ambition justly satisfied, and all his friends were agreed that success had drawn out the best points of his character.[15]

And so Burton agreed to the face-off. David Livingstone was scheduled to deliver a paper on Portuguese involvement in the Central African slave trade. He didn't care for either man and perhaps that would lead to further fireworks.

As the assembled took their seats for the opening session at 11:00 a.m., Burton said he passed in front of Speke. Both made eye contact but did not show signs of recognition. Neither had, in fact, spoken to the other in person for six years. By most accounts, Speke left the meeting around 1:30 p.m. in a somewhat agitated mood, proclaiming, "I can't stand this any longer."[16] When someone asked about his intention to return, Isabel remembered him answering, "I hope not."[17] As events were about to begin the next morning, word reached the committee in charge of the meetings that Speke had died from a self-inflicted gunshot wound the previous afternoon. While he was out hunting partridges in nearby Neston Park his gun discharged as he attempted to climb over a stone fence, the shot hitting him in the chest. According to witnesses, he expired within fifteen minutes. An inquiry ruled his death as accidental, although speculations of suicide swirled about, especially since Speke was an expert with firearms and thus unlikely to be careless enough to leave a loaded gun unsecured in such circumstances. According to Burton, "Even when our canoe was shaken and upthrown by the hippopotamus he never allowed his gun to look at him or others."[18]

Speke might have lost focus if still in an agitated state of mind. The gun was a Lancaster breechloader without a safety. Because no one saw what happened, the matter will forever remain unresolved, although the weight of circumstantial evidence favors the official verdict of accident. Speke was planning a trip to India and had hopes the French would back his Central Africa plan.

Murchison's announcement sent the hall into an uproar. When the din subsided he explained what had happened and then read a brief statement from Burton in which he expressed his "sincere feeling of admiration" for Speke's "character and enterprise" and a "deep sense of loss" at his passing.[19] After regaining a degree of composure, Burton delivered a brief paper on Dahomey scheduled for later in the meetings.

Back in their hotel room that night, Isabel claimed Richard wept "long and bitterly." If he actually did, the question arises, were the tears for Speke or himself? Despite everything, the two men had shared much together in Somaliland and Tanganyika, and later Burton contributed five pounds to Speke's memorial erected in Kensington Gardens. It stands there prominently today, carrying the words "IN MEMORY OF SPEKE VICTORIA NYANZA AND THE NILE 1864." Still, an opportunity for redemption had passed Burton by, and that couldn't have sat well. Illustrative is that within several days he rushed off a letter to the London *Times* disputing Speke's discovery of the source of the White Nile.[20]

Burton presented what he'd planned to say at Bath to the RGS on November 14 under the title "Showing Tanganyika to Be Ptolemy's Western Lake Reservoir."[21] Following a brief gesture to Speke acknowledging "his many noble qualities, courage, energy and perseverance," he went into attack mode by raising a number of objections to the notion that the source of the Nile had been settled.

Burton then criticized the map that had accompanied Speke's brief article in the 1863 edition of the RGS journal, claiming it needed to be modified in three ways. First, Lake Tanganyika should be shown as draining into the Luta Nzege. Burton's support for this is a good illustration of his biases at work. African sources claimed the Rusizi River flowed into the lake, whereas Arab ones said it flowed out. Burton, of course, hadn't visited the river but backed the latter's view: "The African's account of stream-direction is often diametrically opposed to fact: seldom is the Arab's." Well, this time, the Africans got it right, as Livingstone and Stanley proved in 1871. Second, he proposed "converting the Nyanza into a double lake, the northern part fed by rivers from the western highlands, and the southern by small streams from the south to the south-east." Stanley's 1875 circumnavigation would show that only one lake existed. Burton's third change involved "Detaching the Bahari-Ngo from the Nyanza waters." Now known as Baringo, the lake is about a hundred miles east of Lake Victoria, so in this instance Burton was correct. But not in seeing a river called the Asua issuing from it and being "the real White Nile." Indeed, no such river exists, and while fed by two streams, Lake Baringo lacks an effluent.

Burton remained committed to the idea that Lake Tanganyika was at least within the Nile watershed. Indeed, he felt it to be the "western lake-reservoir of Father Nile," a position seemingly strengthened by Livingstone having recently found that no river connected it to Lake Nyasa. There had to be an outlet somewhere because of the lake's fresh, not salty, waters, and as noted above, Burton still put faith in the Rusizi River as the likely one. In the late 1870s Joseph Thomson showed it to be the Lukuga River flowing westward to the Lualaba. Burton, though, would not call Tanganyika a source of the Nile, claiming to follow MacQueen's rather strange view "that a lake, unless it be a mere 'eye' of water, cannot be taken as the head of a river, though the river issues from it." In the end, he concluded that the sources of the Nile remained an open issue and, taking one last shot, proclaimed the "late exploration," meaning that by Speke and Grant, had made them "farther from discovery than before."

Not content to let matters stand as they were, Burton put the paper together with MacQueen's *Morning Advertiser* piece, "Captain Speke's Discovery of the Source of the Nile," in a small, by his standards, book titled *The Nile Basin*, which came out before the end of the year.[22] In a prefatory, he recounted the history of the dispute to show readers Speke's many "errors," even excoriating him for a mistaken partial eclipse of the moon and for not knowing "the use of words." Feeling underappreciated Burton patted himself on the back:

> I led the most disorderly of caravans into the heart of East Africa, and discovered the Tanganyika and Nyanza Lakes. I brought home sufficient information to smooth the path for all those who chose to follow me. They had but to read the Lake Regions of Central Africa and volume xxx. of the Royal Geographical Society to learn what beads, what wires, what clothes are necessary, what guides, escorts and porters are wanted, what facilities offer themselves and what difficulties are to be expected. . . . The labours of the first expedition rendered the road easy for the second. The line has been opened by me to Englishmen, and they had but to tread in my steps.

Even his ardent admirer Donald Young admits that this tome tarnished Burton's image. "It is at once mean-spirited and wrong, and is a sad chapter in what had been a noble story. By allowing bitterness to influence his judgement, Burton was betrayed once again, but this time he had only himself to blame."[23]

Through it all Isabel remained ever faithful, and among other things she continued her campaign to attain a better Foreign Office posting for Richard. He, however, was more interested in hitting the exploration trail again. The source of the Niger River still remained a mystery, and so Burton proposed launching an expedition to find it. As with the Nile, speculation focused on the source being within another large interior lake. The proposal never went anywhere, and in the end Isabel got her way, as Richard wound up being appointed consul in Santos, Brazil, at an annual salary of seven hundred pounds. Although Santos was no more than a village surrounded by a swamp and some two hundred miles distant from Rio de Janeiro, at least she could join him there. Upon further thought, Burton reconciled himself to the prospect, telling Frank Wilson, "I want to see S. America. Plenty of travel there."[24]

They would not be leaving right away, however. A select parliamentary committee had been formed to examine the situation in the West African colonies, and Burton was expected to testify. The basic issues to be addressed were the value of the colonies to British interests and, if maintained, how they should be governed. Hearings didn't begin until March 1865, and while waiting for him to be called, the Burtons socialized a great deal and traveled together, much to Isabel's delight. Richard's day before the committee finally came on April 27. The questions posed ranged from Portuguese activities in Loanda to prospects for the Gambia. As might be expected, Burton came down hard on Sierra Leone, stressing the people's propensity for making trouble throughout the region and their overall unreliability, and he repeated several times his views on the pernicious impacts of the British trade in guns, ammunition, and spirits in the Gulfs of Benin and Biafra. Burton also spoke to the disastrous impacts there of the rise in domestic slavery with the substitution of palm oil exports for those of slaves. As a solution he proposed a "free emigration" to the West Indies of those who could be freed. Since Malthus, emigration had often been urged as good but usually for the metropole. The key to success, Burton thought, was to make labor more valuable so that the remaining slaves would be better treated. At the moment they could be had for only a few shillings each, and thus owners could put their slaves on what amounted to starvation diets and then buy new ones as needed. He felt it wouldn't be hard to identify those best qualified to emigrate, and the chiefs would cooperate under the threat of trade being withdrawn.[25] In the end, the select committee's recommendations produced little effect, other than to reinforce the view, one urged by Burton, opposing the establishment of additional colonies in the region and leaving the door open to possible future withdrawals, save, perhaps, from Sierra Leone.[26]

Burton's opposition to colonies didn't mean a softening on imperialism. He just thought their costs too high, especially given pressing needs for the poor at home. Better reflecting his views at the time are three letters written to the *London Times* in support of the proposal to transport convicts to Cameroon.[27] In the final one he commented,

> Thus will the things of old endure till the Caucasian race, the sons of Japhet, find their way into the heart of Africa and occupy the tents of Ham;—not in colonies like those of Bulama and Sierra Leone, but in

penal settlements where the severest and most dangerous labour will fall upon those who least merit compassion. When the land shall have been prepared for civilization, when the criminal squatters can be moved to the north-east, and when their encampments can be converted into permanent centres of improvement, then the great day of Africa will begin.

As for the mixed race population likely to arise from the loins of the convicts, he went on to note that "My reply is that it would not be permanent. . . . I am convinced that the Mulatto is a *quasi*-mule, whose offspring is generally infecund, and who must presently become extinct or return to the type of either ancestor." So much for the science behind racism.

Burton also spent a considerable amount of time with friends and writing. One outcome of the latter effort was a 3,765-line book in blank verse called *Stone Talk*, the title reflecting a conversation between a sodden Dr. Polyglot and a Fleet Street paving stone, upon which Polyglot fell face down after seeing a beautiful woman. Published under the pseudonym of Frank Barker D. O. N., *Stone Talk* was a full-throttle critique of the times, and most particularly Great Britain, including its beloved heroes. His personal copy at the Huntington Library bears the marginal notation "a pestilent lampoon," which it is and then some, with a mixture of sarcastic humor and anger, fueled, no doubt, by frustration. For example, here is what the stone said about Great Britain compared to Rome:

> Rome's crown and staff were helm and sword,
> Armed with which tools her robber horde
> Went forth, unrecking right and wrong,
> To spare the weak, debel the strong
> It ever was Rome's general rule
> To rob the rich, to strip the fool.
> And so do you. But *she* forgot
> To plunder subjects; *you* do not.
> Lastly, she robbed her fellow-men
> Like warrior—you like highwaymen.
> She scorned to harm a fallen foe;
> You sit upon his breast and show

Your teeth, till, faint with fear and pain,
He lets his bag and baggage be ta'en.
The end, of course, was all the same;
But *she* won fame and *you* win shame.

Toward the end the stone compared the past with the present:

Mourn, Britain, mourn the sad decay
Of honour in thine elder day.
The children of thy younger age,
That race so brave, if not so sage,
Ah, where are they?
Those knights so *débonnaire* and gay,
So fiery in the fight and fray,
That never knew the word of fear,
Brought up from milk on beef and beer,
Ah, where are they?
Like other things they've passed away,
And for their spirits churchmen pray;
Their sword-blades stain the walls with rust,
Their war-steeds, like themselves, are dust:
Ah, gone are they.
A poor and puny race to-day
In vain to take their place essay—
A dwarf'd, degenerate progeny,
Reared on dry toast and twice-drunk tea:
Ah, sad decay!

Isabel knew the book would offend many people and thus do further harm to their career aspirations, should word get out about the real author. Lord Houghton concurred and urged her to buy up and destroy every copy she could find. Only two hundred at five shillings each had been printed, and Isabel's usual thoroughness meant very few people at the time ever saw or even knew of *Stone Talk*. It is very hard to find today.

On April 4, 1865, the Anthropological Society held a dinner to celebrate the election of five hundred new fellows and to honor Burton. Rounds of cheers interrupted Lord Edward H. Stanley's opening remarks. "But no one can dispute this," he said, "that into a life of less than forty-five years Captain Burton has crowded more of study, more of hardship, and more of successful enterprise and adventure than would have sufficed to fill up the existence of a half dozen ordinary men." Burton gave thanks, saying, "The terms of praise which have fallen from your lordship's lips are far above my present deserts, yet I treasure them greatly in my memory as coming from one so highly honoured, not as a nobleman, but as a man." Burton could be generous to those generous to him. Still, with an opportunity at hand, he couldn't resist bringing up Speke. "It has come to my ears that some have charged me with want of generosity in publishing a book which seems to reflect upon the memory of poor Captain Speke. Without entering into the details concerning a long and melancholy misunderstanding, I would here briefly state that my object has ever been, especially on this occasion, to distinguish between personal enmities and scientific differences. I did not consider myself bound to bury my opinions in Speke's grave; to me, living, they are of importance."[28]

Given the context, the gushing over Burton isn't surprising. After all, he cofounded the Anthropological Society, and it tended to attract the like-minded. In other quarters, though, Burton continued to alienate prominent people, among them David Livingstone. Livingstone labeled Burton's frequent comments about Christian missionaries "monstrous and false" and on another occasion called him "an awful ruffian."[29] Burton, for instance, had recently judged missionary efforts in Africa a "complete failure," noting, "There is nothing to cheer us in the conversion of the negro, because when converted he becomes worse than before."[30] Nonetheless, the most important thing for him at this point in time was the opportunity to start a new career in a new land. Perhaps fame and fortune this time would smile.

9

FINAL WANDERINGS

BEFORE HEADING TO BRAZIL, the Burtons spent more than a month together in Lisbon and on tours of the Portuguese countryside. Nothing has emerged from the record to say why they stayed so long, but the answer could be as simple as wanting to vacation in a place where their language skills for the job ahead could be honed. In August 1865 Richard sailed for Santos, while Isabel returned to London to tidy up some loose ends. According to her, they had developed a strategy that had him "start at once *in light* marching order, go forward and prospect the place," while she was left to "settle up our affairs, pay and pack" and bring "up the heavy baggage in the rear."[1]

Far less is known about Richard's activities in South America compared with those in Africa. It's clear he traveled extensively and had plans to write a number of books on the region. Only two ever made it into print, *Explorations of the Highlands of Brazil* (1869) and *Letters from the Battle-Fields of Paraguay* (1870), which dealt with the border war between an outmanned and outgunned Paraguay and the Triple Alliance of Argentina, Brazil, and Uruguay. The Sir Richard Francis Burton Collection at the Huntington Library contains a rough-hewn autograph manuscript titled "Geographical Report of the Province of São Paulo, Part II. Political Geography," with sections on the country's civil divisions (mostly overviews of cities and towns), education, and population, and one labeled "Chronology of Remarkable Events in the Province of São Paulo" beginning with the 1530s. Appended is an even rougher draft of "Part I. Physical Geography." Also in the collection is a disjointed assemblage of scribbles, cross-outs, and inserts called "Drafts and Notes on the Eastern Coast of South America." For whatever reasons, Richard never finished any of these manuscripts. According to Isabel, he had additional projects under way. She mentioned "More Notes on Paraguay," "Lowlands of Brazil," and "South America" as uncompleted manuscripts in *The Life* and elsewhere noted that he planned to write about the River San Francisco and Minas Gerais, as well as produce a general overview of Brazil.[2] Strangely missing is evidence of Burton having conducted any ethnographic research, beyond some study of the Tupi-Guarani languages. Whatever he may have written on such matters disappeared from view long ago. If the pages went up in flames, it would likely have been because they were mere jottings and therefore deemed of little or no value.

Correspondence is another relative lacunae in the historical record. With one exception to be discussed shortly, Richard wrote and received far fewer letters than he did when in West Africa. Isabel, on the other hand, was a busy correspondent, especially with regard to the couple's social life and entreaties on behalf of her husband.[3] Probing deeply into the nearly four years the Burtons spent in South America isn't necessary for the purposes of this book, and besides, I couldn't add anything of much value to what Mary Lovell has related in *A Rage to Live*.

Several matters, though, are worthy of some discussion. One is that Burton continued to look for ways to make additional money. Coffee and cotton offered some possibilities, but mining promised to yield much more. Gold, in particular, fascinated him, as illustrated by the chapter devoted to its history in *Wanderings in West Africa*, and he thought gaining a concession or two might be the very thing to provide a more comfortable life for the two of them, which for him included an ability to pursue interests indebted to no one. As he noted to A. G. Findlay at the RGS, "My great hope is to throw off the Government and become a free man. Then if rich I go to the South Pole, if poor to Africa."[4] Flying in the face of regulations that prohibited consuls from engaging in activities for private gain, Burton formed a mining company. In the end, it came to nothing, and the only concession Burton managed to obtain was an unprofitable one for lead. According to Isabel, he did find some rubies in a streambed, but declined to follow up, feeling the woman who owned the land would ask too much if she knew there were gems on the property. Besides, he considered the place extremely unhealthy.[5]

Annoyingly, Fernando Po wouldn't go away. Burton was still seeking compensation for the expenses incurred in repairing the consular building, and in the meantime another financial matter surfaced. It involved the sale of the *Harriet*, a brig owned by William Johnson, a Liberated African from Sierra Leone who'd died while the *Harriet* was birthed at Santa Isabel in an unseaworthy condition. It's the exception mentioned above about correspondence, as a single Foreign Office file of 190 pages is devoted to the issue.[6] It first came to light when the executors of the Johnson estate sent a letter to Burton on August 13, 1863, granting him power of attorney for the brig's sale and asking that this be done promptly in order to help settle outstanding debts. The letter went unanswered, and so they wrote again on November 13 and followed with another letter dated May 12, 1864, all to no effect. Frustrated, the executors appealed to Lord Russell for assistance in getting compensation. By this time they had obtained a copy of the bill of sale dated November 21, 1863, carrying the signature Richard F. Burton and the consular seal to certify that the brig had been sold to merchants William Brash and James Dick of the Glasgow-based firm William Taylor and Company for 280 pounds. Subsequently, the firm sent them a bill charging the estate 251 pounds for repairs and services (including provisions such as brandy, ale, and claret) rendered the *Harriet* from May 2 to November 3, 1863. That left the estate only 29 pounds.

Meanwhile, William Rainy, a prominent lawyer from Dominica practicing in Freetown, took up the cause of the executors. He documented their case in a pamphlet titled *Censor Censored: Or, the Calumnies of Captain Burton (Late Her Majesty's Consul at Fernando Po) on the Africans of Sierra Leone*. In addition to including the key correspondence, Rainy went after Burton for views expressed in *Wanderings in West Africa*. He called Burton's characterizations a "vile national slander"[7] and took issue with his defense of a Mr. Marston who'd been fined by a black jury for beating a servant. Burton wanted a law enacted that would prohibit or limit such decisions in the future. Rainy concluded by saying,

> I send forth my pamphlet to cheer the upright and honest spirits of Sierra Leone—to chastise the guilty, the truculent, and the fawning. I pronounce punctual, Captain Burton's book to be a disgrace to letters, because it unjustly villifies a people of whom he knew nothing; because

he himself and his pet martyr, Mr. Marston, are the worst examples that could be held forth to a primitive race; because he upholds the conduct of the bad men of the colony; and because he impliedly sanctions measures, upon the part of the government, destructive of the British constitution and the rights of freemen.[8]

Lord Russell did contact Burton about the sale, and to clarify the situation the Foreign Office put a navy commander, W. H. Robinson, in charge of an investigation. His November 1866 report claimed that Burton was indeed present at the November 21, 1863, sale and that Selim acted as auctioneer. Furthermore, he stipulated that Burton never bothered to inquire further into the matter, but instead left it in the hands of Laughlan. Indeed, the signature on the bill of sale seems to be Laughlan's. It certainly isn't Burton's. In sum, Robinson said that Laughlan "appears to have taken unfair advantage of his position" and that many of his charges against the estate were "extravagant and unjust." Although eventually cleared of any official wrongdoing, Burton was judged responsible for the 280 pounds owed the Johnson estate, the amount being deducted from the 407 pounds finally allocated for consul building repairs.[9]

Burton, of course, didn't take this lying down. He protested against the wrongs done to him and Laughlan and about "slander and defamation" coming from the "Negro worshiper," meaning Rainy, noting, "All this fury because I do not hold the black to be equal to the white man, and because I would prefer seeing the missionary at home in Spitalfields than abroad in West Africa!"[10] It all served to "dishonor" the British name. But protest was all he could do, and so once again Africa shorted him. In addition to losing money on the settlement, Burton saw his pay stopped on two occasions pending the outcome of investigations and his reputation further besmirched, both within government circles and in public.

Although not one to enjoy giving formal speeches, Burton did so on at least four occasions in Brazil to audiences that included Emperor Pedro II and Princess Teresa. One recounted the Harar adventure, with, as one might expect, words of self-defense. His final comments, though, are interesting. With regard to the attack at Berbera he said, "The authorities held a Court of Inquiry in my absence, and facetiously found that we and not they were at fault. Lord Delhousie, the admirable statesman then Governing in General British India, declared that they were quite right. I begin to think that they were." The last sentence took another shot at Speke: "Such, ladies and gentlemen, is the plain and unvarnished account of what 'led to the Discovery of the Nile Sources'."[11]

The second speech dealt with Dahomey. Burton spiced it up with accounts of the customs' executions and comments on slavery, which he claimed a "necessary evil" in the "progress of human society." Slaves were at the time still a part of Brazilian life, and this time he sought to avoid offending the audience. A most curious statement involved the "negro." "In the United States every black man is a negro, or, to speak politely, a 'cullured pussun.' Thus the noble races of Northern Africa and the half-Arab Moors, the Nubians and Abyssinians, and the fine Kafir (Caffre) types of South-eastern Africa are confounded with the anthropoid of Sierra Leone, of the Guinea, and of the Congo regions. The families first mentioned differ more from the true negro than they do from the white man."[12]

Another tidbit from the time involving Africa is a recently discovered sketch map by Burton tucked into his personal copy of David Livingstone's *Missionary Travels in Africa* stored at the Huntington Library.[13] The "great traveler," as many called him, had returned to Africa in early 1866 on his antislavery/Nile exploration quests and subsequently disappeared from view. Many in Britain thought him "lost" and thus in danger. Not so Burton, who figured Livingstone quite capable of taking care of himself, and drawing on scattered newspaper reports, he attempted to track where the doctor had been. The effort reveals Burton's obsession with anything related to the source of the Nile: somehow, someway, he needed to be proved right.

The final matter concerns a change that occurred in 1868. For the most part Burton had been in good spirits while in Brazil, calling the country "the garden of South America."[14] The presence of an experienced vice consul in Charles A. Glennie to handle most affairs allowed the couple to be away much of the time, and Isabel could serve as stand-in consul, covering duties including writing reports, if need be, when Richard went off without her. She, however, disliked Santos intensely, telling her mother, " The climate is beastly, the people fluffy. The stinks, the vermin, the food, the niggers are all of a piece."[15] They thus established a second home in much healthier and more pleasant São Paulo, and thereafter stays in Santos were brief, especially since a one-way journey could take

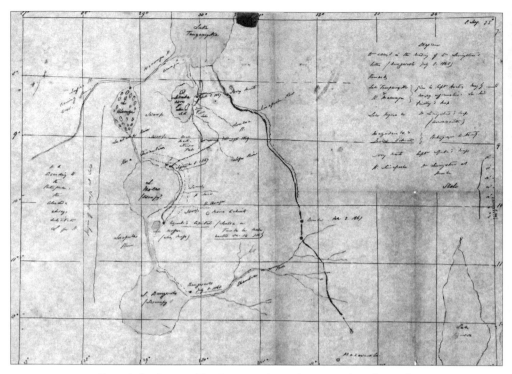

Burton's sketch map of Dr. Livingstone's travels in East Africa during the late 1860s. (Reproduced with permission of the Huntington Library.)

up to a full day. For socializing, they went to Rio. As a now-happy Isabel told Lord Houghton, "This is glorious country and we are very well and very happy in it and find plenty to do. . . . Rio de Janeiro is a very nice place; very hot & very dear to live in but the most beautiful place imaginable, quite like a fairyland. Richard says that it is superior to any place he knows, even the Golden Horn."[16]

In mid-April 1868 Richard developed a fever and bad cough accompanied by severe pains in his side. In spite of Isabel doing her best to treat and comfort him, his condition worsened, as severe paroxysms from alternating sweats and chills shook his body. Desperate for a cure, she called in a Brazilian doctor, who diagnosed a combination of hepatitis and pneumonia. None of his remedies worked, and Richard continued to decline to the point of seeming at death's door. But his tough constitution came to the rescue again. Nonetheless, the episode seems to have driven Burton into deep depression. He blamed it on

Santos. Isabel remembered him believing that "it had given him the illness, it was far away from the world, it was no advancement, it led to nothing."[17]

Still feeling poorly, Burton requested sick leave to last from August 1, 1868, through May of the next year, in order to go to an adjacent country, because, as he told the Foreign Office, "Santos offers small chance of complete recovery after a severe attack of hepatitis and pneumonia and São Paulo has become during this year exceptionally unhealthy." If still not recovered by the end of May, he proposed returning to England for a brief time to convalesce before resuming his duties.[18]

Meanwhile, it was decided that Isabel should go home to see such people as her friend Lord Stanley, who'd become secretary of state for foreign affairs, about Richard being given the consul position in Damascus. A long-held dream for Burton, the position had recently become open. Isabel's departure marks the beginning of a strange odyssey for Burton because, for the most part, he appears to have stopped writing. Letters from August 15 to September 15, 1868, during a field inquiry into the Paraguay/Triple Alliance war mark an exception. That he made the trip shows he was hardly as sick as claimed. On September 5 Burton showed up in Buenos Aires with plans to explore Patagonia and climb Mt. Aconcagua, at 23,081 feet the highest peak in the Andes. He accomplished neither, which didn't surprise a young Wilfrid S. Blunt, who remembered him looking disheveled and "no longer in physical condition for serious work."[19] But Burton did journey west, visiting Cordoba and Mendoza, and during December, with companion William Maxwell, he crossed the Andes. We know Burton was in Valparaíso, Chile, during January 1869 because he wrote a letter there dated the twenty-ninth to the *Valparaíso and West Coast Mail* regarding the Seuda Real through the Andes.[20] Burton also visited Santiago before moving on to Peru. All along the way, he seems to have been drinking heavily, which may explain why he never wrote a book about the journey. If notes for one ever existed, they must have been left behind somewhere.

At Lima, Burton learned he had gotten the Damascus position at one thousand pounds per annum. In no hurry—letters to return home without delay never reached him—he took a ship around the Straits of Magellan and reached Buenos Aires on March 29, 1869. After a quick revisit of the war zone from April 8 to 18 for more interviews, Burton went to Rio to catch the *Duoro* bound for Southampton, where he arrived on June 1. Stunned by his disheveled appearance, Isabel made sure he cleaned up and had new clothes before he saw anyone important.

Some in high places, most notably Henry Elliot, Britain's ambassador in Constantinople and the man to whom Burton would report, expressed concern about the Damascus appointment. In addition to Burton's reputation as a loose cannon, Elliot felt that his Arab/Muslim sympathies and contacts could prove inflammatory, especially to Christian missionaries. Furthermore, Muslims might be unhappy with the presence of a man who'd disguised himself as one of them on the hajj. A subsequent letter from the Foreign Office informed Burton that he might be recalled should his behavior so warrant it. For the moment, though, concerns could be suspended, as he needed some downtime to regain strength. The search for therapy led him to the waters of Vichy, which helped some, although he didn't like the place, calling it a "hideous hole with its jaundices, gauts and diabetes."[21] On the writing front Burton managed to complete final drafts of the two books on South America for Isabel to edit and push to publishers. He also continued working on *Os Lusiadas* and put the final touches to *Vikram and the Vampire, or, Tales of Hindu Devilry*. With these tasks out of the way, he went to Brindisi, crossed the Mediterranean to Alexandria, and then journeyed overland to Damascus. Isabel followed after seeing to her usual activities of packing and paying.

During the interlude, the RGS addressed the Nile issue again. Isabel attended a meeting to hear what people had to say and came away dismayed that Richard's name had been left off the list of those involved in the long history of Nile discovery. She immediately complained to Murchison, who said it was an oversight that would be taken care of in the news release covering the meeting. It's hard to imagine the oversight having been accidental; more likely, it reflected Burton's fall from grace. When the published account failed to make amends, Isabel wrote a letter to the *London Times* about Richard's contributions. In conclusion she wrote, "It is therefore *impossible* to ignore Burton's services in the Nile question. Dr. Livingstone has undoubtedly discovered *the* sources, and must rank the first, but no man can claim the second honour, or the water nearest Livingstone's discovery, but Captain Burton, and so no one can deny the fact that he, so to speak, opened the oyster for the others to get at the pearl."[22] Once again Henry Morton Stanley would have the last word and show both Livingstone and Burton to be wrong. While the doctor didn't live long enough to learn this, Burton did, although it would take him a while longer to admit his error.

New Year's Eve 1869 saw the Burtons reunited. Both were in high spirits, thinking this appointment might lead to others, maybe even the ambassadorship in Constantinople. Almost immediately complaints about Richard began to reach the Foreign Office. The first came from Jewish moneylenders, whom he'd singled out for charging exorbitant interest rates that sometimes put peasants and paupers in jail for failure to pay. The moneylenders reacted by contacting brethren in London, who painted the Burtons as bigoted and anti-Semitic. Such sentiments can be seen in "The Jew," an essay written by Burton in 1875, but only published posthumously because of its content.[23] Soon, various rumors began circulating about both Richard and Isabel, some mere fabrications. She, for instance, supposedly shot an Arab beggar boy for pestering her. It does seem that at least on one occasion Isabel used a horsewhip on a young Muslim man. A missionary couple, the Motts, kept up a constant barrage against Richard, claiming he favored Muslims over Christians. They wrote letters to officials and talked to friends and just about anyone who would listen and likely contributed their share of rumors. Then, while on an archaeological trip in Nazareth, the Burtons' party ran afoul of a group of Copt pilgrims. A fracas ensued, in which a large number of Greek Orthodox parishioners leaving church services jumped in on the side of the Copts. Their Bishop in Nazareth followed up by making claims against Richard. Accusations flew back and forth for months, and although the Burtons were cleared of any wrongdoing, another Syrian constituency had joined the cause against them.

The most devastating attack, however, came from the *wali*, or governor of Syria, Muhammed Rashid Ali Pasha. He, too, opposed the appointment of Burton and found a chance to do some damage over two matters he considered meddling in internal affairs. One involved a visit Burton made to the Sházlis, a Sufi brotherhood, disguised as a member. Because of a vision in 1868, many Sházlis started converting to Christianity, and upon finding out about the visit, Rashid thought Burton somehow involved. It didn't help allay suspicion when Burton proposed establishing a settlement for the Sházlis near Damascus. The other matter was a meeting with some Druze chiefs, longtime foes of the Ottoman regime. Rashid told Burton he was "vexed" by this threat to the country's security, and he wished to express his displeasure formally. Burton registered surprise at the reaction, saying he was "not aware that a simple journey with the object a return visit to copy some inscriptions and to pass through inhabited country (the Diret el Tulul) could have disturbed the security."[24]

Both matters played into Elliot's strategy of having the Foreign Office dump Burton, despite that fact that most Syrians who met Burton, regardless of their religion or ethnicity, liked or at least admired him. That he and Isabel made a point of regularly socializing with them, dressed in appropriate fashion, certainly helped Burton win favor. Elliot, though, succeeded, and on July 22, 1871, Lord Granville (the 2nd) issued the recall, the basic premise being that the Damascus post had been reduced to vice consul status.[25] Later, Isabel would refer to the event as breaking Richard's life.[26] In fact, the cracks were already irreparable.

Four weeks later Richard was on his way back to London. Looking after all the necessary arrangements kept Isabel in Syria until October 14. They, of course, hoped to clear their names and return to Damascus. Shortly after returning home, she wrote a vigorous defense on Richard's behalf, and all allegations in the Druze matter were eventually dropped. In fact, within a month of Burton's recall, Rashid was also recalled over reports of corruption within the government; he continued to serve the Ottoman Empire in other capacities, however. The Burtons didn't shed a tear when they later learned that Rashid had fallen at the hands of an assassin. Still, there would be no reappointment. As longtime acquaintance Baron Redesdale later commented, Burton failed as consul: "He was impatient of any control, had no idea of discipline, and for all conventionalities he simply scattered them to the winds." Isabel didn't help matters according to Redesdale, who noted, "she was not the woman to make diplomatic relations easier" and behaved in a "detestable" way toward Muslims.[27] Whether true or not, his remembrance illustrates the negative opinions about the Burtons then current in some circles.

Now into his fiftieth year, Richard took the recall fatalistically at first, likely knowing his Damascus days were at an end. With no salary, money became a problem. At one point they were down to their last fifteen pounds. Isabel's uncle, Robert Gerard, came to the rescue by providing just enough money to keep them afloat. When an opportunity to join a survey of Iceland's sulfur-mining potential during the summer of 1872 came calling, Richard jumped at it. An offer of two thousand pounds extra if the results proved promising heightened the appeal. He did his job with thoroughness over the course of three months and wrote a favorable report about prospects for future development after returning home on September 14, 1872. Nothing ever came of the project, and thus no bonus was paid to him. Later Burton wrote a book titled *Ultima Thule; Or, A Summer in Iceland* (1875), claiming it was for readers unfamiliar with the island and he wished to promote its development via sulfur mines, fisheries, and emigration. Those few who bothered to read the book found a mishmash of travelogue and facts, interspersed with diversions on such matters as "Note on Stone Implements and Other Prehistoric Remains Found in the Shetland Islands" and "On Human and Other Remains from Iceland." While sulfur received attention in a long appendix, the topics of fisheries and emigration languished.

Burton was also preparing the "Zanzibar" manuscript for publication. At the beginning of chapter 1 he penned an unusually wistful statement:

> I could not believe, before Experience taught me, how sad and solemn is the moment when a man sits down to think over and to write out the tale of what was before the last decade began. How many thoughts and memories crowd the mind! How many ghosts and phantoms start up from the brain—the shreds of hopes destroyed and of aims made futile; of ends accomplished and prizes won; the failures and the successes alike half forgotten! How many loves and friendships have waxed cold in the presence of new ties! How many graves have closed over their dead during those short ten years—the epitome of the past!
> "And when the lesson strikes the head,
> The weary heart grows cold."[28]

One of the ghosts/phantoms was clearly Speke, to whom Burton devoted the final chapter of the book. Titled "Captain Speke," it's a curious mixture of what Carnochan terms "conflicting views," certainly something not out of character.[29] Despite proclaiming, "I do not stand forth as the enemy of the departed," Burton went after Speke at virtually every opportunity. As to his person, he remarked, "My companion had a peculiarity more rarely noticed in the Englishman than in the Hibernian and the Teuton—a habit of secreting thoughts and reminiscences till brought to light by a sudden impulse. He would brood, perhaps for years, over a chance word, which a single outspoken sentence of explanation could have satisfactorily settled. The inevitable result was the exaggeration of fact from fiction, this distortion of the true to the false."

Going back over the incident at Berbera, Burton claimed Speke "had lost his head," and "instead of following me when cutting my way through the enemy, he rushed about, dealing blows with the butt of an unloaded revolver."[30] He bashed Speke's two books on the Nile for such things as their "looseness of the geography," errors of anthropology and ethnography, use of words, and scattered quotations from Scripture. Burton even had the audacity to criticize Speke's use of English place names, instead of native ones, apparently forgetting what he'd done on Mt. Cameroon. Then there's this rather remarkable statement, the truth of which can't be ascertained: "One wise in his generation [meaning Steinhaeuser?] whispered into my ear before returning to England, 'Boldly assert that you have discovered the source of the Nile—if you are right, tant mieux, if wrong, you will have made your game before the mistake can be found out!' I need hardly explain why the advice was rejected, nor does it befit me to complain that Honesty, in my case at least, has not hitherto proved the best policy."[31] No physical wound ever seems to have matched the psychological one opened by Speke.

In the fall of 1872 Burton interviewed Henry Morton Stanley, recently returned from finding Dr. David Livingstone. He labeled him a "right sort" and criticized the RGS for the way some of its members had attempted to demean the accomplishment, commenting that the organization had "as usual put its foot into the wrong hole."[32] Later, though, when reports of Stanley's successful east-to-west crossing of Africa from 1874 to 1877 began to reach the papers, he had some doubts, telling John Kirk, the British consul in Zanzibar, "Of course, you have seen Stanley, who still shoots Negroes as if they were Monkeys. . . . I have somehow or other serious doubts about how far his assertions are to be believed."[33] The reference here is most likely about Stanley having shown Lake Victoria to be one body of water and probable source of the Nile. Burton still believed the area to be a "lake region" with more than single lake as source.[34] Later Burton admitted that while he did not admire Stanley as either geographer or man, Stanley had done something no one else had: he had bisected Africa, which has "given a new base whereupon to operate north and south. *Voila!*"[35] He would have loved for such to be said about him.

Burton also met Verney Lovett Cameron. He, too, had a mission to find and resupply Livingstone, although the doctor died before the expedition could reach him. Upon hearing this news, Cameron decided to see if he could connect with the Congo River and follow it to the coast instead of turning back. As it turned out, conditions along the river forced him to take an overland route to the west coast. Burton and Cameron would form a fast friendship and journey to the Gold Coast together in 1882. Cameron's stock with Burton no doubt was helped when he called *The Lake Regions of Central Africa* "a work which, for minuteness of detail, must ever stand foremost amongst books of descriptive geography."[36]

Despite their poverty, the Burtons did quite a bit of socializing, and Richard gave occasional lectures on one subject or another. Although they attended RGS meetings from time to time, both harbored deep resentments over supposed slights. For example, Richard had this to say after reviewing Murchison's final book: "Since these pages went to print Sir R. I. Murchison has passed away, full of years and honours. I had not the melancholy satisfaction of seeing for the last time our revered Chief, one of whose latest actions was to oppose my reading a paper about the so-called Victoria Nyanza before the Royal Geographical Society; whilst another was to erase my name from the list of Nile explorers when revising his own biography. But peace be to his manes! I respect the silence of a newly made grave."[37]

Replying to the obituary in the *London Times*, Burton remarked in wounded fashion "our lamented President, the late Sir Roderick Murchison, forgot, in his anniversary speech, to couple with the names of Speke, Grant and Baker, that of a man who led the first expedition into the Lake Region, which are now known to send forth the Nile."[38]

Burton still hoped to make some kind of journey of exploration, but that wasn't in the cards just now. Thanks to Isabel's continued lobbying, he instead wound up taking the position of consul at the Austro-Hungarian Adriatic port of Trieste, succeeding Charles Lever, another unconventional sort more or less exiled there. Although the position was a demotion—it paid only six hundred pounds per annum—they needed the money and demands would be few, meaning more time could be spent writing and traveling. In addition, the job might serve as a stepping-stone to a better posting, perhaps the one in Morocco, which both coveted. (An earlier effort to secure the post in Tehran had been rebuffed by the Foreign Office.) Again traveling separately, Isabel and Richard met by chance in Venice. From there they journeyed to Trieste, arriving December 6, 1872. Ethnically a polyglot city of about 150,000 inhabitants, it had a reputation for three winds. "One of these, the Bora, blows the people almost into the sea with its fury, rising suddenly, like a cyclone, and sweeping all before it; the second named the Scirocco, which blows the drainage back into the town; and the third the Contraste, formed by the two first-named winds blowing at once against each other."[39]

The Burtons spent the first six months living in a hotel they thoroughly disliked before finding a ten-room flat to serve as a permanent home. In keeping with expectations, consular matters took up only a couple of hours per day when Richard was on the job, which wasn't all that often. Regular visits to the hill town of Opiçina, only an hour away, provided welcome relief. Venice, too, could be reached quickly. According to Isabel, "When we wanted to go, we just turned the key and left."[40] Her health improved and with it her spirits. As Richard told a friend, "Mrs. Burton much better—Trieste really agrees with her."[41] Henceforth, much of her spare time there would be spent working with and advocating the cause of the Society for the Prevention of Cruelty to Animals.

Burton, though, still longed to be more at center stage. When events in Afghanistan again reached flash points, he felt he could better serve the Foreign Office there in one capacity or another than he could by wiling away time in Trieste. Several letters yielded no response.[42] A request to become governor of West Africa also went nowhere. This particularly bothered Burton in light of renewed war with the Asante Kingdom in the Gold Coast. He felt it could easily have been avoided by showing a stronger hand earlier on and allowing the Asante a post along the Volta River outside the protectorate, something current policy prohibited. According to him, that would have cost only a thousand pounds, whereas now millions might be spent. And with the Fante, whom he labeled "curs" possessed of "all the worst qualities of white and black," as allies, victory seemed questionable.[43] Although the British did prevail militarily, Burton was right about the financial costs involved.

All the while, he kept writing, completing manuscripts for *Ultima Thule*, *Two Trips to Gorilla Land and the Cataracts of the Congo*, *The Lands of the Cazembe*,

A New System of Sword Exercise for Infantry, and *Etruscan Bologna*. Articles and pamphlets flew from his pen as well. In a letter complimenting William T. Saunders for a paper he wrote called "On the Present Aspects of Africa," Burton told him, "Also remember that Islam is a distinct progress over fetishism as slavery was upon mere savagery. And both are like all worldly institutions, temporary and provisional when they have passed their time and cease to do good, they become merely injurious." He claimed being too busy at the moment "to write anything upon this subject for the papers, but some one ought," as his own "books have repeated the matter with little effect."[44]

A staphylococcus infection that spread to the groin felled Burton in the spring of 1874. Suffering intense pain nothing helped to relieve, he became steadily weaker, so weak he was "unable to turn in bed without assistance," according to Isabel, who said she stayed by his side for seventy-eight days straight.[45] But once again he rallied, and an extended leave of absence allowed him to convalesce at a leisurely pace. As the year drew to a close, Burton felt well enough for Isabel to leave for London in order to oversee publications of his books and her own *Inner Life of Syria*. As usual, she also continued lobbying efforts, which included trying to get Richard a knighthood. Burton did his own lobbying:

> The Press are calling me "the neglected Englishman," and I want to express to them the feelings of pride and gratitude with which I have seen the exertions of my brethren of the Press to procure for me a tardy justice. The public is a fountain of honour which amply suffices all my aspirations; *it is the more honourable as it will not allow for a long career to be ignored for the reasons of catechism or creed.* With a general voice so loud and so unanimous in my favour, I can amply console myself for the absence of what the world calls "honours," which I have long done passing well without; nor should I repine at a fate which I share with England's most memorable men and most honourable, to go no further than Gordon and Thackeray. It is certainly a sad sight to see perfectly private considerations and petty bias prevail against the claims of public service, and let us only hope for better things in future days.[46]

Richard reached London some six months after Isabel. He was restless and thought about going to Central Asia, Central Africa, or wherever.[47] A possibility to move arose when the position of consul general in Tiflis became open, but his name never appeared on the list. So, it became clear to the Burtons that in all likelihood Trieste would be the final posting. During July Richard returned to Iceland to look into a new mine and gather evidence for an intended lawsuit over the missing two thousand pounds.[48] The trip was taken in vain. So were his continuing hopes that Lake Tanganyika would be shown to be part of the Nile drainage system, with Victoria turning out to be a "lake region" instead of a single lake.[49] It took until 1881 for Burton to admit his error about Lake Tanganyika, and even then he buried it near the end of *Camoens: His Life and His Lusiads*. A few pages later he made a statement about Livingstone's final effort to find the illusive "Coy Fountains" that equally could be applied to him. "There is a time to leave the Dark Continent, and that is when the idée fixe begins to develop itself. 'Madness comes from Africa' was a favourite and true saying."[50]

Sick once more from lumbago and gout, according to Isabel, Richard spent several weeks in dreaded Vichy, before reuniting with her in London on October 6. They were back in Trieste in time for Christmas but didn't stay long, boarding ship on New Year's Eve for Bombay. It was during this voyage that Richard related to Isabel what she later included in *The Life*. They spent their time in India primarily visiting his old haunts, seeing friends, and taking in the sights. Packed with events, the days passed quickly, and by mid-June they'd returned to Trieste, now a more central post because of escalating tensions in the Balkans. Burton jumped into the fray by writing articles criticizing Britain's siding with Turkey under pseudonyms for the *Times* of India.

Burton also set about the task of writing *Sind Revisited*, with the rather interesting subtitle *With Notices of the Anglo-Indian Army; Railroads; Past, Present, and Future, Etc*. He resurrected Mr. John Bull to be the object of narration, which included events and opinions from the earlier book. All told, it was a disastrous literary effort, probably Burton's worst.

On the way to Bombay, gold once again captured Burton's attention, this time in Midian, a vaguely defined region of the northwest Arabian Peninsula, whose people, the Midianites, Moses commanded be laid waste. Some speculated that it might be the fabled "Land of Ophir." While he was in Cairo in 1853, Burton said a man called Haji Wali showed him sand samples containing what appeared to be flecks of gold. It didn't impress the British consul, who felt at the time that the world already had more than enough gold. Frustrated by such "intolerable bosh," Burton claimed to have said no more about the matter for nearly a quarter century.[51] The existence of ancient ruins in Midian made for an added lure, even though he wouldn't be the first European to see them. With seed money from Isabel's Uncle Robert Gerard in pocket, Burton obtained a short leave of absence and departed Trieste for Egypt on March 3, 1877, in order to gain Khedive Ismail's approval and support for a preliminary reconnaissance. He couldn't have been happier about going back to the desert: "At last! Once more it is my fate to escape the prison-life of civilised Europe, and to refresh body and mind by studying Nature in her noblest and most admirable form—the Nude. Again I am to enjoy a glimpse of the 'glorious Desert;' to inhale the sweet pure breath of translucent skies that show the red stars burning upon the very edge and verge of the horizon; and to strengthen myself by a short visit to the Wild Man [Bedouin] and his old home."[52]

After some initial reluctance, Ismail agreed to the reconnaissance, provided Burton pay the costs up front and then bill the treasury. Early on the last day of March a small party that included Haji Wali, left Suez, destined for Al-Muwaylih on the Arabian side of the Red Sea. From there they coasted northward before striking inland on camels. The animal was the one thing Burton detested about the desert.

> The so-called "generous animal," the "patient camel," whose endurance has been greatly exaggerated, is a peevish, ill-conditioned beast— one of the most cross-grained, vile-tempered, and antipathetic that domestication knows. When very young it is cold, grave, and awkward; when adult, vicious and ungovernable, in some cases dangerous; when old it is fractious and grumbling, sullen, vindictive, and cold-blooded. It utters its snorting moan and its half-plaintive, half-surly bleat even when you approach it. It suspects everything unknown; it roars aloud, like a teeth-cutting child, as each pound of weight is added to the burden. . . . Its vaunted docility is the result of sheer stupidity. It lacks even the intelligence to distinguish poisonous herbs.[53]

They also explored the coastal area south of Al-Muwaylih, and on the way back to Egypt visited the old capital of Midian, Maqná, on the Gulf of Aqaba.

Although the reconnaissance lasted only sixteen days, Burton was encouraged by what he saw and heard, wiring Ismail from Suez about *"succès complet."*[54] In addition to gold, there seemed to be workable deposits of silver, iron ore, tin, lead, and antimony. A vein named the *Grand Filon* looked particularly promising, and Burton proposed going back with a party of engineers to begin blasting operations. But the outbreak of the Russo-Turkish War put the plan to rest, and on May 12 he returned to Trieste in "marvelous good health and spirits."[55]

Burton immediately set about planning a more detailed follow-up survey. He greatly admired Ismail and wanted to help him achieve his ambitious schemes of territorial expansion and economic modernization, which included the building of the Suez Canal. A strained treasury had put the plans in jeopardy, a situation currently made worse by the burdens of the Russo-Turkish War. At some near date, Burton hoped to see Syria joined to Egypt, as he felt this would usher in an age of prosperity, currently "now arrested only by subjugation to Stambúl." It was Egypt's destiny, he predicted, to regain "her birthright" and thereby "spread commerce and civilisation throughout the heart of Africa."[56] Burton also saw an opportunity to make a significant amount of money, which would, he joked—or maybe not—allow him to become "the Duke of Midian."[57] He thus requested three months leave to begin in the latter half of October, adding that absence from Trieste during the season of cold winds would help remedy his current afflictions of lumbago and neuralgia.[58]

After a more than monthlong delay in Cairo, caused mostly by difficulties securing needed funding, an expedition of some sixty strong set off by special train for Suez on December 6, 1877. Storms kept them there for four days, and shortly after they sailed out of the harbor, a boiler problem forced their boat, the *El-Mukhbir*, to turn back. More bad weather delayed the landing at Al-Muwaylih until December 19. These were only the first of a series of problems faced over the course of the next four months. Indeed, hardly a day seemed to pass without one, and even the train from Cairo to Suez, where Isabel waited for Richard, broke down. Still, Richard felt confident about the expedition's results. A large area had been surveyed and mapped, fifteen archaeological sites identified, and numerous botanical specimens collected. Most importantly, Burton claimed having discovered "immense deposits of silver," which, in addition to aiding Egypt, "may open an extensive field to English industry."[59] Sulfur, rock salt, and

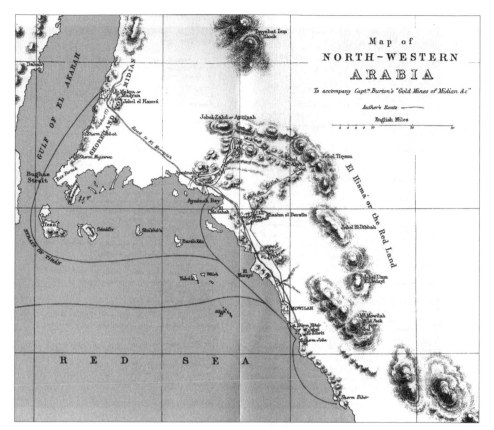

Map of Burton's journey to Midian from Gold-Mines of
Midian. (Reproduced with permission of the Oleander Press.)

gypsum also seemed to exist in workable quantities. In Cairo Ismail put on a
grand reception and organized a three-week-long exhibition of the Midian finds.
With that over, the Burtons left for home to begin the task of finding subscribers
for concessions they hoped the khedive would grant.

In 1875 Charles "Chinese" Gordon had written Burton asking for his
views about how to establish a route between the upper Nile and the eastern
coast of Africa. Gordon was then serving a governor of Equatoria in the Sudan
for the Egyptians and by extension represented the interests of Great Britain. His
main task was to put a stop to the last vestiges of the slave trade. In 1877 Gordon
wrote again, saying he'd asked the khedive to appoint Burton as governor general
of Darfur for two years at a salary of sixteen hundred pounds per year and with

two secretaries to handle administrative tasks. Burton politely refused, believing Midian offered greater financial prospects. Furthermore, he told Gordon, "You and I are too much alike. I could not serve under you, nor you under me. I do not look upon the Soudan as a lasting thing. I have nothing to depend upon but my salary, and I have a wife and you have not." Gordon tried again after meeting the Burtons in Egypt in March 1878. This time he suggested undertaking the task of forming a government encompassing Zeila, Harar, and Berbera, to which he would contribute five thousand pounds. Again Burton declined.[60] Soon thereafter the Sudan was embroiled in the Mahdist uprising, which claimed Gordon's life in Khartoum on January 26, 1885. Strangely Burton refused to believe Gordon had been killed, insisting instead that he'd escaped into the desert and, out of feelings of "betrayal and abandonment" by England, stayed hidden from view.[61]

The assays from Midian proved disappointing. Indeed, they revealed little of value.[62] Burton blamed the man in charge of collecting the rock samples and wrote to Ismail requesting a third expedition to collect new ones so as to interest potential subscribers, who naturally enough had been reluctant to sign on the dotted line. He hoped the work could begin in February.[63]

To handle the business end of the concessions in London, Burton joined forces with entrepreneur John Henry Murchison, cousin of Sir Roderick. Murchison also wanted a concession to build tramways in Alexandria and Cairo. Months passed with no reply from Egypt, beyond a note saying Burton's request would be considered. Murchison became anxious, and in March he suggested both men go to Cairo in the spring to see if work could begin in the coming fall. Murchison then changed his mind, preferring to have concessions in hand before leaving. He asked Burton to find out "how the wind blows."[64] It wasn't blowing favorably, for in June under pressure from Britain and France, Ismail was deposed and his son Tawfiq took the reins of power. Given the resulting political turmoil, the silence from Egypt about Midian continued.

Despite optimism about finding subscribers should concessions be granted, Murchison backed away, and on December 5, 1879, Burton sailed for Egypt by himself. He spent six months there, all the while being ignored by Tawfiq. With abundant time on his hands, Burton inquired into the ongoing slave trade. The hardest hit region was Darfur, where Gordon wanted him assigned, with young women meant for harems and men to be turned into eunuchs in especially high demand. Burton detailed all of this in three letters sent to the Foreign Office. In addition, he purportedly sent a private letter to Lord Granville suggesting himself as the person who could see to the slave traffic's end.

> I would like to have a temporary appointment in the Red Sea as Slave Commissioner. I want a salary of from ƒ1600 to ƒ2000 (ƒ1600 would do if allowed to keep Trieste on half-pay, ƒ350 per annum), the use of a gun-boat, and a roving commission, independent of the Consul-General of Egypt, but to act in concert with a Consul (such as young Wylde) appointed to the Soudan. It is a thing that has long been talked about as a great want in the Red Sea, *if slavery is really to be exterminated*, and Gordon's splendid work to be carried out on the coast. Gordon Pasha has long wished to recommend *me* for this work. As this last appointment would only be *temporary*—say for a couple of years—I would like to keep Trieste to fall back upon when my work is done, and as a home for my wife when she cannot be with me. Other men are allowed to retain their Indian appointments, and still to take temporary service in Egypt: for this there are several precedents. Mr. Brock, Vice-Consul at Trieste, who is thoroughly reliable, would act for me on half-pay, as he has done the last forty years. I guarantee that, placed in such a position, in *two years'* time the Red Sea *shall be as clear of slaves as if slavery had never existed.*[65]

Needless to say, this rather arrogant proposal sparked no interest at the Foreign Office, and should any such commissioner ever be contemplated, Burton would have likely been at or near the bottom of a candidate list.

A mugging ended Burton's stay in Egypt. He lost only a gold rod and signet ring and decided not to report the incident, although it took a while to recover from the physical damages inflicted. In addition to cuts and bruises, he suffered headaches from a blow to the head. There would be no mineral concessions, and he wouldn't even be reimbursed for over five hundred pounds spent out-of-pocket to cover expenses during the previous expedition. In the end, all that resulted from his efforts were two books, *The Gold-Mines of Midian* (1878) and

The Land of Midian (Revisited) (1879). The first actually sold fairly well; the second hardly caused a stir.[66] Nonetheless, Burton didn't give up on Midian, as evidenced during a supper conversation in June 1885 reported by author Bram Stoker, in which he talked about trying again to convince the khedive to reopen the mines.[67] Talking seems to have been as far as matters went, and in point of fact, there was no wealth to be mined in Midian. The valuable deposits had been worked out long ago, just as Burton had been told in 1877.[68]

A project slated for the Juba River Valley in southern Somaliland turned out to be another mining pipe dream. Burton claimed that while in Zanzibar, a man had shown him high-quality quartz crystals purportedly from there, and he felt the sultan would provide needed assistance for getting operations under way.[69] It's not clear whether Burton ever brought the project to the sultan's attention. If he did, the response must have been discouraging, as nothing ever came of it.

Somehow Burton found enough time and energy to continue his literary career. After many years of on-again, off-again work, *Os Lusiadas (The Lusiads)* and *Camoens: His Life and His Lusiads* finally made it into print. The year 1880 also saw the publication of *The Kasidah of Haji Abdu Al-Yazdi*, which Burton noted was "translated and annotated by his friend and pupil F.B." Almost unknown at the time, it's considered by many to be Burton's finest poetic effort, and numerous editions appeared after his death. Increasingly, though, it was erotica that occupied Burton's mind, and before dying, he produced six such studies, highlighted by *The Book of the Thousand Nights and a Night*, which he finally turned to in a serious way in 1879. As he later wrote in the introduction, "This work, laborious as it may appear, has been to me a labour of love, an unfailing source of solace and satisfaction. During my long years of official banishment to the luxuriant and deadly deserts of Western Africa, and to the dull and dreary half-clearings of South America, it proved itself a charm, a talisman against ennui and despondency."[70]

His turn caused Isabel great distress for the rest of her life because in 1857 Great Britain had passed the Obscene Publications Act. Prosecution by its watchdog, the Society for the Suppression of Vice, could mean their complete financial ruin and even jail for Richard. They would, however, escape such fates, largely because Burton and his good friend from Bombay days, Arthur Fitzgerald Arbuthnot, created a fictive Kama Shastra Society headquartered in

Benares, India, as publisher and then sold volumes via private subscription only. Pseudonyms helped provide further cover.

Still, Burton longed for adventure and the illusive thing called fortune, and another opportunity to pursue both came along in 1881 when James Irvine, a palm oil broker from Liverpool who'd moved into mining, approached him about going to the Gold Coast on behalf of his Guinea Coast Gold Mining Company, one of Irvine's many firms. He'd already obtained rights to work a number of properties and told Burton that neither India nor Midian "offer such magnificent results as our Axim mines" and predicted that within a year "we shall surprise the world with the richness of our discoveries." He was after Burton's name because it would "give confidence to the British public" and "open their eyes" to an area hitherto unknown.[71] Burton jumped at the prospect and asked the Foreign Office for three months' leave to begin on November 15, 1881. He justified it by noting the region's "congenial climate" and the opportunity to do "good work by throwing additional light upon the rich gold diggings." Furthermore, he claimed to "know nothing so likely as mining to benefit the Negro," even those in domestic slavery, which was "more terrible perhaps, than the export."[72] A good cover for a hoped-for money-making proposition.

Cameron agreed to be his companion. They shared the belief that Great Britain needed to embark on a more aggressive African policy, and the Gold Coast might provide just such an opportunity, along, of course, with possible riches. Previously, Cameron had requested Burton's help in securing a professorship at Oxford, which he didn't get, and also asked him to join the newly formed Syrian Railways' Founders Association.[73] Then in the late summer of 1881 he paid the Burtons a visit in Trieste. Earlier in the year Cameron had gone out to the Gold Coast on Irvine's behalf and even opened a mine for him, so he knew something about the current situation. They also hoped to explore the Kong Mountains, an east-to-west trending range shown on many maps to be somewhere not too far inland. This plus several reports and his observations of stream flow in the Gold Coast convinced Burton that they existed and would prove to be highly auriferous.[74] Time constraints eventually ruled out making such a journey, and as Burton commented, "Geography is good, but Gold is better."[75] Had the effort been made, they would have found the mountains to be purely mythical, even though some maps continued to show them well into the twentieth century.[76]

On November 18, 1881, Richard and Isabel left Trieste aboard the SS *Demerara*; money being tight she would go only as far as Fiume, now Croatian Rijeka. It was a slow, meandering voyage that saw Richard transfer to the Moroccan Steamship Company's *Fez* at Gibraltar, bound for Lisbon, where he spent a week having a look around. Afterward came a stop at Funchal, Madeira, on December 22 and a fortnight of revisiting well-known places. By this time, the island had lost its reputation as a sanatorium for TB sufferers, bearing out Burton's earlier doubts of its efficacy. Still, he considered Madeira's future promising. Traffic to West Africa was on the upswing, and the "gold boom" promised a future for the island as "kitchen-garden" and place of respite for those involved. "Whatever the traveller from Europe may think of this quasi-tropical Tyrol, those homeward-bound from Asia and Africa will pronounce her a Paradise. They will enjoy good hotels, comfortable *tables d'hote*, and beef that does not resemble horseflesh or unsalted junk. Nor is there any better place wherein to rest and recruit after hard service in the tropics. Moreover, at the end of a month spent in perfect repose the visitor will look forward with a manner of dismay to the plunge into excited civilized life."[77] Despite such amenities, Madeira never realized this function in an important way.

On January 8, 1882, Cameron arrived, and the next day they set off, having to take the SS *Senegal*, basically a cargo ship that called at Tenerife and Las Palmas before reaching Bathurst on January 14. To Burton the place looked unchanged, still a "yellow Home of Pestilence" and peopled with the same sorts as twenty years ago. As for the British, they'd invested next to nothing on improvements. "The whole establishment is starved; decay appears in every office, public and private; and ruin is writ large upon the whole station. An Englishman who loves his country must blush when he walks through Bathurst. Even John Bull would be justified in wishing that he had been born a Frenchman in West Africa."[78]

The next leg to Sierra Leone provided Burton another opportunity to voice his views about the undesirability of white and black mixing aboard ship. "It is a political as well as social mistake," he observed, "to take negro first-class passengers. A ruling race cannot be too particular in such matters, and the white man's position on the Coast would be improved were the black man kept in his proper place. A kind of first-class second-class might be invented for them." To back his claim he went on to parody an incident:

The stewards have neglected to serve soup to some negro, who at every meal has edged higher up the table, and whose conversation consists of whispering into the ear of a black neighbor, with an occasional guffaw like that of a "laughing jackass."

"I say, dadde, I want *my* soop. All de passengers he drink 'im soop; *me* no drink *my* soop. What he mean dis palaver?"[79]

Repeating an earlier refrain, Burton ridiculed their adoption of European styles of dress but saved his most bitter words for general appearance and morals. "It is hardly fair to deride man's ugliness, but the ugly is fair game when self-obtruded into notice by personal vanity and conceit. Moreover, this form of negro folly is not to be destroyed by gentle raillery; it wants hard words, even as certain tumours require the knife. Such aping of Europeans extends from the physical to the moral man, and in general only the bad habits, gambling, drinking, and debauching, are aped."[80]

At Freetown, the two men spent a day walking about the city. Many of the tenements looked dilapidated. This was no surprise to Burton, "in a place where Europeans never expect to outstay the second year, and where Africans, who never yet worked without compulsion, cannot legally be compelled to work."[81] The sight of mulattos once again rankled him. "Inferior in physique to his black, and in morale to his white, he seeks strength by making the families of his progenitors fall out. Had the Southern States of America deported all the products of 'miscegenation,' instead of keeping them in servitude, the 'patriarchal institution' might have lasted to this day instead of being prematurely abolished."[82] Beyond the racist content, it illustrates that while Burton thought the slave trade needed to be abolished, slavery might continue when it served the "best interests" of both society and those enslaved, at least as he interpreted them.

Nonetheless, by this point in time, Burton's racism had softened a bit, for he pointed at misguided policies as the main reason for failures at Sierra Leone:

Most Englishmen know negroes of pure blood as well as "coloured persons" who, at Oxford and elsewhere, have shown themselves fully equal in intellect and capacity to the white races of Europe and America. These men afford incontestable proofs that the negro can be civilized, and a high responsibility rests upon them as the representatives of possible progress. But hitherto the African . . . has not had fair play. The petting and pampering process, the spirit of mawkish reparation, and the coddling and high-strung sentimentality so deleterious to the tone of the colony, were errors of English judgment pure and simple.[83]

The *Senegal* dropped anchor at Axim in the Gold Coast on January 25, 1882. For the next several months it served as the base of operations for Burton and Cameron while they surveyed ongoing mining activities and future prospects in Wassa, just to the north. Here women panned the coastal sands, whereas men dug shafts up to eighty feet deep to reach gold-bearing quartz reefs. The two never got to the interior sites thought to hold greater riches. High costs played a role. As Burton commented, "Apparently one must be the owner of a rich gold-mine to live in and travel on the Gold Coast."[84] Another of their activities involved collecting plants for the Kew Gardens herbarium. Despite "wait-a-bit" thorns, tree snakes, armies of biting ants, "monstrous mangrove-flies," wasps, and bees, they managed to send back quite a few specimens.[85]

During one trip, Burton reflected on the differences between traveling in Africa and Europe, and in the process switched the role of travelers, having Africans coming to England. The text reads like a modern critique of nineteenth-century European travelers and explorers, and illustrates how his mind could operate in multiple worlds.

Fancy a band of negro explorers marching uninvited throughout the Squire's manor, strewing his lawn and tennis-ground with all manner of rubbish; housing their belongings in his dining- and drawing- and best bedrooms, which are at once vacated by his wife and family; turning his cook out of his or her kitchen; calling for the keys of his dairy and poultry-yard, hot-houses, and cellar; and rummaging the whole mansion for curios and heirlooms interesting to the negro anthropologist. Fancy also the bidding him to be ready next morning for sporting and collecting purposes, with all his pet servants, his steward and his head-gardener, his stud-groom and his gamekeeper; and allowing, by way of condescension, Mr. Squire to carry their spears, bows, and arrows;

bitterly deriding his weapons the whole while, as they proceed to whip his trout-stream, to pluck his pet plants, to shoot his pheasants, and to kill specimens of his rarest birds for exhibition in Africa. Fancy them enquiring about his superstitions, sitting in his pew, asking for bits of his East window, and criticizing his "fetish" in general, ending with patting him upon the back and calling him a "jolly old cock." Finally, fancy the Squire greatly enjoying such treatment, and feeling bitterly hurt unless handled after this fashion.[86]

Suddenly on March 4, both men became ill. Burton attributed this to overwork and overconfidence. "Our mornings and evenings were spent in collecting and our days in boating, or in walking instead of hammocking. . . . And we had been too confident in our past 'seasoning;' we had neglected such simple precautions as morning and evening fires and mosquito-bars at night; finally, we had exposed ourselves somewhat recklessly to sickly sun and sweltering swamp."[87]

Cameron recovered within a week, but not Burton, whose poor general health made matters worse. He thus left for the coast, intending to recuperate on Fernando Po. A relapse while waiting for a ship caused him to change plans and head for Madeira instead. After finishing his final survey, Cameron set off from Axim on April 24 to join Burton for the trip home, where they arrived May 20.

While in the Gold Coast, Burton received a letter from the Foreign Office asking if he would look into reports indicating that some chiefs in Cameroon had requested British protection. Normally, he wouldn't have hesitated, but health reasons caused him to decline the opportunity.[88]

Burton waxed enthusiastic about the Gold Coast, calling it the "Land of Gold, in an Old New California."[89] In addition, the area appeared to possess deposits of silver, iron ore, copper, tin, diamonds, and other precious stones, and perhaps even petroleum. But this was hardly an objective observer speaking. Burton had been appointed to the board of West Africa Gold Fields Limited, and although forced to resign by the Foreign Office, he was invested in several other of Irvine's mining ventures. In addition, he actively sought subscribers, even those with as little as fifty pounds to spend. And in 1883 he wrote letter after letter to the journal *Mining World* about the Gold Coast prospects, especially with hydraulic mining techniques. To Burton the major stumbling block to development resided in the work habits of the locals. "I repeat," he said, "their *beau idéal* of life is to do nothing for six days in the week and to rest on the seventh."[90] As a remedy, Burton, following some others, recommended the immigration of Chinese and Indian coolies. "The benefit of such an influx must not be measured merely by the additional work of a few thousand hands. It will at once create jealousy, competition, rivalry. It will teach by example—the only way of teaching Africans—that work is not ignoble, but that it is ignoble to earn a shilling and to live idle on three-pence a day til the pence are exhausted."[91]

As for porters, they could be recruited from the ranks of the Waswahili. Burton didn't stop just with the Gold Coast, claiming that he and Cameron had worked out a plan to supply labor to the whole of British West Africa.[92] They "would like nothing better than to organize a movement of this kind," and if allowed "would willingly do more good to the West African coast than the whole-tribe of so-called benefactors."[93]

Needless to say, the immigration scheme came to naught, and the Guinea Coast Gold Mining Company soon ran into trouble. Its mines, most notably the main one at Izra, had been played out. The locals knew this, and it appears so did Irvine's two agents, William Grant and Robert Bruce Napolean Walker, who arranged the mining rights. When profits failed to materialize, shareholders grew angry, feeling they'd been defrauded. Some complained directly to Burton, hoping he would intervene to put things right. It was beyond his powers, and with lawsuits pending, Irvine liquidated the company in 1885.[94]

In the end, Burton wound up losing money on the deal, just as he had in Midian. And the book he wrote with Cameron, *To the Gold Coast for Gold*, raised little interest, with much of his portion repeating what had been said in *Wanderings in West Africa*. All in all, a sad effort for what would be Burton's last travel book. In addition, the Gold Coast kept following him around. The shareholders of the Guinea Coast Gold Mining Company sought to have the liquidators removed in order to bring an action against the directors and Irvine for "misrepresentation and fraud." Since there was no money left to challenge this in court, Burton and the other former directors were asked to contribute twenty-five pounds each toward cost.[95] It's doubtful he did. Furthermore, Irvine kept popping up like an unwanted guest. Still hopeful about the Gold Coast's prospects he asked Burton to write a letter "pointing out that African mining has never received a fair trial—incompetence and over weaning self-confidence in England and dishonesty in Africa so far accounts for this present want of success."[96] No such letter exists. Desperately short of cash, on another occasion Irvine asked that an advance given in May 1882 be repaid, and in 1889 he sent Isabel a prospectus for the Appalonia Mining Company and hoped she'd bring it to Richard's attention, saying the money-making prospects were bright.[97] Given their finances and knowing Richard's weakness when it came to mining schemes, she probably never made mention of it.

Burton returned to duty in Trieste on August 1, 1882. The delay he chalked up to "African ailments" having laid him low in Paris and Turin. An opportunity to leave again arose when news reached him in September of violence between Muslim sects in India. As Burton told the Foreign Office, "Eastern Intertropical Africa can supply a large number of fighting men who would not sympathize with Egyptians or Indian Mohammedans," and he and Cameron would go to Zanzibar to assemble a force of a thousand such men.[98] Another pipe dream, as it turned out. But then suddenly the next month Burton received a telegram from the Foreign Office asking if he'd assist in a search for Edward Palmer, who'd been on a spy mission for the government in Bedouin country. His two companions were found murdered but hope existed that Palmer might still be alive. Burton had met Palmer in Damascus and again while in the Midian and without hesitation volunteered his services, setting off for Cairo on the first available ship. He needn't have bothered, as the mission was called off with the discovery that Palmer had been killed at the same time as the others. The murders shocked Burton, who claimed, "The Bedawin acted as Bedawin never did before." They might "plunder, strip, beat, wound and turn intruders adrift in the waste" and kill in a fair fight. But he'd never "heard of prisoners being kept for a whole day & then being slaughtered in cold blood."[99]

This turned out to be Burton's last overseas adventure. All the past insults to body began to take their tolls, with episodes of severe pain sometimes producing incapacitation. The most regular and severe attacks were from gout. Isabel, too, suffered. In 1879 she had fainting spells, moments of hysteria, and difficulty walking. These could have been related to a change in life, but she would soon be diagnosed with ovarian cancer, which eventually took her life. Although they'd found a new, more comfortable home in Trieste, Isabel later noted that 1883 marked a turn for the worse: "here we began the last seven years of his life, three and a half years of long gout sicknesses, on and off, without any suspicion of danger, though much suffering, and three and a half years after that, when every moment was a fear."[100]

Nonetheless, Burton wrote on. In 1883 his and Arbuthnot's translation from the Sanskrit of the erotic book of love, the *Kama Sutra*, came out. According to Hindu scholars Wendy Doniger and Sudhir Kakar, Arbuthnot did the bulk of the work, with two Indians, Bhagavanlal Indrajit and Shivaram Parashuram Bhide, even more crucial to the translation.[101] The following year Burton completed *The Book of the Sword*, a massively detailed examination of the weapon throughout history and arguably his most scholarly work, although it was largely ignored at the time. Two intended follow-up volumes never appeared. Instead, he turned attention to completing the translation of *The Arabian Nights*, spurred into action by a version being put together by John Payne, who sent Burton drafts to read. Payne did beat him into print with a ten-volume edition, and Burton apparently went through it page by page while doing his final revisions.[102] The first volumes of what would be an original ten appeared in print on September 12, 1885. He later added six volumes called *Supplemental Nights*. Together they earned a tidy profit of nearly ten thousand guineas. An almost equal sum came from the estate of Isabel's father in April 1886. The money would be mostly used up by the time of Richard's death.

Burton knew that the sexual content of some of the tales would raise Mrs. Grundy's eyebrows. For example, in "The Tale of Ali Shar and Zumurrud" there's the following:

> So he did as she bade him and she mounted upon his back; and he felt what was softer than silk and smoother than cream and he said in himself, "Of a truth, this King is nicer than all the women!" Now for a time she abode on his back, then she turned over on the bed, and he said to himself "Praised be Allah! It seemeth his yard is not standing." The she said, "O Ali, it is of the wont of my prickle that it standith not except they rub it with their hands; so, come, rub it with thy hand till it be at stand, else I will slay thee." So saying, she lay down on her back

and taking his hand, set it to her parts, and he found these same parts softer than silk; white plumply-rounded, protuberant, resembling for heat the hot room of the bath or the heart of a lover whom love-longing has wasted. Quoth Ali in himself, "Verily, our King hath a coynte; this is indeed a wonder of wonders!" And the lust got hold on him and the yard rose and stood upright at the utmost of its height; which then Zumurrud saw, she burst out laughing and said to him, "O my lord, all this happeneth and yet thou knowest me not!" He asked, "And who art thou O King?" and she answered, "I am thy slave-girl Zumurrud." Now whenas he knew this and was certified that she was indeed his very slave-girl Zumurrud, he kissed her and embraced her and threw himself upon her as the lion upon the lamb. Then he sheathed his steel rod in her scabbard and ceased not to play the porter at the door and the preacher in her pulpit and the priest at her prayer niche, whist she with him ceased not from inclination or prostration and rising up and sitting down, accompanying her ejaculations and praise and of "Glory to Allah" with passionate movements and wrigglings and claspings of his membrane and other amorous gestures.[103]

To top it off, he added an explanatory note: "The use of the constrictor vaginae muscles, the sphincter for which Abyssinian women are famous. The Kabázah (= holder), as she is called can sit astraddle upon a man and can provoke venereal orgasm, not by wiggling and moving but by tightening the losing the male member with the muscles of her privities, milking as it were."[104]

Another note spoke of his measuring a Somali man's penis and put his racism on display.

Debauched women prefer negroes on account of the size of their parts. I measured one man in Somaliland, who when quiescent, numbered nearly six inches. This is a characteristic of the negro race and of African animals; e.g. the horse; whereas the pure Arab, man and beast, is below the average of Europe; one of the best proofs by the by, that the Egyptian is not an Asiatic, but a negro partially white-washed. Moreover, these imposing parts do not increase proportionally during erection; consequently, the "deed of kind" takes a much longer time and adds greatly to the woman's enjoyment. In my time no honest Hindi Moslem would take his women-folk to Zanzibar on account of the huge attractions and enormous temptations there and thereby offered to them.[105]

In addition, Burton wrote a lengthy "Terminal Essay," most of which dealt with the history of *The Arabian Nights*, its style, and its social context, plus textual criticism. But toward the end he launched into an extensive discussion of homosexuality, or pederasty, as it was more commonly called at the time. As a part of it, he posited the existence of a "Sotadic Zone," where the practice was supposedly "naturalized," once again claiming climate in an unspecified way as leading to "a blending of the masculine and feminine temperaments." The zone, according to him, started in the western Mediterranean, narrowed in Asia Minor, broadened in East Asia, encompassed the South Sea Islands, and included all of the Americas. "Within the Sotadic Zone," he said, "the vice is popular and endemic, held at the worst to be a mere peccadillo, whilst the races to the north and south of the limits here defined practise it only sporadically amid the opprobrium of their fellows who, as a rule, are physically incapable of performing the operation and look upon it with the liveliest disgust."[106] Many were aghast. This didn't bother Burton one bit. "To these critics who complain of my raw vulgarisms and puerile indecencies I can reply only by quoting what Dr. Johnson said to the lady who complained of the naughty words in his dictionary: 'You must have been looking for them, Madam!'"[107]

Sir Harry Johnston remembered Burton from this time as still having the ability to enthrall audiences. Of a dinner party they both attended in the summer of 1885 he later recounted, "I have seldom heard such conversation: there is nothing like it nowadays. Clever people are too guarded as to what they say, lest they be distributing 'copy'; politicians are afraid of committing themselves or of revealing their gaps of knowledge."[108]

But Burton, the person, does seem to have changed. In the early 1860s journalist and author Justin McCarthy recalled him being

full of irrepressible energy and the power of domination. He was quick in his movements, rapid in his talk, never wanted for a word or an argument, was impatient of differing opinion, and seemingly could not help making himself the dictator of any assembly in which he found himself a centre figure. His powers of description were marvellous; he could dash off picturesque phrases as easily as another man could utter commonplaces; could tell any number of good stories without ever repeating himself; could recite a poem or rattle off a song, could flash out jest after jest, sometimes with bewildering meanings; he was always perfectly good-humoured, and was always indomitably dogmatic.

Two decades later, while still maintaining the "genius, the intellectual power, and the unfailing variety of thought and expression, the quest for new ideas and experiences," Burton was described by McCarthy as having "grown kindly, considerate, patient of other men's opinions, ready to put the best construction on other men's motives, unwilling to wound, though certainly not afraid to strike, in defense of any cause that called for his help."[109] He found the change admirable and attributed it to Isabel's influence. Others preferring the more combative Burton would accuse her of domesticating him for the worse.

The year 1885 saw two people instrumental in Burton's life pass away: his former nemesis Rigby on April 14 and close friend and confidant Milnes/Lord Houghton on August 11. Burton could hardly face Milnes's death, noting when asked to write something, "All I can say of him at present is that, during the course of a long, busy, and fruitful life he never said an unkind word, and he never did an unkind deed."[110] As for the couple, neither was in tip-top condition. According to Isabel, "Dick and I are a pair of old cripples. He poor fellow was laid up 8 months last winter with a complication of diseases, gout, rheumatism, fever and general catarrh of everything. Then we went for 3 months cure to Marienbad and Sauerbrun and he was apparently cured but broke out again 2 months ago with the same but in a milder form without gout."[111]

Thoughts of being posted to Morocco still occupied their minds, and so Richard applied for the position before setting off for Tangier on November 21, 1885, intent on acting the tourist. He found the city disgusting, as did Isabel when she arrived in late January 1886. Word of the appointment would be forthcoming soon, both hoped. It wouldn't be, as once again someone else got the job. A February 5 cable brought some consolation: Lord Salisbury had advised, and the queen approved, Richard being awarded the Knight Commander of the Order of St. Michael and St. George. Peeved over its lateness, he thought about refusing, remarking, "Half gives who late gives."[112] Isabel, who had lobbied for so long on his behalf would not, of course, hear of it.

In October 1886 Burton made one final request of Her Majesty's government—to retire on full pension from the Foreign Service after twenty-five years of service instead of the usual thirty, claiming that the climate in Trieste undermined his health and thus his work. As support, he listed ten accomplishments he thought justified the request:

1. Served nineteen years in the Bombay, nearly ten years on active service, chiefly on the staff of Sir Charles Napier, on the Sind Survey, at the close of the Afghan War, 1842–49. In 1861, was compelled to leave, without pay or pension, by Sir Charles Wood for accepting the Consulship of Fernando Po.

2. Served in the Crimea as chief of Staff of Bashi Bazouk (Irregular Cavalry), and was chiefly instrumental in organizing it.

3. Was author of the Bayonet exercise now used at the Horseguards.

4. Have made several difficult and dangerous expeditions or explorations in unknown parts; notably the pilgrimage to Mecca and Medinah, and afterwards to Harar, now opened up to Europeans, and the discovery and opening up of the Lake Regions of Central Africa, and the sources of the Nile, a country now well known to trade, to missionaries, and the schoolmasters.

5. Have been twenty-five years and a half in the Consular Service, eight to nine years in bad climates.

6. Was sent in 1864 as H. M.'s Commissioner, to the King of Dahomé, and resided with him for three months.

7. Was recalled at a moment's notice from Damascus, under a misrepresentation, and suffered heavy pecuniary losses thereby. My conduct was at last formally approved by the Government, but no compensation was given.

8. Was sent in 1882 in quest of the unfortunate Professor Palmer and his companions, who were murdered by the Bedawi.

9. Have learnt twenty-nine languages, passed Official Examinations in eight Eastern languages, notably Arabic, Persian, and Hindostani.

10. Have published over forty-six works, several of which like "Mecca," and the "Exploration of Harar," are now standard.[113]

Others rallied to the cause, but the Foreign Office didn't know quite what to do. The request was unusual, and concerns were registered about all the leave time Burton had taken. He undoubtedly held the record. In the end he was told that it would be necessary to wait until 1891 to receive full retirement benefits.

While on vacation in Cannes during February 1887, Burton suffered a mild stroke, followed by a severe heart attack, leading Isabel to baptize him for fear of death being near. Bedridden nearly eight months, from this point on he would require constant medical supervision. In failing health as well, Isabel wasn't up to the task alone, and so live-in doctors became a part of life. This, an array of treatments, and travel whenever possible absorbed their money. Burton wrote when he could, finishing the final volume to *Supplemental Nights* in March 1888. He also considered completing his autobiography but repeatedly found reasons to put it off.[114]

All the while, Burton kept an eye on Africa and in December 1888 sent an interesting letter to the *London Times* about events in the Sudan. The British had retaken the port of Suakin from the Mahdists, and Burton cautioned against seeking retribution for the death of Gordon and, in a change of direction, urged Egyptians be kept out in the future. They clearly weren't, in his mind now, the spreaders of "commerce and civilisation throughout the heart of Africa."

> To my countrymen I would say, "Englishmen, at least be humane. The Soudanese tribes never had any quarrel with you. They knew you only as the folk who came among them to shoot big game. They entertained you hospitably, and they freely lent themselves to all your fads. With indescribable levity you attacked these gallant and noble Negroids, who were only doing battle for liberty, for their hearths and homes, and for their freedom from the Egyptian tax-gatherer and from the Turkish despoiler. You threw yourselves, unlike your forefathers, who dearly loved fair play, on the strongest side, and you aided in oppressing the

weak by a most unholy war. With your breech-loading rifles and Gatling guns you attacked these gallant races; but Allah sometimes defends the right, and you have had more than once to flee before men armed with a miserable spear and a bit of limp leather by way of a shield. Your errors were those of ignorance. Do not persist in them now that you have learnt the truth. After dispersing the dervishes, seize the earliest opportunity of showing your magnanimity, and come to terms with the gallant enemy, upon the express condition that no Egyptian official, civil or military, shall ever pollute the land with his presence. And if this step fail (but it will not fail) to restore the peace, you will at least have offered the best atonement for the bloody misdeeds of the past."[115]

The war continued for ten more years before the Mahdist state was finally crushed. In its place stood a condominium called the Anglo-Egyptian Sudan. In 1965 an independent Sudan came into being, cobbled together out of disparate parts. Peace remains elusive.

By this point Burton was consul in Trieste in name only, as he spent even less time there than before. During much of the first half of 1889 the couple visited places nearby, and as the year drew to a close they vacationed in Malta for twenty-three days. Richard wanted to bring out a second translation of *The Perfumed Garden of the Cheikh Nefzaoui*, this time to be called "The Scented Garden." The first, published in 1886, had been based on a French version, and he wanted to find one in Arabic that presumably contained a long erotic chapter missing from the French. So, from Malta, the Burtons journeyed to Tunis and Algiers, with a side visit to Carthage in between, in all spending five months on the hunt and seeing sights. An Arabic copy did turn up, but without a complete version of the missing chapter, and thus one last time Africa thwarted Burton.

In July 1890 the Burtons set off for what had become an annual visit to Switzerland. Richard was unwell much of the time and seemed agitated, although he apparently enjoyed spending several days visiting Henry Morton Stanley and his wife, Dorothy, in Maloja. By now each man had formed a grudging respect for the other. Stanley was worried about Richard, saying he appeared "much broken in health."[116] It was while in Maloja that Richard seriously began to think about his death and posterity. According to Isabel, he signed the following: "In the event of my death, I bequeath to my wife, Isabel Burton, every book, paper, or manuscript, to be overhauled and examined by her only, and to be dealt with entirely at her discretion and in the manner she thinks best, having been my sole helper for thirty years."[117]

Back in Trieste, Burton spent most days working on "The Scented Garden" and his translation from the Latin of *Catullus*. On October 19 Isabel said that

Henry Morton Stanley and Burton together in 1890. (Reproduced with permission of the Royal Museum for Central Africa.)

Final days together in Trieste in 1890. (Reproduced with permission of the London Borough of Richmond upon Thames Art Collection, Orleans House Gallery.)

despite lumbago, he seemed "unusually well and cheerful" and greatly looked forward to an upcoming trip to Greece and Turkey.[118]

That fateful day of reckoning, therefore, came unexpectedly. Did Burton think of Africa during those final hours? If so, the thoughts must have added to his pain. Yes, there were accomplishments to remember, notably in the realms of linguistics and ethnography. And many of his predictions bore fruit. But he'd suffered at its hands, physically, mentally, financially, and professionally. Even being the first European to make it to and from Harar and discovering Lake Tanganyika were soured by their aftermaths. Furthermore, Burton's legacy would be tarnished by his commitments to British imperialism and the racist theories of human differences he advocated. I don't believe he hated Africans, as Frank McLynn has claimed. Rather, it was more a case of disdain for their presumed inherited primitiveness and all that embodied. Furthermore, not all Africans succumbed to his sharp-tongued prejudices. Bearing the brunt were "true" Negroes and mulattos, especially Christianized ones. Warrior types, Muslims, and peoples deviating from the Negro stereotype because of presumed mixing with Semites, and a few others actually earned Burton's admiration on occasion. One might think such ideas combined with many failures would have led to little interest in him today. But, clearly, it's just the opposite. A good part of why has to do with his polymath nature. Few individuals have touched so many fields of interest. To this must be added his irreverent style and complex personality, warts included. How could one as intelligent as he so often been badly mistaken and at times blind? In 1966 Gordon Waterfield wrote, "No one has yet written the final story [of Burton] and perhaps no one can."[119] I would only modify this by leaving out the "perhaps." He thus lives on, and so maybe Captain Sir Richard Francis Burton was successful after all.

NOTES

Introducing Richard F. Burton

1. Quentin Keynes, "Preface," in *The Search for the Source of the Nile*, ed. Donald Young (London: Roxburghe Club, 1999), xi (hereafter cited as *SSN*).

2. Daniel J. Boorstin, *The Exploring Spirit: America and the World, Then and Now* (New York: Random House, 1976), 6.

3. Jonathan Bishop, "The Identities of Sir Richard Burton: The Explorer as Actor," *Victorian Studies* 1 (1957): 119–35.

4. Philip José Farmer, *To Your Scattered Bodies Go: A Science Fiction Novel* (New York: Putnam, 1971); William Rayner, *The Trail to Bear Paw Mountain* (London: Collins, 1974); Win Blevins, *The Rock Child* (New York: Forge, 1998); John Dunning, *The Bookman's Promise* (New York: Scribner, 2004); Iliya Troyanov, *The Collector of Worlds: A Novel of Sir Richard Francis Burton*, trans. William Hobson (London: Faber and Faber, 2008).

5. Richard F. Burton, *The Book of the Thousand Nights and a Night*, ed. Emile Van Vlict (New York: Heritage Press; Limited Editions Club, 1934), 1: xx (hereafter cited as *BTNN*).

6. Gordon Waterfield, ed., *First Footsteps in East Africa* (New York: Praeger, 1966), 4.

7. Richard F. Burton, letter to the *London Times*, January 1, 1863.

8. Greg Garrett, "Relocating Burton: Public and Private Writings on Africa," *Journal of African Travel-Writing* 2 (1997): 70–79.

9. Richard F. Burton, *Sindh, and the Races That Inhabit the Valley of the Indus: With Notices of the Topography and History of the Province* (London: W. H. Allen & Co., 1851), 239, 283.

10. See Edith Sanders, "The Hamitic Hypothesis: Its Origin and Functions in Time Perspective," *Journal of African History* 10 (1969): 521–31.

11. Patrick Brantlinger, *Rule of Darkness: British Literature and Imperialism, 1830–1914* (Ithaca, NY: Cornell University Press, 1988), 11. See also Donald Paul

Nurse's PhD dissertation, "An Amateur Barbarian: The Life and Career of Sir Richard Francis Burton, 1821–1890" (University of Toronto, 1999).

12. Dane Kennedy, *The Highly Civilized Man: Richard Burton and the Victorian World* (Cambridge, MA: Harvard University Press, 2005), 7.

13. W. H. Wilkins, *The Romance of Isabel Lady Burton: The Story of Her Life* (London: Hutchinson & Co., 1897), 1: 151.

14. James A. Casada, *Sir Richard F. Burton: A Biobibliographical Study* (Boston: G. K. Hall, 1990), 19.

15. Isabel Burton, *The Life of Captain Sir Richard F. Burton* (London: Chapman & Hall, 1893), 2: 439 (hereafter cited as *LCSRB*).

16. Ibid., 441.

Chapter 1: The Time Before Africa

1. I. Burton, *LCSRB*, 1: 3.

2. Ibid., 21.

3. See Fawn M. Brodie, *The Devil Drives: A Life of Sir Richard Burton* (New York: Norton, 1967), 25; and Jon R. Godsall, *The Tangled Web: A Life of Sir Richard Burton* (Leicester, UK: Matador, 2008).

4. I. Burton, *LCSRB*, 1: 28–29.

5. Ibid., 69.

6. Ibid., 32.

7. Ibid., 72.

8. Thomas Wright, *The Life of Sir Richard Burton* (New York: Putnam, 1906), 1: 66n.

9. I. Burton, *LCSRB*, 1: 91.

10. See Godsall, *Tangled Web*, 26.

11. Papers signed by Joseph Maitland, copy in Mary Lovell Collection (MLC).

12. I. Burton, *LCSRB*, 1: 81.

13. Ibid., 109.

14. Ibid., 432.

15. See Peter Hopkirk, *The Great Game: On Secret Service in High Asia* (London: Murray, 1990).

16. Burton, "Terminal Essay," in *BTNN*, 6: 3748.

17. Casada, *Sir Richard F. Burton*, 9.

18. William Napier to General Scott, August 19, 1846, National Library of Scotland (NLS), MLC.

19. Godsall, *Tangled Web*, 54.

20. Richard F. Burton, *Goa and the Blue Mountains, or, Six Months of Sick Leave* (New Delhi: Penguin Books, 2003), 64–65.

21. Ibid., 229.

22. I. Burton, *LCSRB*, 1: 147.

23. Ibid., 163.

24. Frank Barker (aka Richard Burton), *Stone Talk: Being Some of the Marvellous*

Sayings of a Petral Portion of Fleet Street, London, to One Doctor Polyglot, Ph.D. (London: R. Hardwicke, 1865).

25. Richard F. Burton, *Falconry in the Valley of the Indus* (London: J. van Voorst, 1852), 61.

26. Cited in Mary S. Lovell, *A Rage to Live: A Biography of Richard and Isabel Burton* (New York: Norton, 1998), 114.

27. See Jon R. Godsall, "Fact and Fiction in Richard Burton's *Personal Narrative of a Pilgrimage to El-Medinah and Mecca (1855–56)*," *Journal of the Royal Asiatic Society*, Third Series, 3 (1993): 331–51.

28. Napier Papers, 49117 f. 214–15, British Library Manuscript Collection.

29. Richard F. Burton, *Personal Narrative of a Pilgrimage to Al-Madinah & Meccah*, Memorial Edition (New York: Dover Publications, 1964), 1: 23.

30. I. Burton, *LCSRB*, 1: 172.

31. To James C. Melville, November 6, 1852, India Office Records, L/P&J/1/62, MLC.

32. Richard F. Burton, "Journey to Medina, with Route from Yambu," *Journal of the Royal Geographical Society* 24 (1854): 209.

33. Godsall, "Fact and Fiction," 349–50.

34. R. Burton, *Personal Narrative*, 1: 14–15.

35. For a concise itinerary see R. C. H. Risley, "Burton: An Appreciation," *Tanganyika Notes & Records* 49 (1957): 257–97; and Godsall, *Tangled Web*, ch. 12, for truth versus fiction.

36. I. Burton, *LCSRB*, 1: 172.

Chapter 2: Among the Somalis

1. Godsall, "Fact and Fiction."

2. R. Burton, "Journey to Medina," 208.

3. R. Burton to Norton Shaw, November 16, 1853, Royal Geographical Society (RGS).

4. R. Burton to Norton Shaw, n.d. but listed as received October 30, 1853, RGS.

5. R. Burton to Norton Shaw, November 16, 1853, RGS.

6. See Norman R. Bennett and George E. Brooks Jr., eds., *New England Merchants in Africa: A History Through Documents, 1802–1865* (Boston: Boston University Press, 1965).

7. Richard F. Burton and J. E. Stocks, "Brief Notes Relative to the Division of Time, and Articles of Cultivation in Sind," *Bombay Government Record*, New Series, 17, Part 2 (1855): 613–36.

8. R. Burton to H. L. Anderson, April 28, 1854, Oriental and India Office Collection (OIOC), British Library, F/4/2570, in Jon R. Godsall, "Richard Burton's Somali Expedition, 1854–55: Its Wider Historical Context and Planning," *Journal of the Royal Asiatic Society*, Third Series, 11 (2001): 163.

9. Richard F. Burton, *First Footsteps in East Africa; Or, An Exploration of Harar* (London: Longman, Brown, Green, and Longmans, 1856), vii.

10. John Hayman, ed., *Sir Richard Burton's Travels in Arabia and Africa: Four Lectures from a Huntington Library Manuscript* (San Marino, CA: Huntington Library, 1990), 68 (hereafter cited as *SRBTAA*).

11. See Henry Salt, *A Voyage to Abyssinia and Travels into the Interior of That Country, Executed Under Orders of the British Government in the Years 1809 and 1810* (London: F. C. and J. Rivington, 1814); and George Viscount Valentia, *Voyages and Travels to India, Ceylon, the Red Sea, Abyssinia, and Egypt in 1802, 1803, 1805, and 1806*, 3 vols. (London: F. C. and J. Rivington, 1809).

12. C. J. Cruttenden, "Report on the Mijjertheyn Tribes of Somallies Inhabiting the District Forming the North-East Point of Africa," *Transactions of the Bombay Geographical Society* 7 (1844–46): 111–26; and "Memoir of the Western or Edo Tribes, Inhabiting the Somali Coast of N. E. Africa; with the Southern Branches of the Family of Darood, Resident on the Banks of the Webbi Shebeyli, Commonly Called the River Webi," *Transactions of the Bombay Geographical Society* 8 (1847–49): 177–210.

13. C. J. Cruttenden, "On Eastern Africa," *Journal of the Royal Geographical Society* 18 (1848): 136–39.

14. R. Burton, *BTNN*, iii.

15. Cruttenden, "Report on the Mijjertheyn Tribes," 181.

16. Richard F. Burton, "Narrative of a Trip to Harar," *Journal of the Royal Geographical Society* 25 (1855): 137.

17. R. Burton, *Personal Narrative*, 2: 252.

18. Richard F. Burton, *Zanzibar: City, Island, and Coast* (London: Tinsley Brothers, 1872), 2: 383.

19. See Stuart Munro-Hay, *Aksum: An African Civilisation of Late Antiquity* (Edinburgh: Edinburgh University Press, 1991); and David W. Phillipson, *Ancient Ethiopia: Aksum, Its Antecedents and Successors* (London: British Museum Press, 1998).

20. R. Burton, *Scinde; Or, The Unhappy Valley* (London: R. Bentley, 1851), 75–76.

21. R. Burton, *First Footsteps*, xxii.

22. John Hanning Speke, *What Led to the Discovery of the Source of the Nile* (Edinburgh: William Blackwood and Sons, 1864), 1–2.

23. J. H. Speke to Captain Hay, October 10, 1854, in Young, *SSN*, 26.

24. R. Burton, *Zanzibar*, 2: 380.

25. Speke, *What Led to the Discovery*, 23.

26. R. Burton, "Narrative of a Trip," 137.

27. Godsall, "Burton's Somali Expedition."

28. C. P. Rigby, "An Outline of the Somauli Language, with Vocabulary," *Transactions of the Bombay Geographical Society* 9 (1849–50): 129–84.

29. Ibn Batuta, *Travels in Asia and Africa, 1325–1354*, trans. H. A. R. Gibb (London: Routledge & K. Paul, 1957), 110.

30. Cruttenden, "Memoir of the Western or Edo Tribes," 182.

31. Norman M. Penzer, ed., *Selected Papers on Anthropology, Travel & Exploration by Sir Richard Burton* (London: A. M. Philpot, 1924), 67.

32. R. Burton, *First Footsteps*, 26.
33. Ibid., 28.
34. Ibid., 74.
35. Ibid., 80.
36. Ibid., 85–86.
37. I. M. Lewis, *A Modern History of Somalia: Nation and State in the Horn of Africa*, rev. ed. (London: Longman, 1980), 36.
38. R. Burton, *First Footsteps*, 37–38.
39. Ibid., n9.
40. Ibid., 132–33.
41. R. Burton, "Narrative of a Trip," 139–40.
42. Hayman, *SRBTAA*, 73.
43. R. Burton, *First Footsteps*, 128.
44. Ibid., 93.
45. R. Burton, "Narrative of a Trip," 140.
46. R. Burton, *First Footsteps*, 142.
47. Ibid., 172.
48. R. Burton, "Narrative of a Trip," 141.
49. I. Burton, *LCSRB*, 1: 203.
50. Hayman, *SRBTAA*, 71.
51. R. Burton, *First Footsteps*, 285.
52. Ibid., 291.
53. Ibid., 294.
54. I. Burton, *LCSRB*, 1: 207.
55. R. Burton, *First Footsteps*, 298–99.
56. Ibid., 363.
57. R. Burton to Norton Shaw, February 25, 1855, RGS, MLC.
58. R. Burton, "Narrative of a Trip," 144–45.
59. R. Burton, *First Footsteps*, 297.
60. Ibid., 322.
61. Ibid., 364.
62. Ibid., 366.
63. Ralph E. Drake-Brockman, *British Somaliland* (London: Hurst & Blackett, 1912), 25.
64. R. Burton, *First Footsteps*, 387.
65. Cruttenden, "Memoir of the Western or Edo Tribes," 186.
66. For the report see Waterfield, *First Footsteps*, ch. 11.
67. R. Burton to Norton Shaw, February 25, 1855, RGS, MLC. In her translation, Mary Lovell mistakenly spelled Shebayli, Shebagli. A more accurate rendition is Webbe Shabeelle, meaning Leopard River.
68. For an assessment of Speke's version see Alexander Maitland, *Speke* (London: Constable, 1971).
69. John Hanning Speke, "Captain Speke's Adventures in Somali Land," *Blackwood's Magazine* 87 (June 1860): 685.

70. John Hanning Speke, "Captain Speke's Adventures in Somali Land," *Black-wood's Magazine* 88 (July 1860): 23.

71. R. Burton to William Coghlan, April 23, 1855, in Young, *SSN*, 29–43.

72. Lewis, *Modern History of Somalia*, 36.

73. Young, *SSN*, 42.

74. See Godsall, "Fact and Fiction."

75. The letter was signed by the acting civil surgeon at Aden, April 22, 1855, Quentin Keynes Collection (QKC), MLC.

76. I. M. Lewis, *A Pastoral Democracy* (London: Oxford University Press, 1961).

77. R. Burton, *First Footsteps*, 107–9.

78. When the emir died has never been firmly established. Waterfield in *First Footsteps* put it in September or October 1856, whereas J. Spencer Trimingham, in *Islam in Ethiopia* (London: Oxford University Press, 1952), wrote that he died a decade later.

79. R. Burton, *First Footsteps*, xxxii–iv.

80. Waterfield, *First Footsteps*, 286.

81. R. Burton, *BTNN*, 5: 1897–98.

82. For modern accounts see Rogaia Mustafa Abusharaf, ed., *Female Circumcision: Multicultural Perspectives* (Philadelphia: University of Pennsylvania Press, 2006); and World Health Organization, "Female Genital Mutilation and Obstetric Outcome: WHO Collaborative Prospective Study in Six African Countries," *Lancet* 367 (2006): 1835–41.

Chapter 3: Interludes and Preparations

1. Wilfrid S. Blunt, *My Diaries: Being a Personal Narrative of Events, 1888–1914* (New York: Knopf, 1921), 2: 129.

2. Frank Harris, *Contemporary Portraits* (New York: Mitchell Kennerly, 1915), 180.

3. Gordon Waterfield, "Burton Attacked in Official Reports," in *First Footsteps*, 260–76.

4. Gordon Waterfield, "The Story Told by Somali and Others," in ibid., 277–84.

5. I. Burton, *LCSRB*, 1: 226.

6. R. Burton to Norton Shaw, August 18, 1855, RGS.

7. McLynn, *Burton*, 127.

8. *London Times*, December 6, 1855.

9. Draft of letter from R. Burton to Norton Shaw, April 1856, in Young, *SSN*, 57–58.

10. Expedition Committee, "Minutebook," vol. 1, April 12, 1856, RGS.

11. A communication from the Church Missionary Society from James [*sic*] Erhardt, titled "Reports Respecting Central Africa, as Collected in Mambara and on the East Coast, with a New Map of the Country," *Proceedings of the Royal Geographical Society* 1 (1855–57): 8–10.

12. Draft of a letter from R. Burton to Norton Shaw, April 19, 1856, in Young, *SSN*, 59–65.

13. *Journal of the Royal Geographical Society* 26 (1856): ccxiii–iv.
14. Dane Kennedy, "British Exploration in the Nineteenth Century: A Historiographical Survey," *History Compass* 5/6 (2007): 1879.
15. May 20, 1856, June 5, 1856, FO 2/37, The National Archives (TNA).
16. Anonymous to R. Burton, September 13, 1856, in Richard F. Burton, *The Lake Regions of Central Africa: A Picture of Exploration* (London: Sidgwick and Jackson, 1961), 2: 420.
17. *Journal of the Royal Geographical Society* 19 (1856): 4–6.
18. R. Burton, *Lake Regions*, 1: xiv.
19. I. Burton, *LCSRB*, 1: 167.
20. R. Burton, *Lake Regions*, 1: 25.
21. R. Burton to the Military Secretary, East India House, November 14, 1856, in *Lake Regions*, 2: 421–22.
22. R. Burton to the Secretary of the Royal Geographical Society, November 14, 1856, in *Lake Regions*, 2: 422.
23. India Office Records (IOR), E/4/1106, MLC.
24. IOR, January 7, 1857, QKC, MLC.
25. R. Burton, *Zanzibar*, 1: 16–17.
26. R. Burton to the Secretary of the Royal Geographical Society, December 15, 1856, in *Lake Regions*, 2: 422–28.
27. Richard H. Crofton, preface to *The Old Consulate at Zanzibar* (London: Oxford University Press, 1935).
28. R. Burton, *Zanzibar*, 1: 35.
29. December 26, 1856, cited in Crofton, *Old Consulate*, 32–33.
30. R. Burton, *Zanzibar*, 1: 37.
31. Ibid., 27–28.
32. Ibid., 180.
33. Ibid., 80.
34. Ibid., 96.
35. Ibid., 85.
36. Ibid., 376–79.
37. Ibid., 408–10.
38. Ibid., 414–17.
39. Ibid., 418–20.
40. Draft of letter from R. Burton to Norton Shaw, January 5, 1857, in Young, *SSN*, 74–76.
41. R. Burton to Norton Shaw, April 22, 1857, in Young, *SSN*, 80–86.
42. I. Burton, *LCSRB*, 1: 259.
43. R. Burton, *Lake Regions*, 1: 15.
44. R. Burton, *Zanzibar*, 2: 3–4.
45. Ibid., 2: 14–15.
46. Richard F. Burton and John Hanning Speke, "A Coasting Voyage from Mombasa to the Pangani River; Visit to Sultan Kimwere; and Progress of

the Expedition into the Interior," *Journal of the Royal Geographical Society* 28 (1858): 191.

47. Batuta, *Travels in Asia and Africa*, 112.
48. I. Burton, *LCSRB*, 1: 260.
49. R. Burton, "Zanzibar; and Two Months in East Africa," *Blackwood's Magazine* 83 (1858): 217 (hereafter cited as "ZTMEA").
50. R. Burton, *Zanzibar*, 2: 79.
51. Draft of letter from R. Burton to Norton Shaw, April 22, 1857, in Young, *SSN*, 80–86.
52. R. Burton, "ZTMEA," 215.
53. R. Burton and Speke, "Coasting Voyage," 194.
54. R. Burton, "ZTMEA," 224.
55. R. Burton, *Zanzibar*, 2: 60.
56. R. Burton, "ZTMEA," 220.
57. Ibid., 222.
58. Ibid., 277.
59. Ibid., 282.
60. R. Burton and Speke, "Coasting Voyage," 204.
61. R. Burton, *Zanzibar*, 2: 162.
62. Ibid., 189.
63. R. Burton, "ZTMEA," 576.
64. R. Burton and Speke, "Coasting Voyage," 214.
65. R. Burton, *Zanzibar*, 2: 221.
66. Ibid., 234.
67. Ibid., 233.
68. R. Burton and Speke, "Coasting Voyage," 216.
69. "Seedi" was a corruption of the Arabic *Sidi*, meaning "My Lord" and used in India for black Africans.
70. R. Burton, "ZTMEA," 587.
71. R. Burton, *Zanzibar*, 2: 257–58.
72. I. Burton, *LCSRB*, 1: 278.
73. R. Burton to Richard M. Milnes, April 27, 1857, Trinity College Library, Cambridge (TCLC), MLC.

Chapter 4: A Tale of Two Lakes

1. See Stephen J. Rockel, *Carriers of Culture: Labor on the Road in Nineteenth-Century East Africa* (Portsmouth, NH: Heinemann, 2006).
2. R. Burton, *Lake Regions*, 1: 69.
3. Ibid., 16, 37.
4. Ibid., 35.
5. I. Burton, *LCSRB*, 1: 280.
6. R. Burton, *Lake Regions*, 1: 50–51.
7. Zungomero is an example of a place name mentioned by Burton that is no

longer used, although Christopher Ondaatje, in *Journey to the Source of the Nile* (Toronto: HarperCollins, 1998), claims to have found its location.

8. R. Burton, *Zanzibar*, 2: 294–95.
9. R. Burton, *Lake Regions*, 1: 51.
10. Ibid., 147–48.
11. I. Burton, *LCSRB*, 1: 281–82.
12. R. Burton, *Lake Regions*, 1: 67.
13. Ibid., 71.
14. Ibid., 110, 112.
15. Ibid., 71.
16. Ibid., 84.
17. I. Burton, *LCSRB*, 1: 282. For a summary of the letters see *Journal of the Royal Geographical Society* 28 (1858): 220–26.
18. I. Burton, *LCSRB*, 1: 271.
19. R. Burton, *Lake Regions*, 1: 91–92.
20. Ibid., 120–21.
21. Ibid., 99.
22. Ibid., 161.
23. Ibid., 162–63.
24. Fragment of letter from R. Burton to Norton Shaw, September 6, 1857, in Young, *SSN*, 96–98.
25. R. Burton, *Lake Regions*, 1: 185–86.
26. Ibid., 187–88.
27. Ibid., 234.
28. Ibid., 248.
29. Ibid., 253.
30. I. Burton, *LCSRB*, 1: 287.
31. R. Burton, *Lake Regions*, 1: 258.
32. R. Burton to consul in Zanzibar, October 1858, in Young, *SSN*, 100–102. The date of the letter reads October 1858, but it should be 1857.
33. R. Burton, *Lake Regions*, 1: 274.
34. Ibid., 278.
35. Ibid., 261.
36. Ibid., 310.
37. R. Burton, *Zanzibar*, 2: 295.
38. R. Burton, *Lake Regions*, 1: 323.
39. Ibid., 328.
40. I. Burton, *LCSRB*, 1: 292.
41. R. Burton, *Lake Regions*, 1: 362.
42. I. Burton, *LCSRB*, 1: 290.
43. R. Burton, *Lake Regions*, 1: 381.
44. Ibid., 387–88.
45. Speke, *What Led to the Discovery*, 201.
46. R. Burton, *Lake Regions*, 1: 403–4.

47. Ibid., 2: 34.
48. Ibid., 42–44.
49. Speke, *What Led to the Discovery*, 202–3.
50. R. Burton, *Lake Regions*, 2: 62–63.
51. Ibid., 69–71.
52. Ibid., 82–83.
53. Ibid., 85–86.
54. Ibid., 154.
55. Ibid., 87.
56. Ibid., 90.
57. Speke, *What Led to the Discovery*, 224–25.
58. I. Burton, *LCSRB*, 1: 302.
59. John Hanning Speke, "Journals," *Blackwood's Magazine* 86 (1859): 391.
60. R. Burton, *Lake Regions*, 2: 106.
61. Ibid., 114.
62. Ibid., 126.
63. Ibid., 130–31.
64. I. Burton, *LCSRB*, 1: 308. Burton didn't mention his father's death in *Lake Regions* but instead inserted the statement in the book after Said bin Salim learned of the death of his only son.
65. R. Burton to Norton Shaw, June 24, 1858, RGS.
66. R. Burton, *Lake Regions*, 2: 170.
67. R. Burton to Norton Shaw, June 24, 1858, *Proceedings of the Royal Geographical Society* 3 (1858–59): 111–12. See also *Athenaeum*, December 11, 1875, 793.
68. R. Burton, *Zanzibar*, 2: 386.
69. Ibid., 384.
70. Fragment of document dated June 1957, in Young, *SSN*, 87–88.
71. James Grant to Samuel Baker, June 26, 1890, QKC, MLC.
72. Francis Galton, *Memories of My Life* (New York: E. P. Dutton and Company, 1909), 199.
73. H. L. Anderson to R. Burton, July 23, 1857, in *Lake Regions*, 2: 428.
74. R. Burton to H. L. Anderson, June 24, 1858, in ibid., 429.
75. R. Burton to Norton Shaw, June 24, 1858, in Young, *SSN*, 104–8.
76. R. Burton, *Lake Regions*, 2: 248.
77. Hayman, *SRBTAA*, 67.
78. R. Burton, *Lake Regions*, 2: 174.
79. Ibid., 175.
80. Arthur Symons, *Dramatis Personnæ* (Indianapolis: Bobbs-Merrill Company, 1923), 242.
81. Speke, *What Led to the Discovery*, 311–12.
82. I. Burton, letter to the *London Times*, January 4, 1891, in *LCSRB*, 2: 424.
83. G. R. Crone, *The Sources of the Nile: Explorers' Maps A.D. 1856–1891* (London: Royal Geographical Society, 1964), 3.

84. Robert O. Collins, introduction to *The Nile Basin by Richard F. Burton and Captain Speke's Discovery of the Source of the Nile by James MacQueen* (New York: Da Capo Press, 1967), xzii.

85. R. Burton, *Lake Regions*, 2: 235.

86. Godsall, *Tangled Web*, 181.

87. Christopher Rigby to H. L. Anderson, November 18, 1860, in *General Rigby, Zanzibar and the Slave Trade*, ed. Lillian M. Russell (London: G. Allen & Unwin, 1935), 266.

88. R. Burton, *Lake Regions*, 2: 274.

89. R. Burton to Norton Shaw, April, 19, 1859, RGS.

90. R. Burton, *Zanzibar*, 2: 345–46.

91. R. Burton, *Lake Regions*, 2: 381–82.

92. Russell, *General Rigby*, 243n.

93. R. Burton to Norton Shaw, June 24, 1858, RGS, and in Young, *SS*94. R. Burton, *Lake Regions*, 1: 177–78.

95. I. Burton, *LCSRB*, 1: 327.

96. R. Burton, *Zanzibar*, 2: 390.

97. R. Burton to Norton Shaw, April 19, 1859, in Young, *SSN*, 135–37.

98. W. B. Carnochan, *The Sad Story of Burton, Speke, and the Nile; Or, Was John Hanning Speke a Cad?* (Stanford, CA: Stanford General Books, 2006).

Chapter 5: Regrouping

1. John Hanning Speke, *Journal of the Discovery of the Source of the Nile* (New York: Harper & Brothers, 1864), 31.

2. *Journal of the Royal Geographical Society* 29 (1859): clxxxiii.

3. H. B. Thomas and Ivan R. Dale, "Uganda Place Names: Some European Eponyms," *Uganda Journal* 17 (1953): 101–23.

4. J. H. Speke to *Blackwell's*, undated, except for Sunday, Inverness, National Library of Scotland (NLS), MLC.

5. I. Burton, *LCSRB*, 1: 328.

6. Young, *SSN*, 147.

7. Dorothy Middleton, "Burton and Speke Centenary," *Geographical Journal* 123 (1957): 414.

8. Dorothy Middleton, "The Search for the Nile Sources," *Geographical Journal* 138 (1972): 216.

9. Russell, *General Rigby*, 230.

10. *Proceedings of the Royal Geographical Society* 3 (1858–59): 217–19.

11. Ibid., 348–58.

12. R. C. Bridges, "Sir John Speke and the Royal Geographical Society," *Uganda Journal* 26 (1962): 23–43.

13. Wilkins, *Romance of Isabel*, 1: 148.

14. I. Burton, *LCSRB*, 1: 330.

15. Ibid., 1: 332–37. Jon Godsall (*Tangled Web*, 191) has uncovered evidence that suggests Isabel wrote this letter at a later date.

16. J. H. Speke to R. Burton, June 17, 1859, in Young, *SSN*, 155–56.

17. J. H. Speke to R. Burton, February 1, 1860, in ibid., 169–70; R. Burton to J. H. Speke, February 3, 1860, in ibid., 170.

18. J. H. Speke to Norton Shaw, February 6, 1860, in ibid., 172–74.

19. J. H. Speke to R. Burton, April 16, 1860, in ibid., 180.

20. B. Speke to Norton Shaw, August 21, 1860, QKC, MLC.

21. Christopher Rigby to H. L. Anderson, July 15, 1859, in R. Burton, *Lake Regions*, 2: 431–34.

22. Government of Bombay to Christopher Rigby, August 19, 1859, in Russell, *General Rigby*, 249.

23. R. Burton, *Zanzibar*, 2: 392.

24. Speke, "Journals," 395, 565.

25. Ibid., 580.

26. For a history of early Nile exploration see John Udal, *The Nile in Darkness*, vol. 1, *Conquest and Exploration, 1504–1862* (Wilby, Norwich: M. Russell, 1998).

27. For an interesting discussion of how the map of the East African Expedition changed see Adrian S. Wisnicki, "Charting the Frontier: Indigenous Geography, Arab-Nyamwezi Caravans, and the East Africa Expedition of 1856–59," *Victorian Studies* 51 (2008): 103–37.

28. J. H. Speke to Christopher Rigby, November 25, 1859, NLS, MLC.

29. R. Burton to East India United Service Club, November 11, 1859, in R. Burton, *Lake Regions*, 2: 434–39.

30. J. H. Speke to the undersecretary of state for India, December 1, 1859, in Russell, *General Rigby*, 249–255.

31. T. C. Melvill to R. Burton, January 14, 1860, in R. Burton, *Lake Regions*, 2: 439–40.

32. R. Burton to T. C. Melvill, in ibid., 2: 440–41.

33. "Leaves from a Notebook 1860," British Library Manuscript Collection (BLMC), MLC.

34. See Lovell, *Rage to Live*, 379–80, for an overview of Burton's finances at this time.

35. I. Burton, *LCSRB*, 1: 337.

36. R. Burton to J. H. Speke, undated, QKC, MLC.

37. "Leaves from Miss A___ B___ 's diary," BLMC, MLC.

38. R. Burton, *Zanzibar*, 1: 14–15.

39. R. Burton, *Lake Regions*, 1: xiii.

40. Ibid., xv.

41. Ibid., xiv.

42. Christopher Rigby to H. L. Anderson, November 16, 1860, in Russell, *General Rigby*, 264–71.

43. Christopher Rigby to Norton Shaw, January 16, in ibid., 273–74.

44. R. Burton, *Lake Regions*, 2: 289–90.

45. Ibid., 2: 324–25.

46. Richard F. Burton, "The Ivory Trade of Zanzibar," *Technologist* 2 (1862): 225–28.

47. Richard F. Burton, *The City of the Saints* (London: Longman, Green, Longman, and Roberts, 1861), 29.

48. R. Burton, *Two Trips to Gorilla Land and the Cataracts of the Congo* (London: S. Low, Marston, Low, and Searle, 1876), 1: 106.

49. R. Burton, *City of the Saints*, 64.

50. Ibid., 9.

51. Ibid., 73.

52. Ibid., 157.

53. Ibid., 187.

54. Ibid., 369.

55. Wilkins, *Romance of Isabel*, 1: 158–59.

56. I. Burton, *LCSRB*, 1: 341.

57. Ibid., 343.

58. R. Burton to R. M. Milnes, March 20, 1861, TCLC, MLC.

59. Correspondence in FO 2/40, TNA.

60. See Godsall, *Tangled Web*, 217–18, for the relevant correspondence.

61. F. R. G. S., *Wanderings in West Africa from Liverpool to Fernando Po* (London: Tinsley Brothers, 1863), 1: 296.

62. I. Burton, *LCSRB*, 1: 344.

Chapter 6: Ports of Call

1. F. R. G. S., *Wanderings*, 1: xiv.

2. Ibid., 21.

3. Ibid., xiv.

4. Ibid., 2: 59.

5. Ibid., 1: 1.

6. Ibid., n13.

7. Ibid., 13.

8. Ibid., 32.

9. Ibid., 54.

10. Ibid., 65–66.

11. Ibid., 99.

12. Ibid., 107.

13. Ibid., 101.

14. Ibid., 143–45.

15. Ibid., 150.

16. Richard F. Burton, "A Trip Up the Congo or Zaire River," with Selim Agha, *Geographical Magazine*, July 1875, 204.

17. F. R. G. S., *Wanderings*, 1: 152.

18. Ibid., 163.

19. Ibid., 165–66.

20. Ibid., 172–73.
21. Ibid., 175–76.
22. Ibid., 180–81.
23. Ibid., 188.
24. Ibid., 254–55.
25. Ibid., 192.
26. W. Winwood Reade, *Savage Africa: Being the Narrative of a Tour in Equatorial, Southwestern and Northwestern Africa* (New York: Harper, 1864), 26–27.
27. See Hollis R. Lynch, *Edward Wilmot Blyden: Pan-Negro Patriot, 1832–1912* (London: Oxford University Press, 1970).
28. F. R. G. S., *Wanderings*, 1: 200.
29. Ibid., 239.
30. Ibid., 211.
31. Ibid., 220.
32. Ibid., 250–51.
33. Ibid., 265–66.
34. Ibid., 288–89.
35. Ibid., 2: 25.
36. Ibid., 1: 300.
37. Ibid., 2: 53.
38. Ibid., 73.
39. Ibid., 130–31.
40. Ibid., 163.
41. Ibid., 76.
42. H. Alan C. Cairns, *Prelude to Imperialism: British Reactions to Central African Society, 1840–1890* (London: Routledge & K. Paul, 1965), 225.
43. F. R. G. S., *Wanderings*, 2: 220.
44. Ibid., 235.
45. Ibid., 227.
46. Ibid., 224.
47. Ibid., 280.
48. Ibid., 280–82.
49. Ibid., 295.

Chapter 7: The Roving Consul

1. FO 84/1147, October 4, 1861, and November 23, 1861, TNA.
2. October 8, 1861, FO 2/40, TNA.
3. Richard F. Burton, *Abeokuta and the Camaroons Mountains. An Exploration* (London: Tinsley Brothers, 1863), 1: vi.
4. Ibid., 5.
5. Ibid., 6–7.
6. Richard F. Burton, "Account of the Ascent of the Camaroons Mountain," FO 84/1176, TNA.

7. R. Burton to Norton Shaw, *Proceedings of the Royal Geographical Society* 6 (1861–62): 65.

8. R. Burton, *Abeokuta*, 1: 26.

9. Ibid., 42–43.

10. Ibid., 45.

11. Ibid., 219.

12. Ibid., 61.

13. Ibid., 68.

14. R. Burton to Norton Shaw, *Proceedings of the Royal Geographical Society* 6 (1861–62): 65.

15. R. Burton, *Abeokuta*, 1: 142.

16. Ibid., 248.

17. Ibid., 202–3.

18. Ibid., 171.

19. Ibid., n300.

20. Ibid., 301, 330.

21. Ibid., 297–98.

22. Ibid., 314–17.

23. Ibid., 2: 12.

24. Sketch Survey of the RIVER OGUN or ABBEOKUTA, FO 925/505, TNA.

25. R. Burton to Lord Russell, January 14, 1862, FO 84/1176, TNA.

26. R. Burton, *Abeokuta*, 2: 29.

27. R. Burton to Lord Russell, January 14, 1862, FO 84/1176, TNA.

28. R. Burton, *Abeokuta*, 2: 103.

29. Ibid., 106.

30. Ibid., 127.

31. R. Burton, "Account of the Ascent."

32. R. Burton, *Abeokuta*, 2: 152–53.

33. R. Burton, "Account of the Ascent."

34. R. Burton, *Abeokuta*, 2: 156.

35. Harry H. Johnston, *The Story of My Life* (Indianapolis: Bobbs-Merrill Company, 1923), 167.

36. R. Burton, "Account of the Ascent."

37. R. Burton, *Abeokuta*, 2: 225.

38. R. Burton, "Account of the Ascent."

39. Foreign Office to R. Burton, April 23, 1862, FO 84/1176, TNA.

40. Richard F. Burton, "Account of the Ascent of the Camaroons Mountain in Western Africa," *Proceedings of the Royal Geographical Society* 6 (1861–62): 235–48.

41. R. Burton, *Abeokuta*, 2: 231– 232.

42. FO 84/1176, January 14, 1862, TNA.

43. Richard F. Burton, *A Mission to Gelele, King of Dahome* (London: Tinsley Brothers, 1864), 1: 22.

44. Richard F. Burton, "Two Trips on the Gold Coast," *Ocean Highways: The Geographical Review* 1 (1873–74): 449.

45. R. Burton, *Two Trips to Gorilla Land*, 1: 15.

46. R. Burton to Lord Russell, April 26, 1862, FO 2/42, TNA.

47. R. Burton, *Two Trips to Gorilla Land*, 1: 28–29.

48. Ibid., 35.

49. Ibid., 40.

50. Ibid., 42.

51. Ibid., 150.

52. R. Burton to R. M. Milnes, April 26, 1862, in "The Selected Correspondence of Sir Richard Burton 1848–1890," by Donald Young (MA thesis, University of Nebraska, Lincoln, 1979), 154–57.

53. R. Burton, *Two Trips to Gorilla Land*, 1: 124–25.

54. Ibid., 71.

55. Ibid., 64–65.

56. Ibid., 196.

57. Ibid., 20.

58. Richard F. Burton, "A Day Amongst the Fans," *Anthropological Review* 1 (1863): 43–54.

59. R. Burton, *Two Trips to Gorilla Land*, 1: 218–19.

60. R. Burton to Lord Russell, April 26, 1862, FO 2/42, TNA.

61. Foreign Office to R. Burton, August 7, 1862, FO 2/42, TNA.

62. R. Burton, *Mission to Gelele* (1864), 1: 10.

63. Foreign Office to R. Burton, May 21, 1862, July 22, 1862, FO 2/42, TNA.

64. I. Burton, *LCSRB*, 1: 376.

65. Foreign Office to R. Burton, May 6, 1862, FO 84/1176, TNA.

66. R. Burton to Lord Russell, May 22, 1862, FO 84/1176, TNA.

67. FO 84/1176, TNA.

68. R. Burton, "Two Trips on the Gold Coast," 450.

69. R. Burton to Admiral Henry Murray, c. mid-January 1863, Scottish Records Office, MLC.

70. R. Burton, "Two Trips on the Gold Coast," 452.

71. Ibid., 455.

72. Foreign Office to R. Burton, FO 84/1176, TNA.

73. F. R. G. S., "My Wanderings in West Africa," *Fraser's Magazine* 67 (1863): 157.

74. Ibid., 277.

75. Ibid., 287.

76. Ibid., 288.

77. Ibid., 407.

78. R. Burton to Lord Russell, August 26, 1862, FO 84/1176, TNA.

79. Richard F. Burton, "An Account of an Exploration of the Elephant Mountain in Western Equatorial Africa," *Journal of the Royal Geographical Society* 33 (1863): 241–50 (hereafter cited as "AEEM").

80. Ibid., 242.
81. R. Burton to Lord Russell, December 18, 1862, FO 84/1176, TNA.
82. See Ronald Rainger, "Race, Politics, and Science: The Anthropological Society of London in the 1860s," *Victorian Studies* 22 (1978): 51–70.
83. Richard F. Burton, "Notes on the Dahoman," in Penzer, *Selected Papers on Anthropology*, 109–10.
84. R. Burton to Lord Russell, January 6, 1863, FO 84/1203, TNA.
85. I. Burton, *LCSRB*, 1: 377.
86. Ibid., 376.
87. Isabel's accounts of their time on Madeira and Tenerife can be found in Wilkins, *Romance of Isabel*, 1: 184–225.
88. "Report by Consul Burton of His Visit to the King of Dahome in May and June 1863," October 1863, FO, 1392A TNA.
89. R. Burton to R. M. Milnes, May 31, 1863, TCLC, MLC.
90. R. Burton, *Two Trips to Gorilla Land*, 2: 1.
91. "Reports by Consul Burton of His Ascent of the Congo River, in September 1863," September 6, 1864, FO 84/1203, TNA (hereafter cited as "RCBACR").
92. R. Burton, *Two Trips to Gorilla Land*, 2: 114–15.
93. Ibid., 201.
94. Ibid., 250. An interesting account, supposedly in part by Selim, is R. Burton, "Trip Up the Congo or Zaire River," 203–7.
95. "RCBACR."
96. Foreign Office to R. Burton, August 20, 1863, FO 84/1203, TNA.
97. R. Burton, *Mission to Gelele* (1864), 1: 27.
98. "Report by Consul Burton of His Visit to the King of Dahome in the Months of December 1863, and January and February 1864," May 30, 1864, FO 84/1221, TNA (hereafter cited as "RCBVKD").
99. Ibid.
100. Richard F. Burton, "The Present State of Dahome," *Transactions of the Ethnological Society of London*, New Series, 3 (1865): 402.
101. R. Burton, *Mission to Gelele* (1864), 1: 164.
102. Ibid., 170.
103. Ibid., 194.
104. Ibid., 277.
105. "RCBVKD."
106. R. Burton, *Mission to Gelele* (1864), 2: 64, 75.
107. R. Burton, "Present State of Dahome," 404.
108. "RCBVKD."
109. Quoted in C. W. Newbury, introduction to *A Mission to Gelele, King of Dahome*, by Richard F. Burton (London: Routledge and K. Paul, 1966), 23.
110. R. Burton, *Mission to Gelele* (1864), 2: 57.
111. R. Burton to Foreign Office, April 15, 1864, FO 2/45, TNA.
112. Melville J. Herskovits, *Dahomey, an Ancient West African Kingdom*, 2 vols.

(New York: J. J. Augustin, 1938). See Newbury, introduction to R. Burton, *Mission to Gelele* (1966), for an assessment.

113. R. Burton, *Mission to Gelele* (1864), 2: 107.
114. Ibid., 119.
115. Ibid., 131–36.
116. R. Burton, "Notes on the Dahoman," 124.
117. R. Burton, *Mission to Gelele* (1864), 1: 14.
118. Ibid., 18, 24.
119. Richard F. Burton, *Wit and Wisdom from West Africa* (London: Tinsley Brothers, 1865), xvi–xvii.
120. R. Burton to Lord Russell, April 15, 1864, FO 84/1221, TNA.
121. Richard F. Burton, "A Mission to Dahome," in Hayman, *SRBTAA*, 93.

Chapter 8: The Great Debate That Never Was

1. *Journal of the Royal Geographical Society* 33 (1863): clxxiv.
2. John Petherick and Kate Petherick, *Travels in Central Africa and Explorations of the Western Nile Tributaries* (London: Tinsley Brothers, 1869), 2: 92.
3. For a semifictionalized biography of Florence see Pat Shipman, *To the Heart of the Nile: Lady Florence Baker and the Exploration of Central Africa* (New York: Morrow, 2004).
4. Petherick and Petherick, *Travels in Central Africa*, 2: 127.
5. Carnochan, *Sad Story*, 86.
6. R. Murchison to J. A. Grant, May 1864, RGS, MLC.
7. *Illustrated London News*, Supplement, July 4, 1863; and *Proceedings of the Royal Geographical Society* 7 (1863): 218.
8. J. H. Speke, *Athenaeum*, January 23, 1864, 121.
9. David Finkelstein, *The House of Blackwood: Author-Publisher Relations in the Victorian Era* (University Park: Pennsylvania State University Press, 2002), 49–69.
10. John Hanning Speke, "The Upper Basin of the Nile, from Inspection and Information," *Journal of the Royal Geographical Society* 33 (1863): 322–46.
11. *Journal of the Royal Geographical Society* 34 (1864): clxxviii.
12. John Milner Gray, "Speke and Grant," *Uganda Journal* 17 (1953): 151.
13. R. Murchison to J. A. Grant, May 1864, RGS, MLC.
14. Maitland, *Speke*, 198.
15. R. Burton, *Zanzibar*, 2: 395.
16. Ibid., 397–98.
17. I. Burton, *LCSRB*, 2: 426.
18. R. Burton, *Zanzibar*, 2: 398.
19. *Bath Chronicle*, September 17, 1864.
20. *London Times*, September 23, 1864.
21. Published as "On Lake Tanganyika, Ptolemy's Western Lake Reservoir of the Nile," *Journal of the Royal Geographical Society* 35 (1865): 1–15.

22. Richard F. Burton and James MacQueen, *The Nile Basin* (London: Tinsley Brothers, 1864).
23. Young, *SSN*, 192–193.
24. R. Burton to F. Wilson, September 24, 1864, QKC, MLC; also in Young, "Selected Correspondence," 178–83.
25. Burton's testimony can be found on pp. 87–107 of "Report from the Select Committee Appointed to Consider the State of the British Establishments on the Western Coast of Africa; Together with the Proceedings of the Committee, Minutes of Evidence, and Appendix," *Parliamentary Papers 1865*.
26. See Christopher Fyfe, *A History of Sierra Leone* (London: Oxford University Press, 1962), 336–39.
27. *London Times*, December 12, 1862, January 9, 1863, and January 21, 1863.
28. Anonymous, "Farewell Dinner to Captain Burton," *Anthropological Review* 3 (1865): 167–82. A slightly different version exists in I. Burton, *LCSRB*, 402–3.
29. David Livingstone to Arthur Mills, May 12, 1865; David Livingstone to Sir Thomas Maclean, May 27, 1865, QKC, MLC.
30. *Journal of the Anthropological Society of London* 3 (1865): ccv.

Chapter 9: Final Wanderings

1. I. Burton, *LCSRB*, 1: 418.
2. Ibid., 2: 455; and R. Burton to Lord Houghton, November 23, 1867, TCLC, MLC.
3. Isabel's papers can be found at the Wiltshire County Records Office. Microfilm versions are part of the Huntington Library Collection.
4. R. Burton to A. G. Findlay, RGS, January 8, 1867, QKC, MLC.
5. I. Burton, *LCSRB*, 1: 425.
6. FO 97/438, TNA.
7. William Rainy, *The Censor Censured, or the Calumnies of Captain Burton* (London: George Chalfont, 1865), 5.
8. Ibid., 41.
9. Lord Stanley to R. Burton, June 4, 1867, FO 13/450, TNA.
10. R. Burton to Lord Stanley, June 5, 1867, FO 97/438, TNA.
11. R. Burton, "First Footsteps in Eastern Africa," in Hayman, *SRBTAA*, 84.
12. R. Burton, "AMD," in ibid., 93, 94.
13. Many thanks to Alan Jutzi at the Huntington Library for bringing this map to my attention.
14. Richard F. Burton, *Letters from the Battle-fields of Paraguay* (London: Tinsley Brothers, 1870), xvi.
15. In Wilkins, *Romance of Isabel*, 1: 250.
16. I. Burton to Lord Houghton, November 23, 1867, TCLC, MLC.
17. I. Burton, *LCSRB*, 1: 453.
18. R. Burton to Foreign Office, June 15, 1868 and July 23, 1868, FO 13/457 TNA.

19. Blunt, *My Diaries*, 2: 129.
20. Copy available at Orleans House Gallery, MLC.
21. R. Burton to R. M. Milnes, September 1, 1869, in Young, "Selected Correspondence," 185–87.
22. I. Burton, *LCSRB*, 1: 464.
23. It's one of three included in W. H. Wilkins, ed., *The Jew, The Gypsy and El Islam*, (London: Hutchinson & Co., 1898). The three topics are unrelated.
24. Rashid to R. Burton, June 7, 1871, Richard Francis Burton Papers, Huntington Library (RFBPHL) 827; and R. Burton to Rashid, June 8, 1871, RFBPHL 315.
25. "The Case of Captain Burton, late H. B. M's Consul at Damascus," Parliamentary Printing Works, Clayton & Co., 1872.
26. I. Burton, *LCSRB*, 2: 256.
27. Algernon Bertram Redesdale, *Memories* (New York: E. P. Dutton, 1916), 2: 563.
28. R. Burton, *Zanzibar*, 1: 1–2.
29. Carnochan, *Sad Story*, 108.
30. R. Burton, *Zanzibar*, 2: 385, 386.
31. Ibid., 321.
32. R. Burton to Lord Houghton, September 23, 1872, TCLC, MLC.
33. R. Burton to John Kirk, October 12, 1876, NLS, MLC.
34. R. Burton, letter to *Geographical Magazine*, November 1, 1875, 354–55.
35. R. Burton to Chaillé-Long, November 4, 1888, in *My Life in Four Continents*, by Colonel Chaillé-Long (London: Hutchinson & Co., 1912), 1: 426.
36. Verney Lovett Cameron, *Across Africa* (London: Daldy, Isbister & Co., 1877), 2: 290.
37. I. Burton, *LCSRB*, 1: 594–95.
38. *London Times*, October 28, 1871.
39. Alfred Bate Richards, Andrew Wilson, and St. Clair Baddeley, *A Sketch of the Career of Richard F. Burton* (London: Waterlow & Sons, 1886), 30–31.
40. I. Burton, *LCSRB*, 2: 17.
41. I. Burton to Mr. Monson, April 27, 1873, Sir Richard Francis Burton Collection, Special Collections Research Center, Syracuse University Library (SUL).
42. Lovell, *Rage to Live*, 592.
43. R. Burton to R. M. Milnes, November 5, 1873, and December 16, 1873, TCLC, MLC.
44. R. Burton to William T. Sanders, March 2, 1874, SUL.
45. I. Burton to Lord Houghton, August 12, 1874, TCLC, MLC.
46. I. Burton, *LCSRB*, 2: 48.
47. R. Burton to R. M. Milnes, June 15, 1875, in Young, "Selected Correspondence," 213–14.
48. See Godsall, *Tangled Web*, 321, for a clarification of the date for this trip.
49. *Proceedings of the Royal Geographical Society* 20 (1875–76): 44–50; and letter to *London Times*, June 21, 1875.

50. Richard F. Burton, *Camoens: His Life and His Lusiads. A Commentary* (London: B. Quaritch, 1881), 2: 514n. 517.

51. Richard F. Burton, *The Gold-Mines of Midian and the Ruined Midianite Cities: A Fortnight's Tour in North-western Arabia* (London: C. K. Paul & Co., 1878), 247–48.

52. R. Burton, Ibid., 1.

53. Ibid., 118–19.

54. Ibid., 371.

55. Ibid., 389.

56. Ibid., 22, 27.

57. I. Burton, *LCSRB*, 2: 123.

58. R. Burton to Lord Derby, September 20, 1877, FO 7/914, TNA.

59. R. Burton to Foreign Office, March 1, 1878, FO 7/977, TNA.

60. Isabel saved the correspondence between Gordon and Burton. It can be found in Wilkins, *Romance of Isabel*, 2: 645–76.

61. Ibid., 675–76.

62. W. A. Ross to R. Burton, September 21, 1878, RFBPHL 780; and Edgar Jackson to I. Burton, October 19, 1878, RFBPHL 835.

63. R. Burton to Ismail, January 20, 1879, RFBPHL 689.

64. J. H. Murchison to R. Burton, March 17, 1879, RFBPHL 753 and May 17, 1879, RFBPHL 757.

65. I. Burton, *LCSRB*, 2: 192–95.

66. In 1979 Oleander Press of Cambridge, UK, released a version of *The Gold-Mines of Midian and the Ruined Midianite Cities* edited by Philip Ward. It included over 1,600 corrections, mostly of Arabic words, that Burton made in the original, which Isabel had edited.

67. Bram Stoker, *Personal Reminiscences of Henry Irving* (London: W. Heinemann, 1906), 1: 357.

68. Alfred G. K. Levick to R. Burton, July 18, 1877, RFBPHL 665.

69. R. Burton to Chaillé-Long in Chaillé-Long, *My Life*, 421–22.

70. R. Burton, *BTNN*, 1: i.

71. J. Irvine to R. Burton, January 24, 1881, RFBPHL 575, and October 27, 1881, RFBPHL 577.

72. R. Burton to Lord Granville, October 8, 1881, FO 7/1026, TNA.

73. V. L. Cameron to R. Burton, March 18, 1878, RFBPHL 326; September 8, 1880, RFBPHL 329.

74. Richard F. Burton, "The Kong Mountains," *Proceedings of the Royal Geographical Society*, New Series, 4 (1882): 484–86.

75. Richard F. Burton and Verney Lovett Cameron, *To the Gold Coast for Gold: A Personal Narrative* (London: Chatto & Windus, 1883), 1: x.

76. Thomas J. Bassett and Philip W. Porter, "'From the Best of Authorities': The Mountains of Kong in the Cartography of West Africa," *Journal of African History* 32 (1991): 367–413.

77. R. Burton and Cameron, *To the Gold Coast*, 1: 107.
78. Ibid., 286.
79. Ibid., 291–92.
80. Ibid., 295–96.
81. Ibid., 341–42.
82. Ibid., 2: 36.
83. Ibid., 6.
84. Ibid., 173.
85. See appendix 2 in ibid.
86. Ibid., 190–91.
87. Ibid., 230.
88. Foreign Office to R. Burton, February 18, 1882; and R. Burton to Foreign Office, April 13, 1882, FO 7/1043, TNA.
89. R. Burton and Cameron, *To the Gold Coast*, 2: 110.
90. Ibid., 328.
91. Ibid., 337.
92. Richard F. Burton, "Gold on the Gold Coast," *Journal of the Society of Arts* 30 (1882): 789.
93. Burton and Cameron, *To the Gold Coast*, 2: 337.
94. See Raymond E. Dumett, *El Dorado in West Africa: The Gold-mining Frontier, African Labor, and Colonial Capitalism in the Gold Coast, 1875–1900* (Athens: Ohio University Press, 1998).
95. Hollams, Son & Coward to R. Burton, April 16, 1877, RFBPHL 556.
96. J. Irvine to R. Burton, January 2, 1886, RFBPHL 616.
97. J. Irvine to I. Burton, June 5, 1889, RFBPHL 573.
98. R. Burton to Foreign Office, September 6, 1882, FO7/1041, TNA.
99. R. Burton to Foreign Office, December 11, 1882, FO 7/1041, TNA.
100. I. Burton, *LCSRB*, 2: 271.
101. Wendy Doniger and Sudhir Kakar, *Kamasutra* (Oxford: Oxford University Press, 2002), l–li.
102. Quentin Keynes, "The Labyrinthine Path of Collecting Burton," in *In Search of Sir Richard Burton: Papers from a Huntington Library Symposium*, ed. Alan H. Jutzi (San Marino, CA: Huntington Library, 1993), 121.
103. R. Burton, *BTNN* 3: 1476.
104. Ibid., 1527.
105. Ibid., 1: 26.
106. Ibid., 6: 3749.
107. Richard F. Burton, *The Sotadic Zone* (New York: Panurge Press, n.d.).
108. Johnston, *Story of My Life*, 146.
109. Justin McCarthy, *Portraits of the Sixties* (New York: Harper & Brothers, 1903), 172–74.
110. *Academy* 28 (August 1885): 68.
111. I. Burton to Albert Tootal, February 19, 1885, RFBPHL 265.

112. R. Burton to Ouida, April 2, 1886, QKC, MLC.
113. R. Burton to Lord Iddesleigh, September 8, 1886, FO 7/1105, TNA. Lovell notes that Isabel wrote the letter.
114. John Hayman, "Burton as Autobiographer," in Jutzi, *In Search of Burton*, 32.
115. I. Burton, *LCSRB*, 2: 367.
116. Quoted in James L. Newman, *Imperial Footprints: Henry Morton Stanley's African Journeys* (Washington, DC: Brassey's, Inc., 2004), 309.
117. I. Burton, *LCSRB*, 2: 439.
118. Ibid., 406–7.
119. Waterfield, *First Footsteps*, 4.

BIBLIOGRAPHY

BOOKS BY BURTON AS AUTHOR, CO-AUTHOR, EDITOR, TRANSLATOR

Abeokuta and the Camaroons Mountains. An Exploration. 2 vols. London: Tinsley Brothers, 1863.

Ananga Ranga: (Stage of the Bodiless One) or, the Hindu Art of Love. Translated by A. F. F. and B. F. R. Benares, India: Kama Shastra Society, 1885.

The Book of the Sword. London: Chatto and Windus, 1884.

Camoens: His Life and His Lusiads. A Commentary. 2 vols. London: B. Quaritch, 1881.

The City of the Saints. London: Longman, Green, Longman, and Roberts, 1861.

A Complete System of Bayonet Exercise. London: William Clowes and Sons, 1853.

Etruscan Bologna: A Study. London: Smith, Elder, & Co., 1876.

Explorations of the Highlands of Brazil. 2 vols. London: Tinsley Brothers, 1869.

Falconry in the Valley of the Indus. London: J. van Voorst, 1852.

First Footsteps in East Africa; Or, An Exploration of Harar. London: Longman, Brown, Green, and Longmans, 1856.

Goa and the Blue Mountains. London: R. Bentley, 1851.

The Gold-Mines of Midian and the Ruined Midianite Cities: A Fortnight's Tour in North-western Arabia. London: C. K. Paul & Co., 1878.

The Gulistan or Rose Garden of Sa'di. With Edward Rehatsek. Benares, India: Kama Shastra Society, 1888.

The Jew, The Gypsy, and El Islam. Edited by W. H. Wilkins. London: Hutchinson & Co., 1898.

The Kama Sutra of Vatsyayana. Translated with F. F. Arbuthnot. Benares, India: Kama Shastra Society, 1883.

The Kasidah of Haji Abdu Al-Yazdi. London: H. J. Cook, 1880.

The Lake Regions of Central Africa. 2 vols. London: Longman, Green, Longman, and Roberts, 1860.

The Land of Midian (Revisited). 2 vols. London: C. K. Paul & Co., 1879.

The Lands of Cazembe:Lacerda's Journey to Cazembe in 1798. Translated and annotated by R. Burton. London: John Murray, 1873.

Letters from the Battle-fields of Paraguay. London: Tinsley Brothers, 1870.

A Mission to Gelele, King of Dahome. 2 vols. London: Tinsley Brothers, 1864.

A New System of Sword Exercise for Infantry. London: William Clowes and Sons, 1876.

The Nile Basin. With James MacQueen. London: Tinsley Brothers, 1864.

Os Lusiadas (The Lusiads). 2 vols. London: B. Quaritch, 1880.

The Perfumed Garden of the Cheikh Nefzaoui: A Manual of Arabian Erotology. Benares, India: Kama Shastra Society, 1886.

A Plain and Literal Translation of the Arabian Nights' Entertainments, Now Entitled "The Book of the Thousand Nights and a Night." 10 vols. Benares, India: Kama Shastra Society, 1885.

The Prairie Traveller, a Hand-book for Overland Expeditions. London: Trübner and Co., 1863.

Scinde; Or, The Unhappy Valley. 2 vols. London: R. Bentley, 1851.

Sind Revisited: With Notices of the Anglo-Indian Army; Railroads; Past, Present, and Future, Etc. 2 vols. London: R. Bentley and Sons, 1877.

Sindh, and the Races That Inhabit the Valley of the Indus: With Notices of the Topography and History of the Province. London: W. H. Allen & Co., 1851.

The Sotadic Zone. New York: Panurge Press, n.d.

Stone Talk: Being Some of the Marvellous Sayings of a Petral Portion of Fleet Street, London, to One Doctor Polyglot, Ph.D. By Frank Baker. London: R. Hardwicke, 1865.

Supplemental Nights to the Book of the Thousand Nights and a Night. 6 vols. Benares, India: Kama Shastra Society, 1886–88.

To the Gold Coast for Gold: A Personal Narrative. With Verney Lovett Cameron. London: Chatto & Windus, 1883.

Two Trips to Gorilla Land and the Cataracts of the Congo. 2 vols. London: S. Low, Marston, Low, and Searle, 1876.

Ultima Thule; Or, A Summer in Iceland. 2 vols. London: W. P. Nimmo, 1875.

Unexplored Syria. With Charles F. Tyrwhitt-Drake. 2 vols. London: Tinsley Brothers, 1872.

Vikram and the Vampire, or, Tales of Hindu Devilry. Adapted by R. Burton. London: Longmans, Green & Co., 1870.

Wanderings in West Africa from Liverpool to Fernando Po. By F. R. G. S. 2 vols. London: Tinsley Brothers, 1863.

Wit and Wisdom from West Africa. London: Tinsley Brothers, 1865.

Zanzibar: City, Island, and Coast. 2 vols. London: Tinsley Brothers, 1872.

Other Editions of Note

Abeokuta and the Camaroons Mountains. 2 vols. Elibron Classics, 2005.

The Book of the Thousand Nights and a Night. 6 vols. Edited by Emile Van Vlict. New York: Heritage Press; Limited Editions Club, 1934.

The City of Saints Among the Mormons and Across the Rocky Mountains to California. Crabtree, OR: Narrative Press, 2003.

First Footsteps in East Africa. Edited by Gordon Waterfield. New York: Praeger, 1966.

Goa, and the Blue Mountains, or, Six Months of Sick Leave. New Delhi: Penguin Books, 2003.

The Gold-Mines of Midian and the Ruined Midianite Cities. Edited by Philip Ward. Cambridge, UK: Oleander Press, 1979.

The Lake Regions of Central Africa: A Picture of Exploration. 2 vols. with introduction by Alan Moorehead. London: Sidgwick and Jackson, 1961.

A Mission to Gelele King of Dahome. 2 vols. Elibron Classics, 2005.

The Nile Basin by Richard Burton and Captain Speke's Discovery of the Sources of the Nile by James MacQueen. New York: Da Capo Press, 1967.

Personal Narrative of a Pilgrimmage to Al-Madinah & Meccah. 2 vols. Memorial Ed. New York: Dover Publications, 1964.

Two Trips to Gorilla Land and the Cataracts of the Congo. 2 vols. Elibron Classics, 2005.

Wanderings in West Africa. New York: Dover Publications, 1991.

Zanzibar: City, Island, and Coast. 2 vols. Elibron Classics, 2005.

ARTICLES, ETC., BY BURTON

"An Account of an Exploration of the Elephant Mountain in Western Equatorial Africa." *Journal of the Royal Geographical Society* 33 (1863): 241–50.

"Account of the Ascent of the Camaroons Mountain in Western Africa." *Proceedings of the Royal Geographical Society* 6 (1861–62), 235–48.

"Ascent of the Ogun, or Abbeokuta River." *Proceedings of the Royal Geographical Society* 6 (1861–62), 49, 64–66.

"Brief Notes Relative to the Division of Time, and Articles of Cultivation in Sind." With J. E. Stocks. *Bombay Government Record*, New Series, 17, Part Two (1855): 613–36.

"A Coasting Voyage from Mombasa to the Pangani River; Visit to Sultan Kimwere; and Progress of the Expedition into the Interior." With John Hanning Speke. *Journal of the Royal Geographic Society* 28 (1858): 188–226.

"A Day Amongst the Fans." *Anthropological Review* 1 (1863): 43–54.

"Gold on the Gold Coast." *Journal of the Society of Arts* 30 (1882): 785–94.

"The Ivory Trade of Zanzibar." *Technologist* 2 (1862): 225–228.

"A Journey from El-Medinà to Mecca Down the Darb el Sharki on the Eastern Road (Hitherto Unvisited by Europeans)." *Journal of the Royal Geographical Society* 25 (1855): 121–36.

"Journey to Medina, with Route from Yambu." *Journal of the Royal Geographical Society* 24 (1854): 208–25.

"The Kong Mountains." *Proceedings of the Royal Geographical Society*, New Series, 4 (1882): 484–86.

"The Lake Regions of Central Equatorial Africa, with Notices of the Lunar

Mountains and the Sources of the White Nile." *Journal of the Royal Geographical Society* 29 (1859): 1–454.

"My Wanderings in West Africa." By F. R. G. S. *Fraser's Magazine* 67 (1863): 135–57, 273–89, 407–22.

"Narrative of a Trip to Harar." *Journal of the Royal Geographical Society* 25 (1855): 136–50.

"On Lake Tanganyika, Ptolemy's Western Lake Reservoir of the Nile." *Journal of the Royal Geographical Society* 35 (1865): 1–15.

"The Present State of Dahome." *Transactions of the Ethnological Society of London,* New Series, 3 (1865): 400–408.

"A Trip Up the Congo or Zaire River." With Selim Agha. *Geographical Magazine,* July 1875, 203–7.

"Two Trips on the Gold Coast." *Ocean Highways: The Geographical Review* 1 (1873–74): 448–61.

"Zanzibar; and Two Months in East Africa." *Blackwood's Magazine* 83 (1858): 214–24, 276–90, 572–89.

REFERENCE BOOKS

Abusharaf, Rogaia Mustafa, ed. *Female Circumcision: Multicultural Perspectives.* Philadelphia: University of Pennsylvania Press, 2006.

Batuta, Ibn. *Travels in Asia and Africa, 1325–1354.* Translated by H. A. R. Gibb. London: Routledge & K. Paul, 1957.

Bennett, Norman R., and George E. Brooks Jr., eds. *New England Merchants in Africa: A History Through Documents, 1802–1865.* Boston: Boston University Press, 1965.

Blevins, Win. *The Rock Child.* New York: Forge, 1998.

Blunt, Wilfrid S. *My Diaries: Being a Personal Narrative of Events, 1888–1914.* 2 vols. New York: Knopf, 1921.

Boorstin, Daniel J. *The Exploring Spirit: America and the World, Then and Now.* New York: Random House, 1976.

Brantlinger, Patrick. *Rule of Darkness: British Literature and Imperialism, 1830–1914.* Ithaca, NY: Cornell University Press, 1988.

Brodie, Fawn M. *The Devil Drives: A Life of Sir Richard Burton.* New York: Norton, 1967.

Burton, Isabel. *The Life of Captain Sir Richard F. Burton.* 2 vols. London: Chapman & Hall, 1893.

Cairns, H. Alan C. *Prelude to Imperialism: British Reactions to Central African Society, 1840–1890.* London: Routledge & K. Paul, 1965.

Cameron, Verney Lovett. *Across Africa.* 2 vols. London: Daldy, Isbister & Co, 1877.

Carnochan, W. B. *The Sad Story of Burton, Speke, and the Nile; Or, Was John Hanning Speke a Cad?* Stanford, CA: Stanford General Books, 2006.

Casada, James A. *Sir Richard F. Burton: A Biobibliographical Study.* Boston: G. K. Hall, 1990.

Chaillé-Long, Colonel. *My Life in Four Continents.* 2 vols. London: Hutchinson & Co., 1912.

Crofton, Richard H. *The Old Consulate at Zanzibar.* London: Oxford University Press, 1935.

Crone, G. R. *The Sources of the Nile: Explorers' Maps A.D. 1856–1891.* London: Royal Geographical Society, 1964.

Doniger, Wendy, and Sudhir Kakar. *Kamasutra.* Oxford: Oxford University Press, 2002.

Drake-Brockman, Ralph E. *British Somaliland.* London: Hurst & Blackett, 1912.

Dumett, Raymond E. *El Dorado in West Africa: The Gold-mining Frontier, African Labor, and Colonial Capitalism in the Gold Coast, 1875–1900.* Athens: Ohio University Press, 1998.

Dunning, John. *The Bookman's Promise.* New York: Scribner, 2004.

Farmer, Philip José. *To Your Scattered Bodies Go: A Science Fiction Novel.* New York: Putnam, 1971.

Finkelstein, David. *The House of Blackwood: Author-Publisher Relations in the Victorian Era.* University Park: Pennsylvania State University Press, 2002.

Fyfe, Christopher. *A History of Sierra Leone.* London: Oxford University Press, 1962.

Godsall, Jon R. *The Tangled Web: A Life of Sir Richard Burton.* Leicester, UK: Matador, 2008.

Harris, Frank. *Contemporary Portraits.* New York: Mitchell Kennerly, 1915.

Harrison, William. *Burton and Speke.* St. Martin's Press, 1982.

Hayman, John, ed. *Sir Richard Burton's Travels in Arabia and Africa: Four Lectures from a Huntington Library Manuscript.* San Marino, CA: Huntington Library, 1990.

Herskovits, Melville J. *Dahomey, an Ancient West African Kingdom.* 2 vols. New York: J. J. Augustin, 1938.

Hitchman, Francis. *Richard F. Burton, K. C. M. G.: His Early, Private and Public Life.* 2 vols. London: S. Low, Marston, Searle & Rivington, 1887.

Hopkirk, Peter. *The Great Game: On Secret Service in High Asia.* London: Murray, 1990.

Johnston, Harry H. *The Story of My Life.* Indianapolis: Bobbs-Merrill Company, 1923.

Jutzi, Alan H., ed. *In Search of Richard Burton: Papers from a Huntington Library Symposium.* San Marino, CA: Huntington Library, 1993.

Kennedy, Dane. *The Highly Civilized Man: Richard Burton and the Victorian World.* Cambridge, MA: Harvard University Press, 2005.

Kirkpatrick, B. J. *A Catalogue of the Library of Sir Richard Burton, K. C. M. G.* London: Royal Anthropological Institute, 1978.

Lewis, I. M. *A Modern History of Somalia: Nation and State in the Horn of Africa.* Rev. ed. London: Longman, 1980.

———. *A Pastoral Democracy.* London: Oxford University Press, 1961.

Lovell, Mary S. *A Rage to Live: A Biography of Richard and Isabel Burton.* New York: Norton, 1998.

Lynch, Hollis R. *Edward Wilmot Blyden: Pan-Negro Patriot, 1832–1912.* London: Oxford University Press, 1970.

Maitland, Alexander. *Speke.* London: Constable, 1971.

McCarthy, Justin. *Portraits of the Sixties.* New York: Harper & Brothers, 1903.

McLynn, Frank. *Burton: Snow Upon the Desert.* London: John Murray, 1990.

———. *From the Sierras to the Pampas: Richard Burton's Travels in the Americas, 1860–69.* London: Century, 1991.

Munro-Hay, Stuart. *Aksum: An African Civilisation of Late Antiquity.* Edinburgh: Edinburgh University Press, 1991.

Newman, James L. *Imperial Footprints: Henry Morton Stanley's African Journeys.* Washington, DC: Brassey's, Inc., 2004.

Ondaatje, Christopher. *Journey to the Source of the Nile.* Toronto: HarperCollins, 1998.

Penzer, Norman M. *An Annotated Bibliography of Sir Richard Francis Burton.* London: A. M. Philpot, 1923.

———, ed. *Selected Papers on Anthropology, Travel & Exploration by Sir Richard Burton.* London: A. M. Philpot, 1924.

Petherick, John, and Kate Petherick. *Travels in Central Africa and Explorations of the Western Nile Tributaries.* 2 vols. London: Tinsley Brothers, 1869.

Phillipson, David W. *Ancient Ethiopia: Aksum, Its Antecedents and Successors.* London: British Museum Press, 1998.

Rainy, William. *The Censor Censured, or, the Calumnies of Captain Burton.* London: George Chalfont, 1865.

Rayner, William. *The Trail to Bear Paw Mountain.* London: Collins, 1974.

Reade, W. Winwood. *Savage Africa: Being the Narrative of a Tour in Equatorial, Southwestern and Northwestern Africa.* New York: Harper, 1864.

Rice, Edward. *Captain Sir Richard Francis Burton: The Secret Agent Who Made the Pilgrimage to Mecca, Discovered the Kama Sutra, and Brought the Arabian Nights to the West.* New York: Scribner's, 1990.

Richards, Alfred Bate, Andrew Wilson, and St. Clair Baddeley. *A Sketch of the Career of Richard F. Burton.* London: Waterlow & Sons, 1886.

Rockel, Stephen J. *Carriers of Culture: Labor on the Road in Nineteenth-Century East Africa.* Portsmouth, NH: Heinemann, 2006.

Russell, Lillian M., ed. *General Rigby, Zanzibar and the Slave Trade.* London: G. Allen & Unwin, 1935.

Salt, Henry. *A Voyage to Abyssinia and Travels into the Interior of That Country, Executed Under Orders of the British Government in the Years 1809 and 1810.* London: F. C. and J. Rivington, 1814.

Shipman, Pat. *To the Heart of the Nile: Lady Florence Baker and the Exploration of Central Africa.* New York: Morrow, 2004.

Speke, John Hanning. *Journal of the Discovery of the Source of the Nile*. New York: Harper & Brothers, 1864.

———. *What Led to the Discovery of the Source of the Nile*. Edinburgh: William Blackwood and Sons, 1864.

Stisted, Georgiana. *The True Life of Capt. Sir Richard F. Burton*. London: H. S. Nichols, 1896.

Stoker, Bram. *Personal Reminiscences of Henry Irving*. 2 vols. London: W. Heinemann, 1906.

Symons, Arthur. *Dramatis Personæ*. Indianapolis: Bobbs-Merill Company, 1923.

Trimingham, J. Spencer. *Islam in Ethiopia*. London: Oxford University Press, 1952.

Troyanov, Iliya. *The Collector of Worlds: A Novel of Sir Richard Francis Burton*. Translated by William Hobson. London: Faber and Faber, 2008.

Udal, John. *The Nile in Darkness*. Wilby, Norwich: M. Russell, 1998.

Valentia, George Viscount. *Voyages and Travels to India, Ceylon, the Red Sea, Abyssinia, and Egypt in 1802, 1803, 1805, 1805, and 1806*. 3 vols. London: F. C. and J. Rivington, 1809.

Wilkins, W. H., ed. *The Romance of Isabel Lady Burton: The Story of Her Life*. 2 vols. London: Hutchinson & Co., 1897.

——— *Wanderings in Three Continents*. London: Hutchinson & Co., 1901.

Wright, Thomas. *The Life of Sir Richard Burton*. 2 vols. New York: Putnam, 1906.

Young, Donald, ed. *The Search for the Source of the Nile*. London: Roxburghe Club, 1999.

ARTICLES, CHAPTERS, AND OTHER SOURCES

Anonymous. "Farewell Dinner to Captain Burton." *Anthropological Review* 3 (1865): 167–82.

Bassett, Thomas J., and Philip W. Porter. "'From the Best Authorities': The Mountains of Kong in the Cartography of West Africa." *Journal of African History* 32 (1991): 367–413.

Bishop, Jonathan. "The Identities of Sir Richard Burton: The Explorer as Actor." *Victorian Studies* 1 (1957): 119–35.

Brantling, Patrick. "Victorians and Africans: The Genealogy of the Myth of the Dark Continent." *Critical Inquiry* 12 (1985): 166–203.

Bridges, R. C. "Sir John Speke and the Royal Geographical Society." *Uganda Journal* 26 (1962): 23–43.

Collins, Robert O. Introduction to *The Nile Basin by Richard F. Burton and Captain Speke's Discovery of the Source of the Nile by James MacQueen*, v–xxvii. New York: Da Capo Press, 1967.

Cruttenden, C. J. "Memoir on the Western or Edo Tribes, Inhabiting the Somali Coast of N.E. Africa; with the Southern Branches of the Family of Darood, Resident on the Banks of the Webbi Shebeyli, Commonly Called the River Webi." *Transactions of the Bombay Geographical Society* 8 (1847–49): 177–210.

————. "On Eastern Africa." *Journal of the Royal Geographical Society* 18 (1848): 136–39.

————. "Report on the Mijjertheyn Tribes of Somallies Inhabiting the District Forming the North-East Point of Africa." *Transactions of the Bombay Geographical Society* 7 (1844–46): 111–26.

Garrett, Greg. "Relocating Burton: Public and Private Writings on Africa," *Journal of African Travel-Writing* 2 (1997): 70–79.

Godsall, Jon R. "Fact and Fiction in Richard Burton's Personal Narrative of a Pilgrimage to El-Medinah and Mecca (1855–56)." *Journal of the Royal Asiatic Society*, Third Series, 3 (1993): 331–51.

————. "Richard Burton's Somali Expedition, 1854–55: Its Wider Historical Context and Planning." *Journal of the Royal Asiatic Society*, Third Series, 11 (2001): 135–73.

Gray, John Milner. "Speke and Grant." *Uganda Journal* 17 (1953): 146–60.

Hayman, John. "Burton as Autobiographer." In *In Search of Richard Burton: Papers from a Huntington Library Symposium*, edited by Alan H. Jutzi, 27–45. San Marino, CA: Huntington Library, 1993.

Jutzi, Alan H. "Burton and His Library." In *In Search of Richard Burton: Papers from a Huntington Library Symposium*, edited by Alan H. Jutzi, 85–106. San Marino CA: Huntington Library, 1993.

Kennedy, Dane. "British Exploration in the Nineteenth Century: A Historiographical Survey." *History Compass* 5/6 (2007): 1879–1900.

Keynes, Quentin. "The Labyrinthine Paths of Collecting Burton." In *In Search of Richard Burton: Papers from a Huntington Library Symposium*, edited by Alan H. Jutzi, 106–31. San Marino, CA: Huntington Library, 1993.

Middleton, Dorothy. "Burton and Speke Centenary." *Geographical Journal* 123 (1957): 413–15.

————. "The Search for the Nile Sources." *Geographical Journal* 138 (1972): 209–24.

Newbury, C. W. Introduction to *A Mission to Gelele, King of Dahome*, by Richard F. Burton, 1–39. London: Routledge and K. Paul, 1966.

Nurse, Donald Paul. "An Amateur Barbarian: The Life and Career of Sir Richard Francis Burton, 1821–1890." PhD dissertation, University of Toronto, 1999.

Rainger, Ronald. "Race, Politics, and Science: The Anthropological Society of London in the 1860s." *Victorian Studies* 22 (1978): 51–70.

Rigby, C. P. "An Outline of the Somauli Language, with Vocabulary." *Transactions of the Bombay Geographical Society* 9 (1849–50): 129–84.

Risley, R. C. H. "Burton: An Appreciation." *Tanganyika Notes & Records* 49 (1957): 257–97.

Sanders, Edith. "The Hamitic Hypothesis; Its Origin and Functions in Time Perspective." *Journal of African History* 10 (1969): 521–31.

Speke, John Hanning. "Captain Speke's Adventures in Somali Land." *Blackwood's*

Magazine 87 (January–June 1860): 561–80, 674–93; and 88 (July–December 1860): 22–36.

———. "Journals." *Blackwood's Magazine* 86 (1859): 339–57, 391–419, 565–82.

———. "The Upper Basin of the Nile, from Inspection and Information." *Journal of the Royal Geographical Society* 33 (1863): 322–46.

Thomas, H. B., and Ivan R. Dale. "Uganda Place Names: Some European Eponyms." *Uganda Journal* 17 (1953): 101–23.

Wisnicki, Adrian S. "Charting the Frontier: Indigenous Geography, Arab-Nyamwezi Caravans, and the East Africa Expedition of 1856–59." *Victorian Studies* 51 (2008): 103–37.

World Health Organization. "Female Genital Mutilation and Obstetric Outcome: WHO Collaborative Prospective Study in Six African Countries." *Lancet* 367 (2006): 1835–41.

Young, Donald. "The Selected Correspondence of Sir Richard Burton 1848–1890." MA thesis, University of Nebraska, Lincoln, 1979.

INDEX

Locations beginning with Lake or Mt. are indexed under their proper names with Lake or Mt. following.

ABOUT THE AUTHOR

JAMES L. NEWMAN is an emeritus professor of geography in the Maxwell School at Syracuse University. Born and raised in Minneapolis, he and his wife, Carole, moved to the "snow capital" of the United States in 1967 and, along with a variety of cats, have remained residents ever since. Dr. Newman's professional career has been devoted to the study of Africa, especially its eastern and central portions, with an emphasis on patterns of population dynamics and change. As Newman is a geographer, maps are always on his mind, as is history. This book, as well as his two previous ones—*The Peopling of Africa: A Geographical Interpretation* (1996) and *Imperial Footprints: Henry Morton Stanley's African Journeys* (2004)— show these influences and also illustrate his long-held conviction that scholars have an educational obligation to make their writings accessible to the wider reading public.